Longman First Certificate Coursebook

Roy Kingsbury

First published 1983
Fifth impression 1985
ISBN 0 582 74345 1

Set in 9/11 Metroset Plantin
Printed and bound in Great Britain by
Hazell Watson & Viney Limited,
Aylesbury

n

dedicated to the memory of Peter Clifford, without whose
siasm it would not have been written.

Author's acknowledgements

I would like to express my sincere thanks to

- Louis Alexander, Roger Scott, Hilary Rees-Parnall, Sheila Ward, Tony Le Proto, Tim Hunt, Annie Bednarska and Judith King for their constant and encouraging constructive criticism while I was writing this book.
- Mrs Pat Hughes and other members of staff and FCE students at the Hinton School of English who tried out all the material and made valuable suggestions for improvement throughout.
- The work of R. A. Close, Randolph Quirk, Michael Swan, and Louis Alexander and other authors of *English Grammatical Structure* (Longman) for their insights into so many aspects of English.
- My own FCE class of autumn 1980 who once again made me acutely aware of so many of the problems for students aiming towards the Cambridge First Certificate in English examination.
- And to my wife Jill and daughter Debbie for putting up with the author's temperament.

Roy Kingsbury, Dorset 1983

Cambridge First Certificate in English

What the examination consists of

Paper 1 Reading Comprehension *1 hour: 40 marks*

This Paper consists of two Sections, A and B. Both are compulsory.
In Section A, you have to answer 25 multiple-choice questions which are designed to test vocabulary, structure and usage.
In Section B, you have to answer 15 multiple-choice questions which are based on three or more texts. These are designed to test gist and detailed understanding of written English.

Paper 2 Composition *1½ hours: 40 marks*

In this Paper you have to write two compositions from a choice of five or more. The choice includes a letter, a narrative, a description, an argument, and one or more based on prescribed reading.

Paper 3 Use of English *2 hours: 40 marks*

This Paper consists of two Sections, A and B. Both are compulsory.
In Section A, you have to do four or five completion, transformation or rewriting exercises which are designed to test active control of the patterns and usage of English.
Section B is always a 'directed writing' task in which you have to read a dialogue, extract from a brochure or a diary, etc., and then assemble and present information in two or more paragraphs.

Paper 4 Listening Comprehension *approx. 30 minutes: 20 marks*

This Paper consists of three or more pieces of spoken English (dialogues, announcements, etc.) which you hear on tape and for which you have a printed question/answer sheet on which you write or tick your answers. The way you mark your answers will take a variety of forms, from ticking true-false and multiple-choice items to filling in blanks and re-ordering pieces of information or pictures.

Paper 5 Oral Interview *approx. 20 minutes: 40 marks*

The Interview consists of three Parts.
In Part 1 you will be shown a picture and asked questions about it. This conversation will also include general discussion.
In Part 2 you will be given a short passage (part of a letter, an announcement, part of some instructions, etc.) which you have to read aloud.
In Part 3 you will have a choice from a small number of optional exercises. You may be asked to give a short talk on a topic of general interest, you may have to take part in a role-playing exercise or some similar kind of activity: you will even have an opportunity to discuss the optional prescribed texts if you have studied them.

Note: The last five Units (26–30) each contain tips on taking the examination together with complete practice Papers (see pp 157, 167, 173, 182 and 188).

Contents

Unit 1

A day in the life of . . .

EXAM FOCUS:
Reading Comprehension

Read and speak

Read this article from *The Sunday Times Magazine* carefully. It was written in March, 1980. Then do these exercises.

1 In pairs, ask and answer these questions:

1 When and where was Buchi born?
2 Where did she grow up and where did she go to school?
3 How old was she when she came to London?
4 When did she separate from her husband?
5 How old are her youngest and eldest children now?

2 Ask and tell each other about her life. Ask:

1 what her father did for a living.
2 what kind of school she went to.
3 when she moved to London.
4 if she was already married then.
5 how many children she's got.
6 if she brings up her children alone now.
7 how she earns a living.
8 when she wrote her first novel.
9 what it was called.
10 what she's writing now.

3 Now ask and answer these questions about her daily routine and habits:

1 When does she normally wake up?
2 What does she usually do when she gets up?
3 What does she generally do when she gets back?
4 How long does she spend cleaning? And then?
5 Where does she sometimes work?
6 How long does she spend writing every day?
7 When does she usually stop? Why?
8 Where does she always go once a week? Why?
9 Where does she nearly always go on Sunday mornings?
10 What does she sometimes do late at night? But generally?

A DAY IN THE LIFE OF

BUCHI EMECHETA

"My day starts around 6 a.m. I am awake an hour or two earlier, but I don't get up: I lie there and plan all I would like to do during the day. We have been a one-parent family since I was 22 and my five children ranged in age from seven months to five years old. Now they are all in their teens.

When I get up, I usually put on my track suit and run round the block, once. By the time I return from jogging, the children are in the kitchen squabbling over breakfast. The children leave for school one after the other. After jogging I feel justified in eating up all my children's leftovers. What do you expect of a Nigerian war baby who spent most of her early life in a mission girls' boarding school, where it was a sin to waste food?

Buchi Emecheta combines a writing career with being the single parent of five teenage children.

Buchi Emecheta, 36, daughter of a railway worker, followed her husband from Nigeria to London in 1962, but was later separated from him and left with five children to bring up alone. She now earns her living by writing and lecturing. She wrote her first novel, In the Ditch, *in 1972 and has since published four more. She also writes books for children.*

I live in this dilapidated North London terrace house, which will be mine in 2001. I have only an hour in the mornings to clean all the rooms, three loos and two baths. I spend a few minutes on myself and carry my Woolworth's portable typewriter into the kitchen: it is the warmest place in the house. On warmer days I work in my bedroom. I write every day, from about 10 a.m. to three in the afternoon. (I am just finishing my first war novel with the working title *Destination Biafra.*) At three I stop writing and dash down to the shops—mainly for bread and vegetables.

I don't go out much in the evenings; but once a week I go to my local church in Crouch End to sing in the choir. I love music, any type of music, but especially church music. I seldom miss Sunday morning Matins at church.

Sometimes late at night I go through what I have written in the day, but in most cases I read other people's work and listen to the radio.

1

Grammar practice 1

The Present Simple with frequency adverbs when talking about routines and habits

REVIEW

I'm	always nearly always often sometimes usually normally generally occasionally hardly ever scarcely ever rarely seldom never	late.
I		get up early.

Note the normal position of frequency adverbs after the verb *be* and before other verbs. Note that *often, sometimes, usually, normally, generally* and *occasionally* can begin a sentence, for example:
Normally I stop work at about 6 p.m.

PRACTICE

1 Make statements about someone else's daily routine and habits, for example:
My brother often goes jogging at 6 in the morning.

2 Ask each other about friends' or relatives' routines or habits, for example:
A: *Does your mother always go to town on Mondays?*
B: *Yes, always.* or *No, she doesn't always go on Mondays. She occasionally goes on Fridays.*

3 Read about Buchi again and say what she always does, sometimes does, never does, etc. every day or every week, on Sundays, etc.

Grammar practice 2

The Simple Past with regular verbs . . .

REVIEW

start	started /id/: expected, visited, waited, rested, landed
plan	planned /d/: returned, lived, listened, ranged, played, carried
work	worked /t/: stopped, finished, dashed, missed, typed

and irregular verbs

REVIEW

bear	bore	born/borne	grow	grew	grown
swear	swore	sworn	blow	blew	blown
tear	tore	torn	know	knew	known
wear	wore	worn	throw	threw	thrown
begin	began	begun	do	did	done
drink	drank	drunk	eat	ate	eaten
ring	rang	rung	go	went	gone
sing	sang	sung	lie	lay	lain

PRACTICE

Make statements about Buchi's past. Then say what she did yesterday and last Sunday.

ABOUT YOU

Tell another student what you did yesterday. (Use the verbs above where you can.)

Vocabulary

Formation of nouns with suffixes

Words describing people (profession, etc.) are often formed with a suffix *-er, -eer, -ist, -ess,* etc. For example, Buchi Emecheta is a *writer* (a *novelist*) and *lecturer.* Her father was a *railway worker.*

1 Study these words carefully, and then play the game.

Nouns mainly from nouns

-ster	gangster, youngster
-eer	engineer, mountaineer, volunteer
-er	footballer, golfer, teenager, widower
-ess	manageress, waitress, actress, (air-)hostess
-ist	novelist, dramatist, pianist, guitarist, (hair)stylist, violinist, manicurist, chemist, typist

Nouns mainly from verbs

-er	writer, lecturer, worker, singer, driver, dancer, swimmer, teacher, (tennis-)player, photographer, builder, employer, robber, owner, songwriter, busdriver
-or	inventor, inspector, instructor
-ar	beggar, burglar, liar
-ant	assistant, applicant, participant, accountant, informant, inhabitant
-ee	employee, trainee, divorcee, absentee, refugee, referee

Note the difference between *an employer/a trainer* (=a person who employs/trains other people) and *an employee/a trainee* (=a person who is being employed/ trained). The word *referee* is used both for a person who referees e.g. a football match, and a person who gives a reference to an applicant for a job (see Unit 3).

2 Game: *What's my line?* (see Teacher's Guide p 16)

Discussion

1 In groups, ask and tell each other about your life and daily routine. Ask and/or say things like this:

- when you were born (and where).
- where you grew up.
- when and where you went to school.
- whether you are single, married, engaged, etc.
- what you do now (for a living).
- what you did when you were younger, at school or at college.
- when you usually wake up and get up.
- if you go jogging or do any other kind of exercise (and for how long).
- what you normally have for breakfast and lunch.
- when you generally leave home for work or school and get home from work or school.
- what you usually do in the evenings.

2 Now ask and tell each other about someone you know well, a good friend or relative. Tell each other about the person's life and their daily routine.

1

Exercises for homework

See if you can do these exercises in 60 minutes.

1 Use of English

Read this passage and for each numbered blank supply the past tense of the appropriate verb from the list below.

The railway station was one of those small ones in the middle of the countryside where trains only stop once or twice a day. A party of about twenty of us had been out walking for the whole day and had arranged to get there in time to catch the train back into the city. We got there early. We ___(1)___ that the train wasn't due for another hour, so we ___(2)___ our rucksacks on to the ground, ___(3)___ down on the grass by the track and ___(4)___. We were all hungry and thirsty, so we ___(5)___ and ___(6)___ what was left of the food and drink we had taken. After a while Dennis, who always took his guitar everywhere, ___(7)___ to play and we all joined in and ___(8)___ a few songs. Then someone said: 'Ssh! I think I can hear the train.' We all ___(9)___ and ___(10)___.

begin eat lie stop know listen wait throw sing drink

2 Composition: Letter

As part of your first letter to a new pen-friend in an English-speaking country, write two short paragraphs. In the first give a brief life story, saying when and where you were born, where you grew up, where you went to school, what you do now, etc. In the second, describe briefly your normal daily routine. (Each paragraph should be about 50 words in length.) Wherever possible, use language that you have practised in this Unit.

3 Use of English: Directed writing

Write a brief summary (about 100 words) of Buchi Emecheta's life and daily routine, using these questions and joining words:

Is Buchi Emecheta a teacher or a writer?	Buchi Emecheta is . . .
Where was she born? What kind of school did she go to?	. . . who . . . where . . .
When did she follow her husband to London?	She . . .
Since they separated, how many children has she brought up alone?	. . . but . . .
Where has she brought them up? (i.e. Where is the house?)	. . . in a house . . .
Does she have a set daily routine or not?	She . . .
Does she get up early or late every morning?	She . . .
Does she always go jogging, or only occasionally?	. . . and . . .
When does she clean the house? (Where have the children gone?)	She . . . when . . .
Does she generally write from 9 to 4, or from 10 to 3?	She . . .
Does she go out much? What does she like singing in? When?	She . . . but . . .

TEST: READING COMPREHENSION

Time: 15 minutes

Choose the word or phrase which best completes each sentence.
Write your choice for each (A, B, C or D) on a separate piece of paper.

1 The boss of the firm gave all his ________ an extra week's holiday.
A payees B employees C referees D refugees

2 We go to the cinema about three or four times a year: in other words, just ________.
A usually B normally C generally D occasionally

3 Mary ________ in an old terrace house in South London.
A leaves B inhabits C lives D visits

4 Their three children ________ in age from 10 to 17.
A account B ring C grow D range

5 All the athletes were wearing ________ suits when they came into the stadium.
A track B running C sports D jogging

6 He had to ________ down the road to get something he had forgotten earlier.
A blow B return C train D dash

7 Because Shakespeare mainly wrote plays, he is always thought of as ________.
A a writer B a novelist C a dramatist D an author

8 The man next door has been a ________ since his wife died ten years ago.
A widower B divorcee C single D widow

9 The woman they finally chose was much older than the other ________ for the job.
A informants B participants C applicants D consultants

10 She has to take great care of her hands, so she has them done by a ________ once a month at a beauty salon.
A stylist B handyman C manicurist D hostess

11 Some writers take a lightweight ________ typewriter with them wherever they go.
A carrying B portable C bearable D weighing

12 If you want to be a driving ________, you have to have a lot of patience!
A instructor B informant C trainee D assistant

13 He ________ most of his early life in a small village in Scotland.
A grew up B brought C did D spent

14 She's got a very interesting job. She earns her ________ working as a secretary for a Member of Parliament.
A life B profession C living D line

15 When I went into the room, the children were ________ over the last piece of cake.
A discussing B squabbling C participating D consulting

Unit 2

Nothing to write home about

EXAM FOCUS:
Composition (Letter)

Read and speak

Read this letter carefully.
Then do the exercises opposite.

Inver Cottage,
Glenvalley,
Sutherland,
Scotland

2nd May 198-

Dear David and Ann,

I imagine you've been wondering why we haven't written since we left London. I know we said we would write very soon, but I'm sure you understand what it's been like. We've been so busy just settling into the cottage up here that there isn't really anything 'to write home about'.

You know we couldn't wait to move. I was looking forward to doing a different job, and the family to getting away from the noise and dirt of London. Well, we've certainly done that, I assure you! And more. We've got away from everything! As you'll see from the enclosed photos, the cottage is charming, but miles from anywhere. There's nothing much to do, nowhere to go (unless we drive into the nearest town 20 miles away to the one cinema!), and nobody to talk to. Jill and the children feel more cut off than I do, of course. At least I go off to work every day, but the children have got no one else to play with, and Jill hasn't got anyone to talk to all day except the children. And conversation with 4- to 5-year-olds tends to be somewhat limited!

The one good thing is that I know we are all healthier than we were in London - but I'm afraid we're far from happy. I expect we shall think seriously about coming back down south again quite soon.

I meant it when I told you just before we left to come up and stay with us. It's ideal for relaxing. The air's fresh and clean, the mountains and valleys are magnificent, there's no noise - and you won't have to worry about anything. What do you say? We'd all love to see you.

We look forward to hearing from you soon.

With best wishes,

Chris & Jill, Jamie & Pauline

1 In pairs, ask and say:

1 where Chris and Jill used to live.
2 where they are living now.
3 how long you think they have been living there.
4 why they haven't written to David and Ann before now.
5 what Chris and the family were looking forward to before they left London.
6 if there is a lot to do or a lot of places to go to.
7 why Jill and the children feel more cut off than Chris.
8 if there is *anything* good about the family's new life in Scotland.
9 what Chris expects they will think seriously about quite soon.
10 when Chris invited David and Ann to go up and stay with them.

2 Discussion

In his letter, Chris wrote: 'I expect we shall think seriously about coming back down south again quite soon.' What do you think they should do—stay or move? Express opinions with: *I think . . .*, *I feel . . .*, *I'm afraid . . .*, *I imagine . . .*, etc.

3 About you

If you live in a town or city, would you like to move to the country? Why?/Why not? If you live in the country, would you like to go and live in a town or a city? Why?/Why not?

2

Grammar practice 1

Compound indefinite pronouns formed from *some, any, no* and *every*

REVIEW

I'd like / Here's — someone/somebody to talk to. / something to do. / somewhere to stay.	I haven't got / Have you got — anyone/anybody to talk to./? / anything to do./? / anywhere to stay./?
I've got / There's — no one/nobody to talk to. / nothing to do. / nowhere to go.	You've met everyone/everybody now. I've done everything I can. We've looked everywhere for the children.

Note a) the other *some-* compounds: *somehow, sometimes, sometime, somewhat.*
Note b) the other *any-* compounds: *anyhow* and *anyway.*

PRACTICE

Read this passage and supply suitable words from the boxes above.

Before we got to the town, __(1)__ had told us that we could get __(2)__ to eat in a little backstreet. We looked __(3)__ but couldn't find __(4)__ that looked like a restaurant or café. And strangely we couldn't find __(5)__ to ask: the streets were deserted. So there we were, with __(6)__ to eat or drink, __(7)__ to ask and apparently __(8)__ to get a meal. Just then an old man appeared. 'Excuse me,' I said. 'We're looking for __(9)__ to get a good meal. Is there __(10)__ you can recommend?' He looked at me for a second, shook his head, and just walked away without a word!

Grammar practice 2

Verbs generally used in the simple form to express opinions and feelings

REVIEW AND PRACTICE

Study these sentences about Chris and his family, noting carefully the verbs that are used. Then express your own feelings with these verbs about the situation Chris and the family find themselves in.

Assumption: I assume/imagine / suppose/think (that) Jill's rather unhappy.

Certainty: I know (definitely) / firmly believe (that) they've made a mistake.

Uncertainty: I expect/somehow feel (that) they'd like to see some old friends.

Ignorance: I (honestly) don't know / (really) have no idea whether they'll go back to London or not.

Deduction: I gather/understand (that) they've got no one to talk to.

Hope: I hope (that) they learn to like the place.

Regret: I fear/I'm afraid (that) they're not very happy.

Doubt: I doubt whether they'll stay there very long.

Grammar practice 3

More irregular verbs

REVIEW

Study these verbs and then do the exercise below.

creep	crept	crept
dream	dreamt	dreamt (dreamed)
feel	felt	felt
keep	kept	kept
lean	leant	leant (leaned)
leap	leapt	leapt (leaped)
leave	left	left
mean	meant	meant
meet	met	met
sleep	slept	slept
sweep	swept	swept

bring	brought	brought	drive	drove	driven
buy	bought	bought	ride	rode	ridden
catch	caught	caught	rise	rose	risen
fight	fought	fought	write	wrote	written
teach	taught	taught			
think	thought	thought			

PRACTICE

Put in the Simple Past tense of the verb in brackets.

1 He (*leave*) for work at 6 a.m. yesterday.
2 We (*sleep*) in a tent on our holiday.
3 Chris (*write*) to them from Scotland.
4 I (*catch*) a cold last week.
5 She (*sweep*) the path this morning.
6 I (*meet*) them at the football match.
7 I (*mean*) to write to them, but I forgot.
8 I first (*ride*) a bike when I was four.
9 She (*buy*) a new dress last week.
10 He (*lean*) against the table as he spoke.

Exercises for homework

1 Use of English: Directed writing

See if you can do this exercise in 20 minutes.

A friend has written to ask for news about Chris and his family. Using the beginning and ending of the letter and the prompts given below, write a summary of Chris's letter (p 7).

Dear Paul,

In your last letter, you wanted to know if I had any news of Chris and his family. I had a letter from them only the other day. They have moved to Scotland, as they said they would, but I doubt whether they'll stay there very long. You see, . . .

1 they/live/charming cottage/but/it/miles/anywhere.
2 I/afraid/they/not only/get away/city/but/everything else/too.
3 I/somehow/feel/they/not/very happy.
4 As Chris/say/nothing/do/nowhere/go/no one/talk to.
5 I/imagine/they/go back/London/quite soon.

Well, that's all for now. I hope you and the family are well.

Kindest regards,

David

2 Study section: Writing a personal letter

One of the Composition subjects in the First Certificate (Paper 2) is nearly always a letter. In any letter, just as much care must be taken with the lay-out as with the content. Look at the letter on page 7 again and notice how carefully it is laid out on the page. Now study this letter and the information about lay-out and conventions. Ingrid Jones put an advertisement in an international magazine for a pen-friend. Sue, a Swedish girl, has answered the advertisement, and this is Ingrid's reply.

1
2 22, North Road,
Harlow,
3 Essex,
England

5 4 1st May 198- 5

6 Dear Sue,

7 What a nice surprise it was to receive a letter from you. I didn't expect an answer to my advertisement so soon. And thank you for telling me so much about yourself. I feel I know you a little already.

Now I must tell you something about myself. My name is Ingrid Jones. I'm 19 and I'm a hair-stylist. I was born and grew up in London. My father's a policeman and my mother's a teacher. I like swimming and music. When I was younger, I sang in the church choir, but I don't now. I work in a hairdresser's not far from my home in Harlow. I work from 9 to 6, six days a week, but I have a free half-day every Tuesday or Wednesday.

I look forward to hearing from you again soon. Perhaps I can send you some English books.

8 With best wishes,
Yours sincerely,
Ingrid

9 P.S. I enclose 2 photos of myself taken last year.

1 You do not put your own name at the top. Your signature at the end of the letter is enough.
2 The address and date are written in the top right-hand corner.
3 The address is absolutely necessary, and the order is: (name of house), house number and street, town/city, county/region, country. Note where commas are used.
4 The date is written *1st May 198–* or *May 1st 198–*. Remember the abbreviated dates: 1st, 2nd, 3rd, 4th, 5th, etc. Abbreviated months which can be used are: Jan., Feb., Aug., Sept., Oct., Nov., Dec..
5 Leave a good margin down both sides.
6 The salutation: most letters begin with *Dear* (*+first name*) or *Dear Mr/Mrs/Miss/Ms* (*+surname*), depending on how well you know the person you are writing to.
7 The body of the letter should have: a clear introduction; the purpose or message; and a conclusion. The introduction refers, for example, to a letter you have received; the middle part gives the message (and may be one or more paragraphs); and the conclusion rounds off the letter politely.
8 The subscription nearly always uses *Yours*, or *Yours sincerely*—the former is much more common nowadays—and is often preceded by a phrase such as *With best wishes, Kindest regards, All the best,* etc. Note where capital letters and commas are used in the subscription. Your signature: most people sign a personal letter with just their first name.
9 If you have forgotten something and wish to add it, add a post-script (P.S.).

TEST: COMPOSITION

Time: 30 minutes

Write **one only** of the following composition exercises. Your answer must follow exactly the instructions given, and must be about 120 words in length.

Either

1 You have recently moved to another town. Write a letter to a friend describing briefly what you are doing now and the place in which you are living, and giving your opinion of the town. The beginning and ending should be as for an ordinary letter, but the address is not to be counted in the number of words.

Or

2 You have just received the first letter from a pen-friend in an English-speaking country. In it he/she introduced himself/herself and told you about his/her studies or occupation, when and where he/she was born, something about his/her family, and his/her interests and normal daily routine. Write your first letter back, telling the pen-friend the same kinds of things about yourself. The beginning and ending should be as for an ordinary letter, but the address is not to be counted in the number of words.

(*Note:* For this Test you may refer back to Units 1 and 2 in this coursebook to help you.)

Unit 3
Who'll get the job?

EXAM FOCUS:
Use of English

Read, listen and speak

Jane and Michael have both applied for the job of Senior Secretary in a medium-size firm. Both are the same age and have had the same training and similar experience.

1 Read both references carefully. Then, in pairs, ask and say:

1 how good Jane is as a secretary.
2 how good Michael is at his job.
3 if they are both good typists.
4 how well they speak French.
5 if they both dress well.
6 what Jane is like as a person.
7 what Michael is like as a person.
8 how well they both mix with other people.
9 what kind of temperament each has got.
10 what each of them is interested in.

Ask each other more questions if you can.

2 Now listen to part of Jane's interview with the Personnel Manager and Mr Toms. Then answer these questions:

Does Jane think she is conscientious? Why?
Did she leave her last job because they were making changes?

3 Now listen to part of Michael's interview with the Personnel Manager and Mr Toms. Then answer these questions:

Do you think Mrs Grey was worried that Michael 'tended to be impatient'?
How often does Michael play football and golf?

Applicant's full name

Jane Sarah LANGLEY

Referee's name

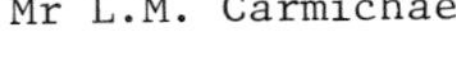

Mr L.M. Carmichael

Company

Sparks & Co.

Position

Personnel Manager

PLEASE COMMENT AS WELL AS YOU CAN ON THE FOLLOWING:

Skills, work ability and potential

Miss Langley is an enthusiastic, efficient secretary who always works carefully. She is very experienced in all office procedures and can adapt quickly to change. She is an excellent typist, and can speak and read French quite well.

Appearance

She is a girl who takes pride in her appearance. She dresses well and sensibly - never untidily.

Character, temperament, manners, etc.

She is a sincere, conscientious person who is always courteous to clients. But at times she is almost overconfident. I imagine she could be somewhat bossy if she were given a position of responsibility.

Ability to work with others

She mixes well with people both in the office and outside, and is very even-tempered.

Sport and other interests

To the best of my knowledge, she has no interest in sport, but she is a keen amateur actress and singer.

Applicant's full name

Michael John JAMES

Referee's name

Mr R.H. Smith

Company

All Office Trading

Position

Personnel Manager

PLEASE COMMENT AS WELL AS YOU CAN ON THE FOLLOWING

Skills, work ability and potential

While Mr James is an enthusiastic young man who is experienced in most office procedures, he tends to be a little impatient at times. This is due to a desire to 'get on with the job'. He types wells, is an excellent driver, and speaks and reads both French and German fluently.

Appearance

I feel sure that he does his best to look smart, but he does tend at times to dress rather sloppily.

Character, temperament, manners, etc.

Mr James is a clear thinker and tends to work very quickly. Because of this he can lose his temper with colleagues with less insight into the work. With clients, however, he is always patient and polite.

Ability to work with others

He has never mixed very well with the other employees in the company. But he would make a good 'team leader'.

Sport and other interests

He is a young man who enjoys sport immensely. He is a keen footballer and a first-class golfer.

4 Discussion

In pairs or small groups, compare and discuss Jane and Michael as applicants for the job. At the end of your discussion, say who you would give the job to, and why. Use sentences like these in your discussion:

Michael's a fluent French and German speaker, but Jane can only speak French 'quite well'.

(I think that) Jane's a nicer/more sincere person than Michael (is).

As a person, Jane's nicer/more sincere than Michael.

Michael doesn't always dress as well as Jane (does).

Jane mixes better with people in the office than Michael (does).

Michael's more enthusiastic about sport than Jane (is).

Michael isn't as good a typist as Jane (is).

5 Now listen to the Personnel Manager and Mr Toms discussing Jane and Michael after they have interviewed them. Then answer these questions:

Who are they going to give the job to? Why?
Do you agree or disagree? Why?

3

Grammar practice 1

Comparative adjectives

REVIEW

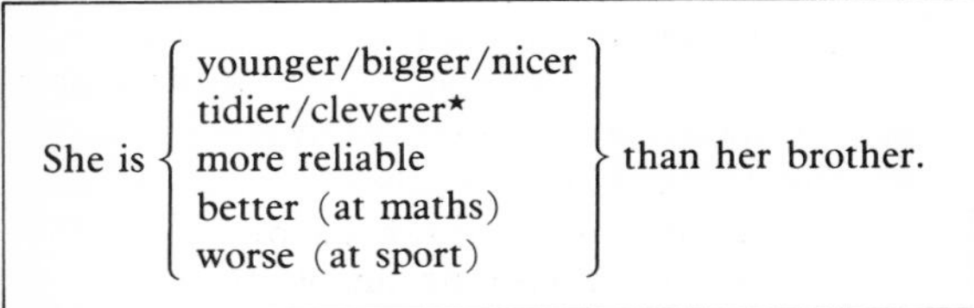

She is { younger/bigger/nicer | tidier/cleverer* | more reliable | better (at maths) | worse (at sport) } than her brother.

Remember that adjectives form their comparatives with (*adjective*) *-er* or *more/less* (+*adjective*), or irregular *better, worse,* etc.

*Note other two-syllable adjectives which form the comparative with *-er*: *busy, easy, pretty, funny, silly, healthy, polite, quiet, common, stupid, gentle, narrow.*

ABOUT YOU

Think of people you know and compare them using sentences like these:

1 (I think that) Erica is { much | far } { nicer | more responsible | less pleasant } than Sue (is).

2 In my opinion, John is a { much | far } { nicer | more reliable } person than Peter (is).

3 Mary isn't as/so young as Bill (is).

4 Jim isn't as good a tennis-player as Mark (is).

5 Jane's a good dancer, but I don't know a better dancer than Pat.

Grammar practice 2

Comparative adverbs

REVIEW

Note that many adverbs of manner are formed by adding *-ly* to the adjective:

fluent→*fluently* (and in the same way: *quickly, slowly, efficiently, badly, carefully, loyally, occasionally, usually, generally*).

enthusiastic→*enthusiastically* (and in the same way: *automatically, scientifically*).

(*un*)*tidy*→(*un*)*tidily* (and in the same way: *busily, angrily,* (*un*)*happily*).

Adverbs ending in *-ly* form their comparative with *more* (+ *adverb*):

> They both work carefully, but Jane works more carefully than Michael (does).

Remember the comparative adverbs *better* and *worse.*

> Mary and Jane both type well/badly, but Mary types better/worse than Jane (does).

Remember that certain adverbs have the same form as their adjective. They are: *fast, hard, early, late, high, low, straight,* for example:

He's a { *hard* | *fast* } *worker.* → *He works* { *hard.* | *fast.* }

Remember the other adverbs *lately* (=recently) and *hardly* (=almost not, as in *I can hardly wait for my birthday*).

Adverbs with the same form as their adjective form their comparative with *-er*:

> He got up earlier/later than I did.
> She works faster/harder than he does.
> The plane flew higher/lower than it should have done.

PRACTICE

Look at the information about Jane and Michael on pp 13–14 once again and compare them using sentences like this:

Jane generally dresses better than Michael does.
Michael speaks French more fluently than Jane does.
Jane tends to mix with people (much) better than Michael does.

1
What you did was ________ and ________!
You are a/an ________, ________ man!
You are ________, ________ and ________!
I am going to send you to prison for three months!

Vocabulary

Adjective opposites with prefixes

Many adjective opposites are formed with the prefixes *dis-*, *un-*, *im-*, *in-*, *il-* and *ir-* Study these words carefully, then do the exercise below.

dis-	dishonest, disagreeable, disloyal, discourteous
un-	unreliable, unpleasant, unhappy, untidy, unenthusiastic, unable
im-	(before *m/p*) impatient, impolite, immoral, impractical
in-	inefficient, insincere, inaccurate, inexperienced
il-	(before *l*) illegal, illogical, illegible
ir-	(before *r*) irresponsible, irrational, irreplaceable

Now cover the box and use appropriate words from it to complete what the people below are saying:

2
I know I may be ________, but I haven't got time even to try and read this. It's ________ and almost ________!

3

Exercises for homework

See if you can do these exercises in 50 minutes.

1 Use of English

Supply the correct form of the word in brackets—comparative adjective, adverb or comparative adverb.

1 John's ________ than Bob. (*clever*)
2 He swore at me ________. (*angry*)
3 He threw the book ________ at me. (*straight*)
4 He's a ________ swimmer than she is. (*bad*)
5 She works extremely ________. (*careful*)
6 I got there ________ than I said. (*early*)
7 He spoke ________ than usual. (*polite*)
8 He works ________ than he used to. (*hard*)
9 You paint ________ than I do. (*good*)
10 He behaves very ________ at times. (*odd*)

2 Use of English

Read this paragraph from a short story. Then for each numbered blank supply the negative form of the corresponding numbered adjective in the list given below.

I have yet to meet a more ___(1)___, ___(2)___ man than Julius Higgins. Everything he does is ___(3)___. That is not to say that he is in any way ___(4)___ or ___(5)___, of course, for all his criminal activities are conducted with the utmost efficiency. But having decided to pursue a life of crime, it would have been ___(6)___ or ___(7)___—I'm not quite sure which—for him not to have made a success at it. He is indeed one of those who would soon have made himself ___(8)___, whatever profession he had decided to enter. Perhaps he could even have been a medical man: his handwriting is as ___(9)___ as that of any doctor's that I have seen! But, seriously, I do not feel that, with a character as ___(10)___ as his, he could really have done anything but enter a life of crime.

1 honest 2 moral 3 legal 4 efficient 5 experienced
6 practical 7 rational 8 replaceable 9 legible 10 pleasant

3 Use of English: Directed writing

Write, as in a short report, brief descriptions of Michael and Jane (pp 13–14) as prospective candidates for the job. Use the following 'starters', questions and joining words. Each paragraph should be about 50 words in length.

Jane Langley is just the sort of person we want for the job.

How does she dress? What sort of a person is she?	. . . and . . .
How does she behave towards clients?	who . . .
What sort of a secretary is she? How does she work?	. . . who . . .
How does she get on with people?	. . . and . . .
I am however a little concerned about Michael James because. . .	
How does he dress at times? How does he work?	. . . and . . .
Is he a clear thinker, or not? What sort of a driver is he?	At the same time, however, . . .
How well does he speak and read French and German?	. . . and . . .
How well does he mix with others in the office?	Unfortunately, . . .
Does he tend to act patiently or impatiently at times?	. . . and . . .

TEST: USE OF ENGLISH

Time: 20 minutes

Answer all questions. Write your answers **in ink on the paper provided by the teacher.**

1 The word in capitals at the end of each of the following sentences can be used to form a word that fits suitably in the blank space. Supply the correct form of the word.

1 This book is much ________ than the last one he wrote. BAD
2 It's odd that she's so sloppy at home, because she does her work in the office very ________. CONSCIENCE
3 He knew he'd never get the job: there were over 200 ________. APPLY
4 She's so ________ that she loses her temper at the slightest little thing. PATIENT
5 Thieves are ________ people. HONEST
6 His handwriting is so bad it's almost ________. LEGIBLE
7 That boy behaves rather ________ at times. STRANGE
8 Those tomatoes are far ________ than the ones we bought last week. GOOD
9 That girl plays the piano very ________. GOOD
10 Our last Hoover cleaned a lot more ________ than this new one. EFFICIENT

2 Finish each of the following sentences in such a way that it means exactly the same as the sentence printed before it.

1 She's a fluent Italian speaker.
She speaks..
2 George is older than Mary.
Mary isn't..
3 He drives extremely dangerously.
He's an..
4 Jane's far more sensible than Sue is.
Sue's much..
5 Bob's the best footballer in the club.
No one in the club..
6 I got up earlier than you did yesterday morning.
You got up..
7 They were very irresponsible.
They behaved..
8 Jack's the most reliable worker they've got.
They haven't got..
9 She's normally an early riser.
She normally..
10 John's a poor swimmer, but Tom's much worse.
Tom's a..

Unit 4
'I hate tidying up'

EXAM FOCUS:
Listening Comprehension

Listen and speak

We interviewed these four people in the street. Listen and do the exercises.

1 The first thing we asked each of them was: 'Have you got any pet hates; things that you hate doing?' Listen, and say whether these statements are true or false, or whether you can't tell (from what you hear).

1 The boy doesn't like tidying up.
2 The boy doesn't mind having his hair cut.
3 The man detests filling in forms.
4 The man hates driving.
5 The man likes politicians.
6 The girl loathes copying out school notes.
7 The girl likes watching people at bus stops.
8 The girl enjoys cracking her knuckles.
9 The woman doesn't mind cleaning up after meals.
10 The woman slurps her tea.

2 Then we asked the same four people: 'What do you like doing most?' Listen, and then in pairs ask and say:

1 what the boy enjoys doing most.
2 what the man enjoys doing most.
3 what else he likes doing, and why.
4 if the girl likes watching films.
5 if the girl reads much.
6 why the girl likes going shopping.
7 what else the girl enjoys doing.
8 what the woman enjoys most.

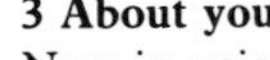

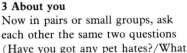

3 About you
Now in pairs or small groups, ask each other the same two questions (Have you got any pet hates?/What do you enjoy doing most?) and discuss your pet likes and dislikes.

Grammar practice 1

The gerund or *-ing* form after verbs to express preferences, likes and dislikes for activities in general

REVIEW

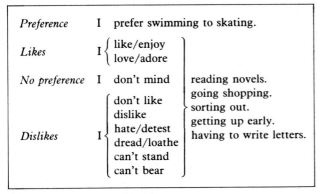

Preference	I	prefer swimming to skating.	
Likes	I	like/enjoy love/adore	
No preference	I	don't mind	reading novels. going shopping. sorting out. getting up early. having to write letters.
Dislikes	I	don't like dislike hate/detest dread/loathe can't stand can't bear	

Note how general preferences are expressed: *I prefer sleeping to working.*
Note, too, the gerund *having to* (from *have to/must*) in, for example:
I loathe having to get up early (from *I have to/must get up early: I loathe it.*).

ABOUT YOU

1 In pairs or small groups, tell each other about the preferences, likes and dislikes of friends and/or relatives, for example:

My father hates clearing out the garage./My sister adores going shopping.

2 Tell each other about your own pet hates and favourite activities using this model:

The thing / *What* } *I hate/enjoy doing most is ____ing . . .*

Grammar practice 2

Verbs *would like, would love, would prefer, hate, dread* and *can't bear* + to + infinitive for likes and dislikes regarding specific events

REVIEW

> I'd like to/I'd love to help you, but I can't.
> I'd prefer to stay at home this evening.
> I hate to tell you/to say this, but you've got to tidy up the classroom.
> I dread to think what the baby's doing.
> I can't bear to watch an animal in pain.

ABOUT YOU

Express your own wishes about tonight, next weekend, the summer, next year, etc. with *I'd like to . . ., I'd love to . . .* and *I'd prefer to . . ..*

4

Grammar practice 3

The gerund or *-ing* form after *How about, What about* and *Do you fancy* for a suggestion or invitation

REVIEW

How about What about Do you fancy	playing tennis tomorrow? a game of tennis tomorrow?

Note that *How/What about (playing) tennis?* (after other questions about likes and dislikes) can also mean *How/What do you think about (playing) tennis?* i.e. *Do you like it?*

PRACTICE

In pairs, practise and adapt this dialogue with the prompts given:

A: *How about going to the cinema?*
B: *That's a good idea. I enjoy going to the cinema.*
or *No, I don't think so. I don't really like going to the cinema.*

go to the theatre
go out to eat on Sunday
stay at home this evening
drive up to London next week
go shopping on Wednesday

Vocabulary

Verbs + adverb particles *away, down, out, up,* etc.

All the verbs in this section consist of a verb + adverb particle. Note how the transitive verbs (= those that can have an object) can transpose the particle:

He took away the car./He took the car away./He took it away. (NOT He took away it.)

1 Verb combinations such as *take away* are very common in English. Both verb and particle retain their original meanings. Study these verbs, then do the exercise.

away	(= direction away, departure, etc.) go away stay away keep away take/throw/put/give sthg away
down	(= direction downwards) go down sit down come down drive down jump down take/bring/put/carry sthg down
up	(= direction upwards) come up go up jump up walk up hold/put/hang/throw sthg up
out	(= exclusion) keep out stay out get out
in	(= to do with entering) go in come in walk in drive in

Express likes and dislikes for activities in general with the verbs above, for example:
I hate throwing things away or *I hate throwing away things.*

2 Sometimes, with a verb like *tidy up,* the adverb particle has a secondary meaning. In this case, *up* suggests a completion of the act of tidying. Study these verbs, then do the exercise.

up	(= completion) tidy/clean/finish/eat/ drink/break/wrap/fill/cut sthg up
out	(= completeness) sort/tidy/clean sthg out (= clarity) call/read/write/copy sthg out
down	(= to do with writing) write/copy/take/get sthg down (=destruction) cut/knock/pull/take/burn sthg down
on	(= attachment) sew/put/stick/pin/tie/screw sthg on
off	(= removal) take/pull/knock/shake/break sthg off

Express likes and dislikes for activities in general with the verbs above, for example:
I love wrapping up presents./I can't stand having to tidy up my room.

3 **Game:** *Mime it!* (see Teacher's Guide p 24)

4 Read the strip cartoon below. (The characters are George and Gaye.) Then tell the story of the cartoon round the class. Student A begins with: 'One day last week George was reading in the lounge when . . .'

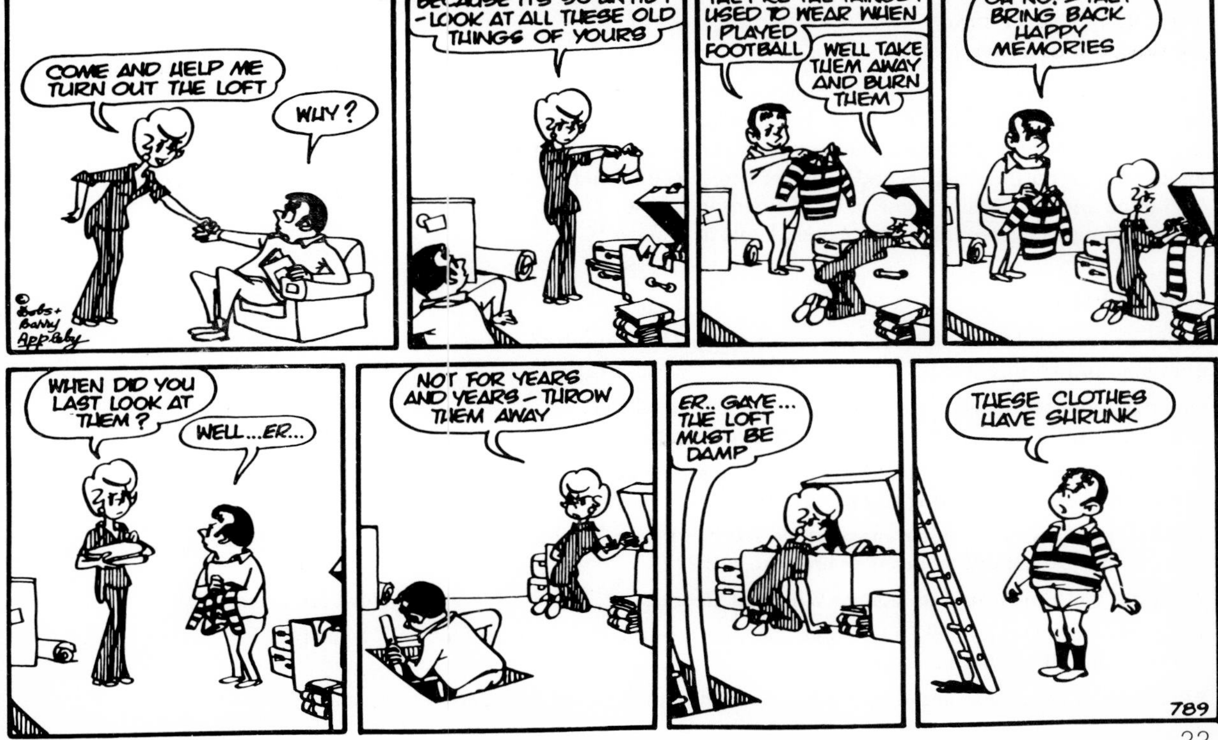

4

Exercises for homework

See if you can do these exercises in 80 minutes.

1 Use of English

Finish each of the following sentences in such a way that it means exactly the same as the sentence printed before it.

1 Sorting out cupboards at home is the thing I detest doing most.
What I ....
2 Would you like to go to Scotland in August?
How about ....
3 He doesn't want to stay home this evening and watch television.
He doesn't fancy...
4 She often has to do the washing-up and she can't stand it.
She can't stand ....
5 Given a choice of swimming or skating, I prefer skating.
I prefer ....
6 I can't help you, although I'd love to.
I'd love...
7 She goes jogging every morning, and enjoys it.
She enjoys...
8 I have to tell you that you're wrong, even though I hate to.
I hate ....
9 Getting up earlier than I have to is something I loathe.
I loathe ....
10 I see people waste so much and I can't bear it.
I can't bear...

2 Composition: Letter

You have received a letter from an English-speaking pen-friend in which he/she told you about some of the things he/she likes and hates doing. Write a reply (about 150 words, not counting the address) telling him/her about your favourite activities and your pet hates. You should make the beginning and ending like those of an ordinary letter (see Unit 2) and use as much language from this and previous Units as you can.

3 Use of English

Write an account of the Gambols cartoon story (p 22) using these 'starters', questions and joining words.

One day last week George was reading in the lounge when . . . Who came in? What did she ask him to go and help her do?	. . . and . . .
Who went up into the loft first? Who climbed up after her? What was she already pulling things out of?	. . . and when . . .
Did he like the idea of taking away his old football things and burning them, or not? What did he say they brought back?	. . . because . . .
What did Gaye insist on him doing? What did George do?	However, . . . so . . .
What was Gaye still doing? Did George come back to the top or to the foot of the ladder? What did he call out?	. . . when . . . . . . and . . .
What had he gone away and done? What, according to him, had happened?	. . . and . . .

TEST: LISTENING COMPREHENSION

Time: approx. 10 minutes

You will hear a conversation between a man and a woman twice (on cassette or read by the teacher), and you will be given time to mark your answers. Before you listen for the first time, look carefully at the pictures and statements below. Then, as you listen, write in the numbers of the activities which 'He hates, but she likes', 'She hates, but he likes', etc. The first one has been done for you. Check your answers while you are listening for the second time.

He hates, but she likes	4
She hates, but he likes	
They both hate	
They both love	
Neither of them mind, but they're not keen on	
They didn't even mention	

Unit 5
'A Heath Robinson affair'

EXAM FOCUS:
Oral Interview

Look, listen and speak

You are going to hear a short lecture. Listen carefully and do the exercises.

1 In pairs, ask and tell each other:

1 what 'a Heath Robinson affair' or 'a Heath Robinson contraption' is.
2 what kinds of people often begin with 'Heath Robinson contraptions'.
3 what people sometimes say when they've got over a problem by tying something together with string.
4 when and where Heath Robinson was born.
5 in what way he took after his father.
6 what books he illustrated.
7 what his name stands for.
8 why his drawings are so funny.
9 when he died.
10 what he left behind him when he died.

2 Look at the picture opposite, and in pairs, ask and tell each other what will (probably) happen if . . .

1 the policemen manage to get free.
2 the dog manages to get out of its kennel and get the hood off its head.
3 the car runs out of petrol!
4 the balloon bursts!
5 the burglar in the armchair moves!

3 Discussion

1 What would you do to prevent burglars from entering your home and stealing things?

2 What would you do if you came home and discovered a burglar there who turned on you and attacked you?

◁ *William Heath Robinson*

De Luxe Outfit for the Cat Burglar

5

Grammar practice 1

Conditional sentences with *will/shall do . . . if/unless does*, and *had better (not) do* for warnings and advice

REVIEW

> If you move, you'll fall off.
>
> You'll fall off if you move.
>
> Move, and you'll fall off.
> (= If you move, . . .)
>
> Don't move, or (else) you'll fall off.
>
> You'd/You had better not move—
> or (else)/otherwise you'll fall off.

Note that *unless* can replace *if . . . not* in a sentence like: *He'll be all right—if the balloon doesn't burst/unless the balloon bursts.*

PRACTICE

1 Look at the cartoon on p 26 again and make as many statements as you can using the models above, for example:
If the balloon bursts, the whole thing will collapse.
The policemen had better escape soon, otherwise they won't be able to stop the burglars.

2 Make statements of warning or advice to other people with these prompts, using *If . . .* or *You'd better (not) . . .*:
go out without an umbrella/catch a cold
hurry/miss the bus
copy this down/forget it
(you) not put these things away/ (I) throw them out

3 **Game**: *Get out of that!* (see Teacher's Guide p 28)

Grammar practice 2

Conditional sentences with *would do . . . if/unless did* for advice or to describe present and future unlikely, but not impossible, situations

REVIEW

> If you did that, you'd/you would regret it.
>
> You'd/You would regret it if you did that.
>
> If I were you, I wouldn't do that.
>
> I wouldn't do that if I were you.
>
> Supposing / Suppose / Imagine } (that) you had an accident in your car, what would you do (then)?

ABOUT YOU

In pairs, ask and tell each other what would happen *or* what you would do (first) if . . .
1 you were late for school/work very often.
2 you saw a bad road accident near you.
3 you won a holiday for two in a competition.
4 there was a fire in your house/flat in the middle of the night.
5 you saw a friend shoplifting.

Vocabulary

Phrasal verbs

Unlike the verbs + adverb particles in Unit 4 in which the verbs retain their original meanings, there are many phrasal verbs in English, the meanings of which are much different from the meanings of the two parts. For example, *stand for* can mean 'represent', and has nothing to do with *stand* or *for*. Study these phrasal verbs (sometimes called 'Type 1') and then finish the sentences on the right in your own way. (Because these verbs can have other meanings, learn them in the sense given here.) These verbs take an object, but the verb and particle cannot be separated:

If I bump into him/John, I'll go into it/the matter with him.

ask after sby (= enquire about health)	Please ask after the family if/when . . .
break into (= enter by force or for robbery)	If a thief broke into that office, . . .
bump into sby (= meet by chance)	If you bump into Mary, . . .
come across sby/sthg (= meet/find by chance)	If you come across that book, . . .
get at sby (= criticise)	He was getting at me when he said . . .
get at sthg (= mean, imply)	What was she getting at when she said . . .?
get over sthg (= overcome e.g. a problem)	I think you'll get over the problem if . . .
(= recover from an illness)	He'd get over his operation quicker if . . .
go for sby (= attack, physically or verbally)	The dog went for me as . . .
go into sthg (= investigate, study carefully)	If you go into the history of it, . . .
look after sby/sthg (= care for)	You'd better look after yourself, or . . .
look into sthg (= investigate)	If you look into it carefully, . . .
make for (somewhere) (= go towards)	They were making for the river when . . .
run into sby (= meet by chance)	If you run into John, . . .
run into difficulties (= meet difficulties unexpectedly)	You'll run into difficulties if . . .
see to sthg (= put sthg right, attend to)	If you don't see to this broken lawn mower soon, . . .
stand for sthg (= represent)	Heath Robinson's name stands for . . .
take after sby (= look or behave like sby)	Who does she take after— . . . ?
take to sby (= begin to like)	You'll probably take to him if . . .
take to sthg (= get used to, begin to like)	I'm sure you'd take to jogging if . . .
turn out (to be) (= happen (to be) in the end)	The day turned out (to be) . . .

5

Exercises for homework

See if you can do these exercises in 40 minutes.

1 Reading Comprehension

Choose the word or phrase (A, B, C or D) which best completes each sentence.

1 If you ________ Mary, could you tell her I'd like to see her?
A go into B look after C run into D look into

2 You'd better ________ that broken chair as soon as you can.
A see to B get at C stand for D bump into

3 Don't move, or the dog will ________ you!
A come across B go for C take to B bump into

4 It's said that very young babies will ________ swimming like ducks to water.
A break into B turn out C take to D make for

5 John's finally ________ his operation now and is back at work.
A come across B looked after C seen to D got over

2 Use of English: Directed writing

On the right are some notes written down by a student during the lecture about Heath Robinson. Write them out in full, as if for a short magazine article, using the 'starters' and suggested joining words on the left.

The phrases 'a Heath Robinson affair' . . . . . . which . . . . . . and which . . . . . . but which . . . It is also . . . You might hear someone say . . .	'Heath Robinson affair'/'Heath Robinson contraption'—used to describe any piece of machinery—looks ingenious, complicated, unsafe—tied together with string—but works! Often used as apology when someone's got over a problem. 'A bit Heath-Robinsonish, but it'll do.'
William . . . . . . who . . . He . . . . . . who was also . . . He . . . . . . and . . .	William Heath Robinson—cartoonist, illustrator—born 1872. Took after father . . . also illustrator. Illustrated many books—became world-famous before 1914, particularly for cartoons and humorous illustrations.
His name now . . . . . . which . . . In the same way others caricatured people. . . and his inventions . . . The people . . . so . . . that they . . .	Name stands for any invention—'absurdly ingenious and impracticable'. Caricatured machinery—designed often for ridiculous purposes. People in them—so serious—add to humour.
When he . . ., he . . . . . . and . . . A good example is . . .	Died 1944—left behind kind of humour people still enjoy + word to describe complicated machines tied together with bits of string. Good example—cartoon called the 'De Luxe Outfit for the Cat Burglar'.

Oral Interview preparation

Part of the First Certificate Oral Interview is a conversation with the examiner based on a photograph. Look at this photograph and then answer the questions below.

About the photograph

1 These men, standing on a cliff-top, are about to go hang-gliding. How would you describe the hang-glider itself?
2 What are the men wearing? Why?
3 One man's facing us. What do you think he's doing? What would happen if he didn't do that?
4 How do you think the pilot will get into the air?

General

1 Do you think you could take to hang-gliding? Why?/Why not?
2 What's your favourite sport or hobby? Why do you like it?
3 People who do a sport like hang-gliding say that it's 'no more dangerous than walking along the road'. What do you think?

Unit 6

It's easy to get to from London

EXAM FOCUS:
Reading Comprehension

Read and speak

This information appeared in a National Trust Touring Guide of famous houses to visit within 60 miles of London. Read it carefully and study the map. Then do the exercises.

Chartwell, Kent: The home of Sir Winston Churchill from 1924 until the end of his life in 1965. The rooms, left as they were in his lifetime, strongly evoke the career and wide interests of this remarkable man. Every phase in his long life is represented by pictures, maps, documents, photographs, books and personal mementos which in their way summarise the history of Britain during the twentieth century. Two rooms are given over to a museum, where gifts received from all over the world are displayed, as well as the uniforms of his many offices. The house was remodelled for Sir Winston and Lady Churchill by the architect Philip Tilden; its fine position commands distant views of the Weald and terraced gardens descend towards the lake with its famous black swans. Sir Winston's garden studio containing many of his paintings is also open to visitors.
Location: 2m S of Westerham, fork left off B2026 after 1½m.
Open: House: March to end Nov: weekdays except Mon & Fri 2–6 (but open Bank Holiday Mon). Sat, Sun & Bank Holiday Mon 11–6. Tues mornings reserved for pre-booked parties only (apply to the Administrator, tel. Crockham Hill 368). Car park open from 10.30 on days when house is open. Garden & studio: April to mid-Oct: same times as house.
Admission: House & garden £1.70. Garden only 70p. Studio 40p extra (no reduction for children or parties in studio). Pre-booked parties £1.20, Tues mornings only. Dogs admitted to grounds if on lead. Indoor photography by permission only. Shop.
Refreshments: Licensed self-service restaurant (no spirits) open 10.30–5.30 on days when house is open.

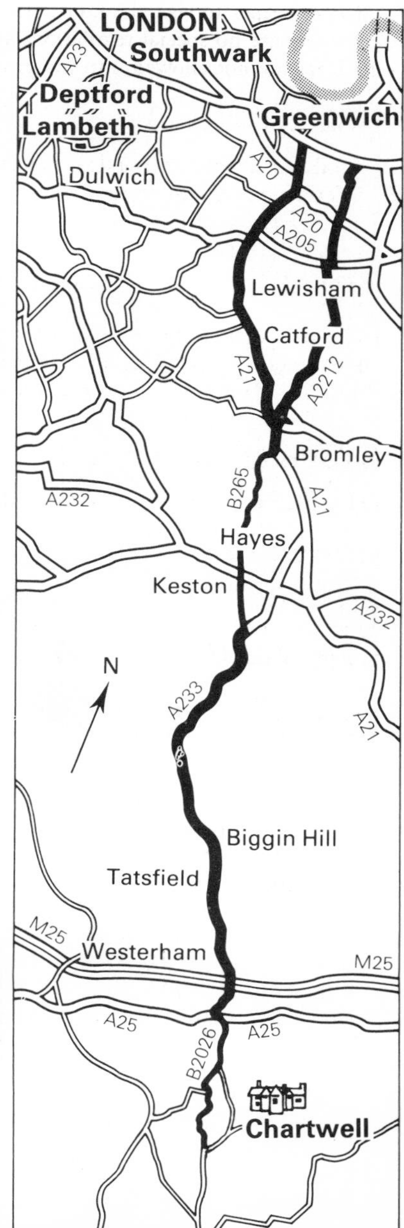

1 From the information given about Chartwell (opposite), are these statements true or false, or don't you know?

1 Everything in Chartwell is exactly as it was when Churchill lived there.
2 Books, pictures and documents show that the house is over 200 years old.
3 All you can see from the gardens is the lake.
4 The house is a short drive north of the village of Westerham.
5 You can't visit the house in December.
6 You can only visit the house on a Tuesday morning if you are in a party.
7 Car parking is free.
8 It's cheaper to visit the house if you go with a pre-booked party.
9 There are no special regulations about taking photographs in the house.
10 Dogs are not allowed into the grounds at Chartwell.

2 Role play (in pairs)

While on holiday in London you decide to visit Chartwell and go to an information bureau to ask for information. Another student plays the part of the assistant. He or she refers to the text for answers to your questions (e.g. Where is it? How do I get there by car? When is it open? How much does it cost to go in? etc.). You should *not* refer to the text.

3 In pairs or small groups, tell each other all about a large house, castle, monument or building worth visiting in your country, and explain how to get there from the nearest big town.

Grammar practice 1

Prepositions of location (*Where (at)?*) and direction (*Where to?*)

REVIEW

Here are some of the prepositions we use to say where places are or to give directions. Revise them with the intensifiers *right, almost, nearly, directly* and *straight.* Then do the exercises over the page.

Location only

It's	right / almost / nearly	at . . . near . . . next to . . . by (= next to) . . . in . . ./on . . . at the end of . . . on the corner of . . . opposite . . . in front of . . .
It's	directly	opposite . . . in front of . . .

Direction only

Go / Walk	straight	(along) / (up) / (back) to . . . by (= past) . . . through . . . on to . . . into . . . towards . . . out of . . .
Go / Walk		as far as . . .

Direction and location

Go / Walk / It's	right	along . . . down . . . up . . . across . . . past . . . over . . . under . . . (a)round . . . between . . .

6

PRACTICE

Study this map of Canterbury carefully and practise this dialogue. (You are outside East Station.)

A: Excuse me. Sorry to trouble/bother you. Where's /the Royal Museum/, please?
B: It's /in the centre of the town, on the corner of High Street and Guildhall Street/.
A: And could you tell me how to get there (from here)?
B: Yes. /It's quite a long walk, but it's quite easy to find./ This is Station Road East. /Go along here and you'll come to a big roundabout. Turn right there and walk up Castle Street. Keep going until it becomes St Margaret's. Walk on up, then turn left into the High Street and first right into Guildhall Street. The Royal Museum's on the left./ You can't really miss it.
A: Thank you very much (indeed).

Now adapt the dialogue as necessary to ask where these places are and to give directions on how to get there:

1 the Post Office; 2 the Castle; 3 the Tourist Information Centre; 4 the Cathedral; 5 West Station; 6 the Odeon Cinema; 7 Westgate Gardens; 8 the ABC Cinema

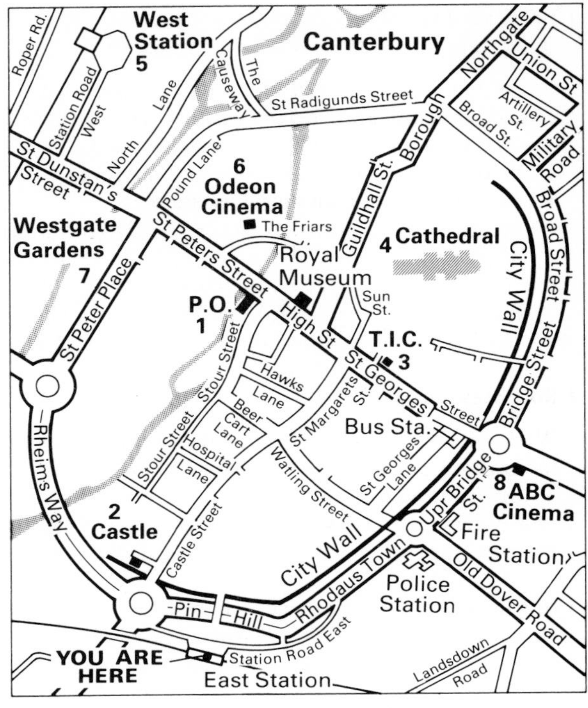

ABOUT YOU

In pairs, ask and say where places are in this town, and ask for and give directions to get to those places from the building you are in now.

Grammar practice 2

Verbs + prepositions (with special reference to location and direction)

REVIEW

Verb + preposition + object

allow for /heavy traffic/
(be) prepare(d) for /hold-ups/
watch out for /signs to London/
look (out) for /the sign which says . . ./
decide on /a route/
know of /a good road from A to B/
You must/should beware of /the by-pass/

Verb + object + preposition + object

ask sby for /a route/
show /our appreciation/ for sthg
blame sby for sthg
compare /this route/ with /that one/
discuss sthg with sby
explain sthg to sby
mistake sthg for sthg else
provide sby with /a good route/
save sby from /a lot of trouble/
supply sby with /a map/
thank sby for sthg
warn sby of/about sthg

PRACTICE

Supply the correct prepositions in this extract from a letter:

'When we explained __(1)__ you where we were heading, you were kind enough to provide us __(2)__ a good route. But you did warn us __(3)__ the road through Hightown, so at least we were prepared __(4)__ a long hold-up. We'd like to thank you __(5)__ all your help and advice.'

Vocabulary

Nouns from verbs

Nouns are formed from verbs in many ways. Some have the same form as the verb, while others add a suffix, for example *-tion, -ation, -ing* (not a gerund), or *-al.* Study these and then do the exercises.

No change

to aim—an aim	to mistake—a mistake
to blame—the blame	to rest—a rest
to delay—a delay	to stay—a stay
to drive—a drive	to travel—travel
to fine—a fine	to trouble—trouble
to garage—a garage	to walk—a walk
to hold up—a (traffic) hold-up	to work—work
to journey—a journey	

Nouns from verbs (e.g. *solution* comes from the verb *to solve*)

-tion	attention, construction, description, direction, junction, solution
-ation	accommodation, appreciation, confirmation, destination, explanation, information, operation, preparation, recommendation
-ing	belongings, a booking, a crossing, a sailing, a turning, a warning, a saving, upbringing, a recording
-al	arrival, (dis)approval, refusal, revival, survival

1 Rephrase these sentences using words from the box above and making any changes necessary.
For example:

Traffic lights *are operating* there.→ There are traffic lights in operation there.
This is an old song *they've revived.*→ This is a revival of an old song.

1 It took an hour *to journey* from X to Y.
2 They showed *they appreciated* the talk.
3 He quickly *solved* the problem.
4 We *turned* third left into Green Street.
5 They *fined* him £50 for speeding.
6 They *prepared carefully* for the journey.
7 He collected *everything that belonged to him* and left.
8 'I shan't *warn you* again,' she said.
9 He *described* the man to the policeman.
10 She *explained* the problem to us very well.

2 Game: *Make up a story* (see Teacher's Guide p 31)

6

Exercises for homework

See if you can do these exercises in 45 minutes.

1 Use of English

Read this paragraph, then for each of the numbered blank spaces supply words formed from the corresponding numbered verbs.

'The __(1)__ of the new road system which is under __(2)__ at the moment is to prevent the long __(3)__ caused by vehicles waiting to take the __(4)__ to the right at the __(5)__ of High Street and Mill Road in the __(6)__ of Hightown.' This __(7)__ was given yesterday by the Roads Committee Chairman after repeated expressions of __(8)__ by members of the Council. He went on, 'There will unfortunately be __(9)__ while the __(10)__ is being carried out, and temporary traffic lights will be in __(11)__, but we are sure that the __(12)__ is the right one. And we have paid great __(13)__ to the __(14)__ made by the Town Planning Department.' Further detailed __(15)__ about the new road system can be obtained from the Town Hall.

1 AIM
2 CONSTRUCT
3 DELAY
4 TURN
5 JOIN
6 DIRECT
7 EXPLAIN
8 DISAPPROVE
9 HOLD UP
10 WORK
11 OPERATE
12 SOLVE
13 ATTEND
14 RECOMMEND
15 INFORM

2 Use of English: Directed writing

As if part of a letter, write three short paragraphs about Chartwell. Refer to the text and map on p 31 and use the 'starters', questions and joining words below.

Chartwell is a beautiful house in Kent.	
Who did it belong to? For how long? What is it full of?	 . . . and . . .
Is there a museum? What does it contain? Is there a studio? What does it contain?	There is also . . . which . . . . . . and . . . which . . .
It's quite easy to get there from London by car.	
Which direction do you go from the centre of London? Where do you head for? On which 'A' road?	Go . . . . . . and . . . or . . .
Which 'B' road do you take from Bromley? To where? Which 'A' road does it join?	Then . . . . . . until . . .
In which direction do you follow that? Towards where and past what?	Follow . . .
Which road do you take out of Westerham? After how many miles do you fork left?	Take . . . . . . and . . .
How much does it cost to see the house and gardens? Although the studio is extra, is it worth it or not?	When you get there, ... and although . . .
I must warn you about one thing.	
Must you check the opening times carefully before or after you go?	Check . . .

TEST: READING COMPREHENSION

Time: 20 minutes

Read this passage carefully. Then choose which you think is the best suggested answer or way of finishing the statement in each item below—A, B, C or D. Write your answers on a separate piece of paper.

As I jogged over the bridge and round the corner on my regular early morning run, he was standing opposite the jeweller's looking extremely suspicious. But the moment he saw me, instead of trying to avoid me, he came straight across the road as I drew level with the jeweller's. Halfway across he began addressing me: 'I thought you said you were going to . . .'—but his voice trailed away as he received no reply and no sign of recognition from me. It was quite obvious that he had mistaken me for someone else. But he started up again as if nothing had happened. 'Good morning,' he said. 'Nice to bump into someone so early. Someone to talk to. I've taken to talking to myself on this job.'

I loathe meeting people when I'm out early, and I was almost out of breath, so I just paused in my stride, nodded in a friendly manner, and went on up the road. The stranger had spoken quietly, and quite slowly. And I had noticed that he was well dressed, too. But if *he* looked suspicious dressed like that at that time of the morning, what about *me*? I was in a track suit, with a sloppy old sweater round my shoulders and a beret on my head. As to his odd remark about 'talking to himself on the job', I hadn't paid any attention to it, although now it began to worry me. Was he perhaps a plain clothes policeman? At the time I somehow felt he was.

I had just turned the corner into the High Street when I heard the sound of breaking glass somewhere behind me, and I thought the sound came from the street I had just left. I stopped dead and almost without thinking looked back around the corner. The 'stranger' was not there, but almost immediately an alarm bell in the jeweller's began ringing furiously.

I found out later that a burglar had broken into the jeweller's shop and stolen watches and rings worth about £5,000. The police are still looking into the matter, but I'm afraid to go and tell them what I know now because they might even suspect *me* of committing the crime, and it might be difficult for me to prove my innocence. After all, I haven't offered my assistance as a witness, and the only other person around that morning was the 'stranger' who had spoken to me.

1 The writer
A always goes past the jeweller's.
B goes jogging regularly.
C meets a few people every morning.
D often sees a policeman in the High Street.

2 The stranger
A was waiting for someone to talk to.
B hated talking to people in the morning.
C thought he recognised the writer.
D had bumped into the writer before.

3 Why did the stranger seem suspicious?
A He was far too friendly.
B He was dressed too well for that time.
C He was about to go into the jeweller's.
D He talked to himself a lot.

4 If the writer hadn't turned the corner,
A he might have been badly injured.
B the stranger wouldn't have broken the window.
C he wouldn't have heard the alarm bell.
D he would have seen what happened.

5 The writer hasn't told the police what little he knows because
A he is afraid they might arrest him.
B he thinks the stranger is innocent.
C the stranger hasn't asked him to be a witness.
D the burglar didn't steal very much.

Unit 7

How far do you let your children go?

EXAM FOCUS:
Composition (Description)

Read and speak

Read this article carefully.
Then do the exercises.

The Taylors with Wendy, Susan and Ian

'Our children have had a free rein. It's worked with the girls—my only worry is Ian'

When it comes to bringing up children, some experts say discipline produces a happy, well-balanced child; others believe that freedom brings greater understanding. But can anyone really tell you what's best for *your* child?

PEARL TAYLOR of Clapham, London, and her barman husband Buck, have been married for 26 years. They have four children: June, 25, and Wendy, 22, both married, Susan, 18, and Ian, 11. They've brought them up in a remarkably free atmosphere.

'Our children have had a free rein and we've never had any trouble with the girls. Nothing's ever locked away. There's plenty of alcohol around and we say to the children: "If you want a drink, help yourself." Funnily enough, they hardly touch it. Their friends are always welcome, and if they want a party, we leave them to it. Yet they've never used our drink—or touched drugs.

'Money is always left lying around. Buck tells the children to help themselves if they want something, but they're never greedy. Ian recently came back from a school trip and handed back £1.70 of the £4 we gave him.

'I've always let the girls go out as they like, to dances, discos or weekends away with friends. They never say: "Can I go?" They say: "I am going," because they know I won't mind. Sometimes I set a time for them to come in, but I'd never argue. Of

1 In pairs, ask and tell each other:

1 how long Pearl and Buck have been married.
2 how the Taylors have brought up their children.
3 if they have always locked alcohol away.
4 what the Taylors do about giving their children money.
5 what the Taylors' attitude is to the girls going dancing or going away.
6 what they thought when Wendy wanted to get married, and what they did.
7 how Pearl Taylor was brought up.
8 if Pearl is strict with her children.
9 which daughter went to Sardinia, and why.
10 what Pearl said about it.
11 how Pearl describes her children.
12 why Pearl worries about Ian.
13 if Pearl has ever smacked him, and how she feels about doing it.
14 what Wendy thinks of the way she was brought up.
15 what she said about the girl whose parents were very strict.

Continue to ask more questions in the same way about the rest of the article.

2 Role play

Imagine you are one of the Taylor children still living at home. Tell another student about the way your parents treat you and the way they have brought you up. What's their attitude to
1 drink and drugs?
2 money?
3 your going out?
4 sex?
5 bringing your friends home?

3 Discussion/About you

If you are still living with your parents, how have they brought you up? Strictly?—or have they given you 'a free rein'? If you have left home, how did your parents bring you up? Strictly?—or did they give you 'a free rein'?

---

course I worry. But I'd never let them see it. They know, anyway. They always say where they're going without me having to ask.

'Buck and I thought Wendy was too young to get married at 18, but if we'd said no, she would only have resented it.

'There's nothing we've felt we couldn't discuss in front of the children and sex comes up naturally. I've always been able to trust the girls with their boy-friends.

'If you are strict, children will go against you, but they won't if you show trust in them. My mother died when I was young, and I was brought up very strictly by an aunt. Now I want my children to have everything I never had. I wouldn't have dreamed of objecting when Susan went to work in Sardinia—I wish I'd been able to do the same.

'They are all considerate and independent. Perhaps in some families children would take advantage of our kind of freedom—we're lucky.

'My only worry is Ian. Being the only boy and the last one at home, he is very spoiled. He usually doesn't want to eat the same food as us, so I get something different for him.

'He's getting a bit cheeky and he needs a jolly good hiding at times. I've even had to stop letting him have all his friends in because they jumped on the furniture. Now they only come in one at a time.

'It upsets me, having to discipline Ian. Whenever I've smacked him, I go away and cry afterwards. He needs his father's hand, but with his job, Buck's only here at weekends. I'm hoping things will be better when Ian goes to secondary school. It has a reputation for being strict.'

Daughter Wendy Taylor enjoys the honest and open family relationship—but believes discipline must be used when necessary.

'There's never been a division here between us, the children, and them, the adults. My husband couldn't get over seeing all of us join in decorating the flat, or go out to dinner together. Freedom has made us close.

'I went out every night, probably only to a friend's house. I was never told not to. I came home at the right time, although I knew I wouldn't really get told off if I didn't.

'I knew a girl whose parents were very strict and it made her a liar. I told my mum if we were going to a dance, but she would pretend she was coming over to my house.

'I remember when I wanted to smoke. Mum said "no" but I kept on till she said yes. Other kids did it behind their parents' back, but it would have upset me to do anything sneaky. I still hate letting anyone down. My parents have been right. For instance, if the drink had been locked away it would have been a challenge for us to get at it. I've never wanted to do anything to upset my parents. Mum and Dad have always put us first, and I think this consideration in turn comes to you.

'Though I think Ian is getting out of hand. When I have children, I want to be able to tell them just once, and that's it. Sometimes I think if I could smack Ian on the bottom, he would stop. But perhaps it wouldn't work.'

7

Grammar practice 1

Present Perfect Simple (*has/have done*) and Simple Past (*did*)

REVIEW

Compare the ways people talk about their past (recent and distant):

Someone in his/her teens and still living with parents

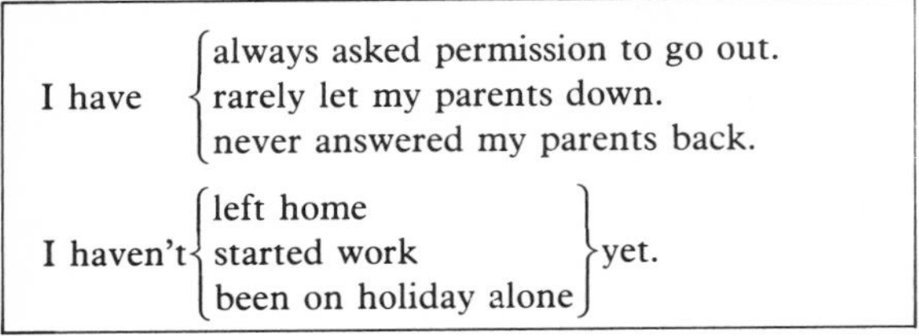

I've { been at my present school / had a part-time job / been able to go out to /discos/ } since { /1978/. / last /May/. / I was /12/. } for { (/5/) years. / a long time. / ages.

Someone older who has left home

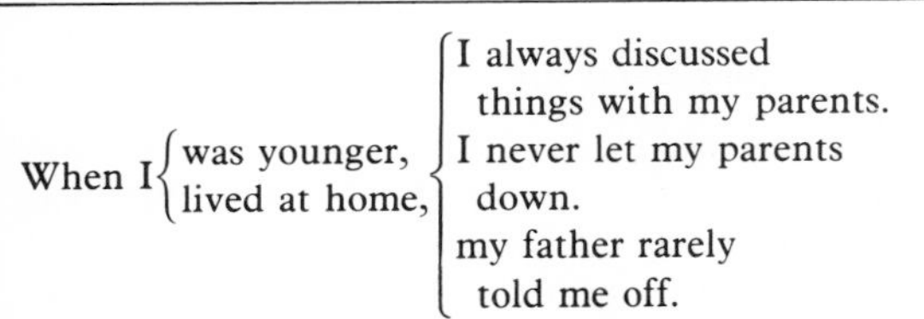

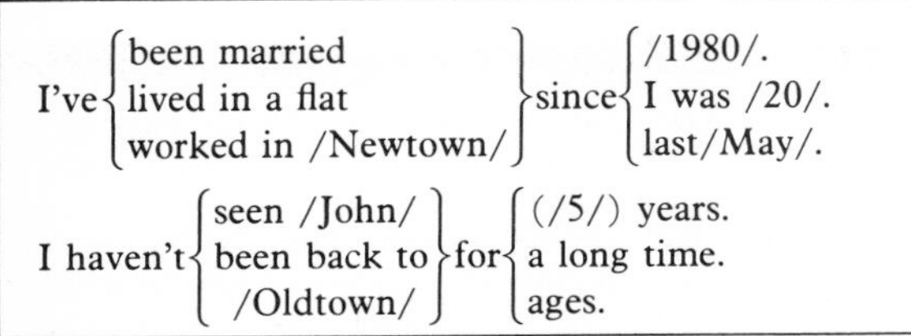

ABOUT YOU

In pairs or small groups, discuss your upbringing.
a) If you are still at school, how have your parents brought you up? What have they (always/never) done for/to you? What have you (not) done for/to them?

b) If you have left home, do you think your parents brought you up well? What did they (always/rarely/never) do for/to you? What did you do for/to them?

Grammar practice 2

More irregular verbs

REVIEW

Study these verbs and then do the exercise below.

bet bet bet bid bid bid cost cost cost The following verbs operate in the same way: burst cast cut hit hurt let put quit set shut split spread	sell tell	sold told	sold told
	become come run	became came ran	become come run
	shake take	shook took	shaken taken

ABOUT YOU

Using irregular verbs as much as you can from those above and from Units 1 and 2, ask and tell each other about past experiences with this model:

A: Have you ever /sung in a choir/?
B: No, I haven't./No, never./No, (strangely enough) I've never done that.
or Yes, (of course) I have.
A: Oh? When was that?/When did you last /sing in one/?
B: /About 10 years ago.//It was about 10 years ago, when we lived in Newtown/.

Vocabulary

Phrasal verbs

There are a large number of phrasal verbs which are sometimes called 'Type 3'. Some are practised here, and more in Units 8 and 9. Study those below (with their meanings), then rephrase the sentences below with phrasal verbs. Like those in Unit 5 (p 28), these verbs take an object, but the verb and particle can be separated. The particle is stressed when it follows the object:

1 They brought their children up very well. *They brought them up very well.*
2 They brought up their children very well. (BUT NOT They brought up them.)

Those marked '!' can only be used in pattern 1 in the meaning given here.

!answer sby back (= reply rudely)
put sthg back (+ time) (= delay by + time)
pay sby back (= repay; have revenge)

break sthg down (= overcome; analyse)
!cut sby down to size (= reduce sby to his/her true importance)
let sby down (= disappoint; not support)
!run sby down (= criticise)
turn sby/sthg down (= refuse)

back sby up (= support)
bring sby up (= raise, care for, educate)
!call/ring sby up (= telephone)
hold sthg up (= delay)
make sthg up (= invent e.g. a story)

break sthg off (= cancel; interrupt)
call sthg off (= cancel)
cut sby/sthg off (= interrupt, stop)
let sby off (= not punish)
let sthg off (= explode e.g. a firework)
put sthg off (= postpone)
put sby off (= discourage; distract)
!set sby off (= make/persuade sby to start laughing/talking)
shake sthg off (= escape from; get rid of e.g. a cold)
!take sthg off (= deduct; give oneself a holiday (from work))
take sby off (= imitate, impersonate)
tell sby off (= scold, blame)

1 I've never *replied rudely* to my father.
2 His illness *delayed* his education *by* a year.
3 I *repaid* him for what he did to me.
4 We shall have to *analyse* these figures.
5 I hate *disappointing* my friends.
6 Her teachers often *criticise* her.
7 She can't *refuse* a request for help.
8 His wife has always *supported* him in his career.
9 I was *raised* in a small village.
10 A friend *telephoned* me last night.
11 He often *invented* stories when he was a boy.
12 We had to *cancel* the party last week.
13 The teacher *didn't punish* me when I stole a pencil.
14 But she *scolded* me.
15 I once *exploded* a firework in class.
16 Let's *postpone* the meeting till Monday.
17 I laughed a lot at school, and one girl always *made me do it* by making faces.
18 I've had flu for a month now: I just can't *get rid of* it.
19 She *gave herself a holiday* last Friday.
20 He *did an impersonation of* the President.

7

Exercise for homework

Study section: The descriptive/narrative composition

The First Certificate Paper 2 often contains a descriptive composition and a narrative which we shall deal with in Unit 12. If you were asked, however, to describe your upbringing and/or your early childhood, your composition would not be a straightforward description or series of events. It would be something between the two. A composition describing a period of your life, then, with memories, impressions and so on, is best planned like the example below. Study the subject, the plan and ideas, and the composition. Then plan and write your own composition on this subject.

SUBJECT

'Choose a skill or special ability that you possess. Give an account of when you first noticed you had this skill or ability, and how it developed.'

Plan and ideas

The following plan and ideas would produce this account, slightly adapted from an account written by Mike Yarwood, a famous English impersonator.

Introduction

1 I can take people off—started when young.

2 Easy to imitate people.

Development

3 Popular with family and friends; not with teachers.

4 Impersonated teachers in playground and in class.

5 Teachers caught me—extra homework. Didn't put me off.

6 Sometimes felt teachers were pleased with my ability to take off other pupils and teachers.

Conclusion

7 Example—farewell party.

8 Teachers' reactions—and people's reactions since.

I believe I have always been able to 'take people off'. It certainly started at a very early age, because I always seemed to be able to imitate the voice and mannerisms of almost anyone I met.

It made me quite popular with my family and my school-friends, but sometimes not quite so popular with others. The more important 'others' were the teachers at the last school I attended. Without consciously thinking about it, I found it quite easy to 'take off' most of them; all teachers have exaggerated mannerisms, and our teachers were no exceptions. My friends were delighted and I had to do my impersonations for them in the playground. It must have gone to my head somewhat, because I allowed them to persuade me to do impressions in class when the particular teacher taking us did not appear to be watching.

As you know, all teachers also seem to have eyes in the back of their head, and I was often caught. This led to unpleasant things like extra homework and other punishments, but this still did not put me off, because I could not resist the urge to mimic what I saw. However, I was quite sure that, when I was not impersonating them, a lot of the teachers were quite pleased with my ability to impersonate their colleagues.

My belief was borne out when the time came for me to leave the school, at the age of 14. There was a little farewell party for the school-leavers. Suddenly, the restraint of the past two or three years was broken down. The teachers actually encouraged, indeed insisted, that I did my impersonations of the staff. It was an amazing afternoon. I took off all the teachers one by one. Each 'take-off' set everybody off laughing and clapping, but I noticed that the 'victim' in each case stayed strangely silent. And I have noticed ever since then that, although most people enjoy impersonations of others, they do not like being impersonated themselves.

TEST: COMPOSITION

Time: 40 minutes

Write **one only** of the following composition exercises. Your answer must follow exactly the instructions given, and must be about 120 words in length.

Either

1 Write an account of an event in your childhood which shows how your parents brought you up. First of all, briefly describe how your parents tried to bring you up, and then relate the event to that.

Or

2 'Children nowadays are not brought up strictly enough.' What do you think? Give reasons for the opinions you express, perhaps referring to your own upbringing.

(*Note:* For this Test you may refer back to Units in this coursebook to help you.)

Unit 8
The Loch Ness Monster: what could it be?

EXAM FOCUS:
Use of English

Read and speak

Perhaps you have heard of the Loch Ness Monster? Loch Ness is a large, deep lake in Scotland, and since a road was constructed along the side of it in 1933, hundreds of people have seen, or think they have seen, something strange in the loch. That 'something' is called the Loch Ness Monster. This photo was taken in 1934 by a London surgeon and many people believe that it *is* the Monster. But what do *you* think it might be? A black swan perhaps? The large branch of a tree floating in the water? Could it be a seal or a fish of some kind? Or is it really the Loch Ness Monster?

Read this report of a sighting by Mr Torquil MacLeod, an artist and full-time investigator at Loch Ness. Then do the exercises.

At approximately 3.30–3.45 p.m. on February 28th, 1960, I was driving towards Fort Augustus from Invermoriston when, approximately 2½ miles *from* Invermoriston, I had occasion to pull up, and my attention was attracted by a slight movement upon the opposite shore (there is no road along this 8-mile stretch). The weather was dull and overcast, with a drizzle drifting down the loch.

Upon turning my binoculars on the moving object, I saw a large grey-black mass . . . and at the front there was what looked like an enormous elephant's trunk. Paddles were visible on both sides, but only at what must have been the rear end, and it was this end . . . which tapered off into the water. The animal was on a steep slope, . . . the 'trunk' being at the top and to the left, and the tail at the bottom, in the water, to the right.

I was able to pinpoint both my own and the animal's position on the map, the distance between us being approximately 1,700 yards.

For about 8 or 9 minutes the animal remained quite still, but for its 'trunk' (I assume neck, although I could not recognise a head as such) which occasionally moved from side to side with a slight up-and-down motion—just like a snake about to strike—but quite slowly. It seemed to be scanning the shores of the loch in each direction.

In the end it made a sort of half-jump, half-lurch to the left, its 'trunk' coming right round until it was facing me, then it flopped into the water and appeared to go straight down—so it must be very deep close inshore at that point. As it turned I saw distinctly a large squarish-ended flipper

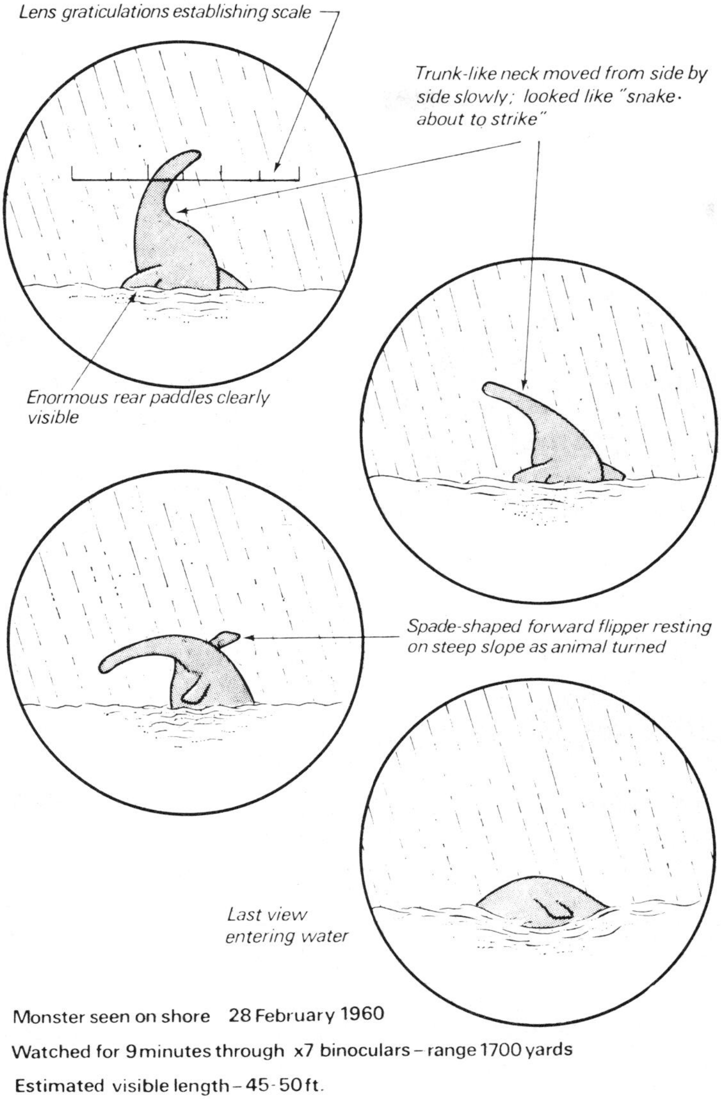

Lens graticulations establishing scale

Trunk-like neck moved from side by side slowly; looked like "snake about to strike"

Enormous rear paddles clearly visible

Spade-shaped forward flipper resting on steep slope as animal turned

Last view entering water

Monster seen on shore 28 February 1960

Watched for 9 minutes through x7 binoculars – range 1700 yards

Estimated visible length – 45-50 ft.

Figure 17 Sketch drawn by Torquil MacLeod of his sighting, 28 February 1960.

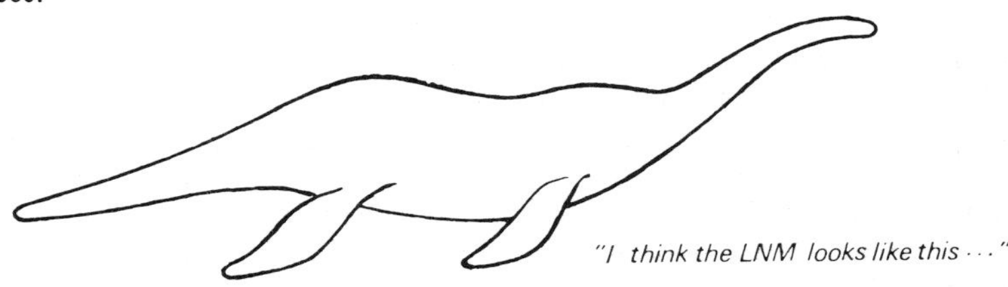
"I think the LNM looks like this . . ."

Figure 18 Torquil MacLeod's impression of the Monster.

forward of the big rear paddles, or flippers—call them what you will, but *not* legs. I did not see the end of the tail at any time, but the animal looked something like this (*see left*).

My binoculars are Ross 7 × 50 and have graticulations—degrees and minutes of arc as hairlines—and I looked up the Almanac tables and was able to establish the animal's length at approximately 45 ft, possibly 50 ft or so in length—*the visible parts only, remember.* I have no idea of the length of its tail and its neck.

That's about all I can tell you, and conditions were by no means ideal. I think the L.N.M. looks like this (*see left*).

---

1 In pairs, ask and tell each other about Mr MacLeod's experience. Ask and say:

1 when it happened, and where.
2 what he was doing and what he did.
3 what the weather was like.
4 what the 'animal' looked like.

2 Discussion

What do you think Torquil MacLeod must (or might) have seen? Why do you say that? What do *you* think the Loch Ness Monster could be? Why?

8

Grammar practice 1

Modal verbs *can, must, may, might, could, should,* etc.

REVIEW AND PRACTICE (Present)

Two people are looking at this scene. There seems to be something in the water. Read the models, then cover and repeat them looking only at the picture.

Ability	I can see something, but I can't make out what it is.
Permission	Can/May I borrow your binoculars? Yes, of course you can/may.
Obligation	We must try to get a photo of it. We have (got) to tell someone about it.
Assumption	It must be a large fish of some kind. It can't be the 'monster'.
Possibility	It may/might/could be a large fish (but I don't know for sure).
Advice/ Suggestion	(I think/believe/feel (that)) we ought to/should keep quiet about this. We shouldn't tell anyone about this. I don't think/believe we should say anything about this to anyone.

REVIEW AND PRACTICE (Past)

The same two people saw something similar yesterday. Read what they say, then cover and repeat the statements.

Ability	I couldn't believe my eyes when I saw it.
Obligation	We had to tell someone, didn't we?
Assumption	It must have been a large sea bird. It can't have been the 'monster'.
Possibility	What we saw yesterday may/might/could have been the branch of a tree.
Regret	We ought to/should have taken a photo of it.

Grammar practice 2

'Stative' verbs *look, seem, appear, look like* and *look as if/as though*

REVIEW

Appearance

He looks/seems/appears ill.

He seems/appears to be ill.

He looks like my cousin.

He looks as if/as though he's had some bad news.

PRACTICE

1 Practise this dialogue and then adapt it as necessary to talk about the other people in the same way.

A: Look at Sue. She must be ill
B: Well, she might/could be ill, I suppose.
A: I'm sure she can't be well. She looks dreadful. She looks as if she's got a headache or something.
B: Yes, she does.

2 Now cover the pictures and practise this dialogue, adapting it to talk about the people as if you saw them yesterday.

A: Did you see Sue? She must have been ill.
B: Yes, she can't have been well. In fact, she looked dreadful.
A: I thought she looked as if she had a headache.
B: Yes, I thought so, too.

Vocabulary

Phrasal verbs (cont.)

Here are some more 'Type 3' phrasal verbs. Refer back to p 40 for the patterns in which these verbs are used. Those marked '!' can only be used in pattern 1 (see p 40). Study the verbs, then play one of the games below.

get sthg across (=communicate, explain)
put sthg across (=communicate, explain; perform sthg well)

bring sthg about (=cause to happen)

!give sby away (=betray)
!give sthg away (=make known, intentionally or unintentionally)

bear sthg/sby out (=confirm, support)
carry sthg out (=fulfil, complete, do)
find sthg/sby out (=discover)
knock sby out (=eliminate; make unconscious)
leave sby/sthg out (=omit)
make sthg/sby out (=understand; see)
pick sby/sthg out (=choose)
think sthg out (=find a solution)
try sthg out (=test)
work sthg out (=solve)

hold sby/sthg up (=delay)
!look sby up (=visit)
look sthg up (=consult sthg in a reference book)
!pull sby up (=stop, interrupt)
wind sthg up (=bring to an end)

Game: *You mean . . . ?* (See Teacher's Guide p 36) or *Make up a story* (See Teacher's Guide p 31)

8

Exercises for homework

See if you can do these exercises in 60 minutes.

1 Reading Comprehension

Choose the word or phrase (A, B, C or D) which best completes each sentence.

1 It's a true story. If you want confirmation, Bob will ____ me ____.
A find . . . out B give . . . away C bear . . . out D pull . . . up

2 The weather is so bad we'll have to ____ the match until tomorrow.
A leave out B put off C make out D tell off

3 Can you try to ____ what time the concert starts on Saturday?
A pull up B pick out C hold up D find out

4 What ____ the thief ____ was the fact that he had left his fingerprints everywhere!
A brought . . . about B gave . . . away C picked . . . out D let . . . off

5 He might ____ his ideas much better if he planned what he wanted to say.
A put across B carry out C look up D make out

2 Use of English

Read the following passage and for each numbered blank supply *one* suitable word.

'If I've worked this __(1)__ properly,' John said, 'the answer __(2)__ be fifteen. But I __(3)__ have made a mistake somewhere. Sometimes I'm good at maths, sometimes I'm awful. My maths teacher just can't __(4)__ me out!'

'Well,' said Jane, 'I think fifteen __(5)__ be wrong! I'm still __(6)__ it out, and I'll let you know soon what *I* think it __(7)__ to be. But I'm sure the answer's not fifteen, What do *you* think, Alison?'

'__(8)__ me out of it,' said Alison. 'It looks as __(9)__ you two will solve it between you. Anyway, I always have to __(10)__ up the answers in the back of the book!'

3 Use of English: Directed writing

Read the eye-witness report of the Loch Ness Monster again (pp 43–44) and write a brief account of Torquil MacLeod's experience (in about 120–150 words) as if for a newpaper report the day after the event. Give the article a suitable headline (title) and begin like this:

Was the thing that Mr Torquil MacLeod saw yesterday afternoon the Loch Ness Monster? It might have been.

He was driving . . .

TEST: USE OF ENGLISH

Time: 25 minutes

Using the information given in the following conversation, continue each of the two paragraphs below. Use no more than 50 words for each paragraph. Write your answer on a separate piece of paper.

PETER: Did you read that report from the Himalayas in yesterday's paper about the abominable snowman?

RAY: No, I didn't. But it's the old 'yeti' story again, is it?

PETER: Yes. A climber on this latest Everest expedition says that he saw what looked like a large ape. They were about 4,000 metres up when they saw it, he and another climber.

RAY: Oh, yes. What did it look like?

PETER: Well, it must have been enormous. According to their description, the creature was about three metres tall, had a white face, and the rest of its body seemed to be covered with dark reddish hair. They said it looked as if it was walking upright all the time.

RAY: I find all these stories almost impossible to believe. How could a creature survive in the snow and ice up in the Himalayas? By the way, did the climbers manage to take any photos?

PETER: Unfortunately not. By the time they got out a camera, the 'yeti' had gone.

RAY: So nothing to back their story up—not even photos of its footprints!

PETER: No. Almost immediately, according to the report, there was a bad snowstorm. But they obviously saw something strange. The creature had very long arms, they said. Almost down to its knees. Just like others that have been seen.

RAY: I still don't believe it. I know that some quite famous mountaineers have photographed unusual footprints in the snow, but they've usually turned out to be the tracks of bears or wolves.

PETER: I admit that, but not all of them have been explained that easily. And this 'thing' couldn't have been a bear or a wolf. It was too big, and walking upright.

RAY: It might have been a 'sadhu'. In fact, it probably was.

PETER: What's a 'sadhu'?

RAY: A 'sadhu' is a Hindu holy man. They often live in altitudes up to 5,000 metres and often go naked, or almost naked. And they let their hair grow long.

PETER: That still doesn't mean that there isn't such a thing as a 'yeti'. After all, I'm sure scientists haven't discovered *every* creature on earth yet.

RAY: True, but there is a large monkey in the Himalayas, too. It's called a 'langur', and what your climbers saw could well have been one of those.

PETER: But apparently the Sherpas saw it too, and their story bears out what the climbers said they saw.

RAY: I'm afraid that doesn't convince me, either. The 'yeti' seems to be part of their religion and mythology—so of course anything they see can be a 'yeti'.

PETER: But to go back to the question of footprints for a moment, some have been photographed in recent years which cannot be explained.

RAY: Yes, I know, you're right. But I still think it's strange that no one has ever photographed or shot one of these things.

Peter seems convinced that 'yetis' exist. . . .

Ray, on the other hand, does not believe that 'yetis' exist. . . .

Unit 9
What I'd really like . . .

EXAM FOCUS:
Listening Comprehension

Look, listen, write and speak

1 Listen to three people discussing this menu in a restaurant and then giving their order to the waitress. As you listen, write down the complete order that the waitress took back to the kitchen.

The Old Windmill Restaurant
25 Green Street *Tel:* 397421

MENU

3-course business lunch £3.75

STARTERS
Fruit Juice
Soup of the day
Home-made Paté
Egg Mayonnaise

MAIN COURSE
Steak and Kidney Pie
Roast Lamb
Roast Beef and Yorkshire Pudding
Fried Fillet of Plaice

Beef, Ham or Chicken Salad

All main courses served
with vegetables of the day

DESSERT

Apple Pie and Cream
Trifle
Assorted Ice Cream

OR

Cheese and Biscuits
(Cheddar, Stilton
Edam or Camembert)

Coffee

Prices include VAT but not service.
Gratuities at your own discretion.

2 Role play
(*Group of 4: 3 customers + 1 waiter/waitress*)

Using the same kind of language that you heard on the tape, discuss what you would like from this menu, and then give your orders to the waiter or waitress.

9

Grammar practice 1

Expressing wants and needs, and making requests

REVIEW

Practise these patterns with the items below. You are in a general store:

Stating wants and needs

I (really) want/need I'd (really) like I'm (really) looking for	some brown sugar

What	I really need/want I'd really like I'm really looking for	is a bottle of red wine.

Making requests

May/Might/Can/Could I have a tube of toothpaste, please?

I wonder if Do you think	I	might could	have a melon?

I don't suppose I could have some sugar, could I?

You wouldn't have I don't suppose you'd have	any brown sugar by any chance, would you?

bottle of white wine   bananas   French coffee   rice   tins of soup   spaghetti   soap   black shoepolish   Indian tea   Cheddar cheese

PRACTICE

Practise asking for the following things in the following places:

1 *In an accommodation bureau:*
a small flat—living room, bedroom, kitchen, bathroom

2 *In a travel agency:*
a week's holiday in /Paris/ for four (two adults, two children)

3 *In a clothes shop:*
WOMEN a /jacket and skirt/ with blouse to match
MEN a lightweight summer suit—blue—not too expensive

Grammar practice 2

Reporting requests and demands

REVIEW

'I'd like roast beef, please.'
→He says (that) he'd like roast beef.

'Can I have roast beef, please?'

→He wants to know	if whether	he can have roast beef.

'I need some soap'

→He	told me said	(that) he needed some soap.

'Can I have some soap, please?'

→He	wanted to know asked (me)	if whether	he could have some soap.

PRACTICE

Report the following, beginning with the words in brackets:

1 'I'm looking for a dress.' (*She said . . .*)
2 'I'd like some grey socks.' (*He says . . .*)
3 'Can I have a glass of water?' (*She asked . . .*)
4 'I wonder if they have any melon?' (*She wondered . . .*)
5 'Might I have a vanilla ice cream?' (*He wants to know . . .*)
6 'I want a glass of wine.' (*He told me . . .*)
7 'What I really want is a glass of water.' (*She said that . . .*)
8 'Can I have some sugar, please?' (*She wanted to know . . .*)

Grammar practice 3

Passing on demands and requests

REVIEW

Please tell {him / her} (that) I'd like beef.
→'He'd/She'd like beef, please.'

Please tell {him / her} to take it away.
→'Take it away (please).'

Please ask {him / her} {if / whether} I might have beef.
→'Might he/she have beef, please?'

ROLE PLAY

'Please interpret for me'

In groups of four, role-play the restaurant scene again (p 50), *but this time*, while one student plays the part of the English-speaking waiter/waitress, two others speak English, and the third customer speaks in his or her own language. The other two between them interpret for the waiter/waitress and the third friend.

Vocabulary

Phrasal verbs (cont.)

Here are some more 'Type 3' phrasal verbs. Like those on pp 40 and 46, most can be used in either pattern—*1 May I turn the radio up?* or *2 May I turn up the radio?*—except where marked 1 or 2, when they are *usually* used in that particular pattern. Study the verbs, then rephrase the sentences below using phrasal verbs.

1 keep/put sthg by (= reserve, put aside)

lay sthg in (= store)
run sthg in (= use a new machine carefully)
take sthg in (= understand)
take sby in (= deceive)
throw sthg in (= supply as an extra without a charge)

1 get sthg over (= finish)
run sby over (= knock down, in traffic)
2 go/run through/over sthg (= rehearse, read quickly)
take sthg over (= assume responsibility for)

1 bring sby round (= persuade)

call sthg/sby up (= mobilise)
1 catch sby up (= come up from behind, draw level with)
do sthg up (= repair, redecorate)
draw sthg up (= compile e.g. a list)
get sthg up (= organise)
mix sby/sthg up (= confuse)
set sthg up (= establish)
2 step up sthg (= increase)
take sthg up (= start e.g. a new hobby)
turn sthg up (= increase the volume of)

1 Could you *reserve* this book for me?
2 I couldn't *understand* all of it.
3 Could we *finish* the meeting soon?
4 May I *read* your orders again *quickly?*
5 She's *assumed responsibility for* my job.
6 They've *mobilised* all young men over eighteen.
7 I must *redecorate* the kitchen soon.
8 Please don't *confuse* our orders.
9 Do you think you could *increase* production?
10 You're never too old to *start* a new sport.

9

Exercises for homework

See if you can do these exercises in 60 minutes.

1 Use of English

Finish each of the following sentences in such a way that it means exactly the same as the sentence printed before it.

1 Could I have another piece of cake, please?
I don't suppose ....

2 I'm really looking for something a little more interesting.
What ....

3 Might I have a clean knife, please?
I wonder ....

4 Have they got any seats for Saturday night's performance by any chance?
They wouldn't have ....

5 Would she like her steak well done? Please ask her.
Please ask ....

6 'Can we go through the figures again?' he asked.
He wanted to know ....

7 She'd really like a glass of ice-cold water.
What ....

8 I'm quite sure the vegetables weren't fresh.
The vegetables can't ....

9 John thinks they probably missed the bus.
John thinks they must ....

10 You started work here last August, didn't you?
You've ....

2 Composition: Dialogue

(Later in the course we shall practise writing the kinds of dialogues you might be expected to write in the Composition Paper 2. This is an exercise which will begin to help you.)
Write a dialogue between a woman customer and an assistant in a watchmaker's and jeweller's shop. The woman wants a wristwatch. Begin like this, giving the name of each speaker followed by the words spoken:

ASSISTANT: Good morning, madam. Can I help you?
MRS QUICK: Good morning. Yes, I'm looking for a wristwatch. What I really want is something small and neat, and not too expensive.

Then continue the dialogue using these prompts:

ASSISTANT: of course. /wonder—you—look—these?
MRS QUICK: may I ask—how much?
ASSISTANT: certainly. /range—price—£50–£100.
MRS QUICK: no—sorry—far too expensive. /wouldn't have—about £20?
ASSISTANT: well, yes—this—£19.99.
MRS QUICK: exactly what—want. /you think—keep it by—me? /You see—never carry money!

TEST: LISTENING COMPREHENSION

Time: approx. 10 minutes

You will hear one passage twice (on cassette or read by the teacher), and you will be given time to choose your answers to the five questions below. Before you listen to the passage for the first time, read the questions and suggested answers below carefully. Read them again as you listen and before the second reading and choose which you think is the correct answer (A, B, C or D). Write your answers on a separate piece of paper. Check your answers while you are listening to the passage for the second time.

---

1 By profession, Uncle Janus was really
- A an accountant.
- B a diplomat.
- C a tailor.
- D a salesman.

2 Uncle Janus always
- A argued with his customers.
- B told his customers they were wrong.
- C persuaded his customers he was right.
- D spoke rudely to his customers.

3 Uncle Janus had to do a good job because
- A he was afraid his customers would go somewhere else.
- B he knew that he had to make a good profit.
- C his customers knew exactly what they wanted.
- D otherwise, his customers would run him over.

4 The man who walked into Uncle Janus' shop
- A wanted Janus' advice.
- B said he needed a red three-piece suit.
- C was already a valued customer.
- D had already decided what he wanted.

5 Uncle Janus is certainly . . . now than he used to be.
- A a lot richer
- B less critical of his customers
- C visited more often by pop stars
- D taken in by clients more often

Unit 10
A full-time job

EXAM FOCUS:
Oral Interview

Look, listen and speak

You are going to hear a short talk about the work of a zoo. Look at the pictures and listen, then do the exercises below.

1 In pairs, ask and tell each other:

1 why looking after animals in a zoo is a full-time job.
2 how often different animals are fed and watered.
3 how and when the dolphins are fed at the Seaquarium in Miami.
4 why some young animals are hand-reared, why they are weighed regularly, and what sort of records are kept.
5 what cleaning and repair jobs have to be done regularly in a zoo.
6 what happens if an animal falls ill.
7 what is done if they have to put an animal down in a zoo.
8 what is extracted from snakes in some zoos and what is done with it.
9 why many zoos now have a 'zoo school'.
10 what are shown to pupils in lessons at the Cologne zoo school.

2 Look at each picture and make statements, like this:

The dolphins are being fed by a diver.
They are fed several times a day.
They were last fed a few hours ago.

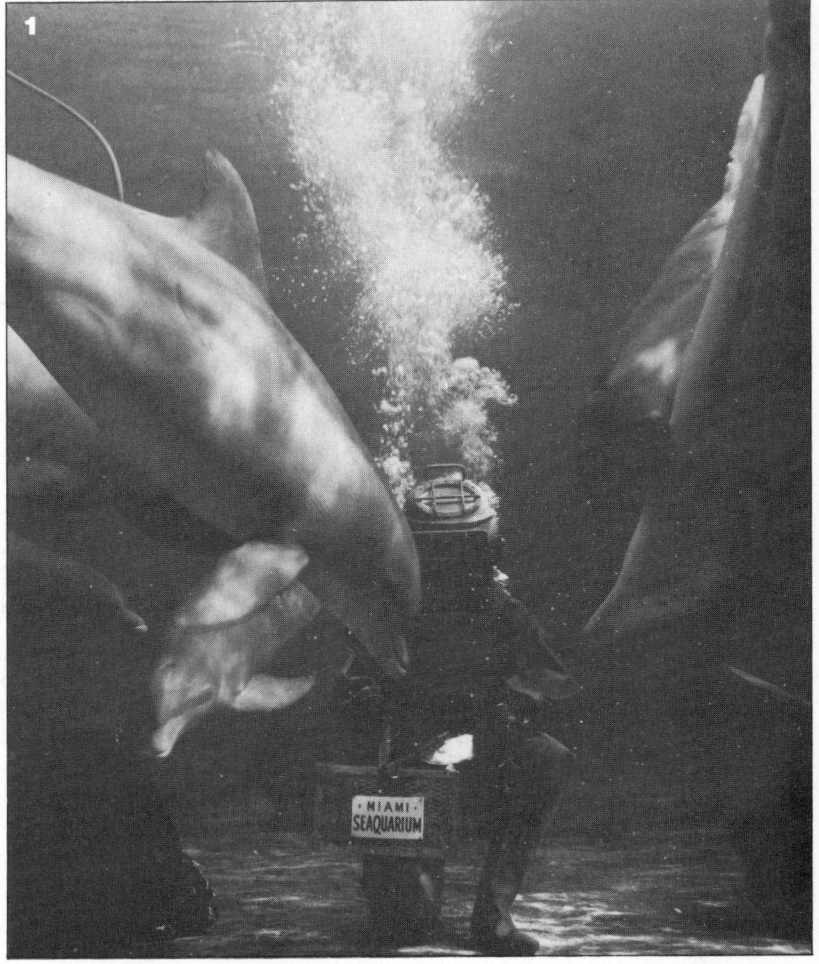

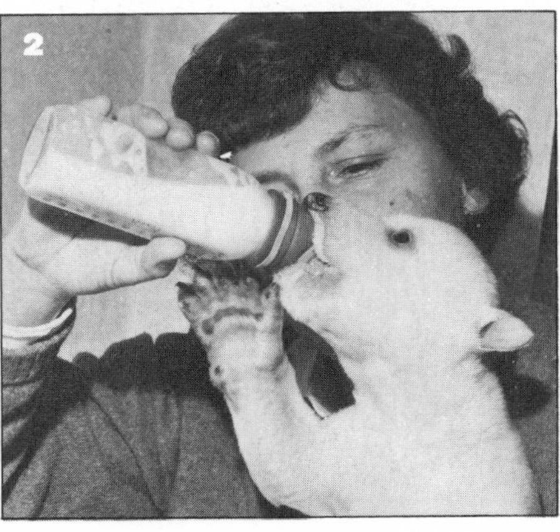

4

5

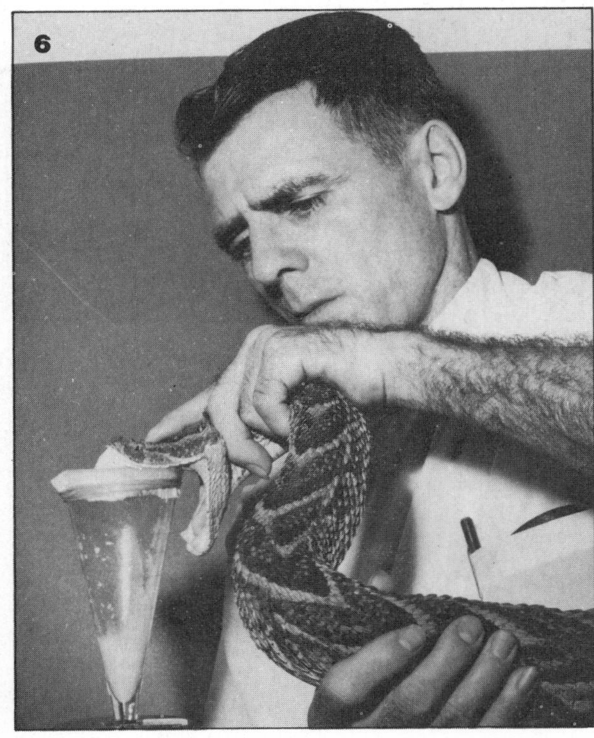
6

7

10

Grammar practice

The Passive: Present (*is/are done, is/are being done*) and Past (*was/were done, was/were being done*), and *has to/must be done*

REVIEW

Present

Someone repaints the house every year.	⟶	The house is repainted every year.
Someone cleans the windows once a week.	⟶	The windows are cleaned once a week.
Someone is renovating the roof (now).	⟶	The roof is being renovated.
Someone is planting some young trees.	⟶	Some young trees are being planted.

Past

Someone redesigned the garden five years ago.	⟶	The garden was redesigned five years ago.
Someone put up some new signs yesterday.	⟶	Some new signs were put up yesterday.
When I visited the house last Monday,		When I visited the house last Monday,
someone was cutting the grass	⟶	the grass was being cut
and someone was feeding the horses.	⟶	and the horses were being fed.

has to be done/must be done

Someone has to/must cut the grass.	⟶	The grass has to/must be cut.
Someone has to/must empty the litter bins every day.	⟶	The litter bins have to/must be emptied every day.

PRACTICE

1 Look at this picture and make as many statements as you can about what is being done at the moment, and guess how often these things are done or have to be done.
For example:
The lawn is being cut. I expect/imagine/assume (that) it's cut/it has to be cut once a week.

2 Now cover the picture and imagine you went there last week. Say what was being done while you were there. Then guess when each of the jobs was last done.
For example:
While I was there last week, the lawn was being cut. I expect/imagine/assume (that) it was cut the same time the week before, too.

Vocabulary

Adjectives with suffixes

Adjectives are formed in many ways, most commonly by adding a suffix to a noun (for example, danger→dangerous) or a verb (for example, to attract →attractive). Study these adjectives carefully, then do the exercise and play one of the games below.

-ive	attractive, sensitive, talkative, productive, extensive
-ous	dangerous, famous, marvellous
-ious	furious, curious, conscientious, ambitious
-eous	courteous, erroneous
-ar	polar, muscular, circular, rectangular
-al	educational, criminal, tropical, musical, critical, philosophical, cultural, rational, zoological
-ic	scientific, tragic, athletic, aquatic, atomic, specific, dramatic, electronic, enthusiastic

Note carefully the difference between these pairs of adjectives ending in *-ic* and *-al*:

economic (=connected with the economy): *an economic miracle/problem*
economical (=not expensive to run): *an economical machine/car*

historic (=to do with or making history): *a historic house/moment/monument*
historical (=to do with the study of history): *historical research*

comic (=connected with comedy): *a comic opera/masterpiece*
comical (=funny, laughable): *a comical hat/situation*

electric (=powered by electricity): *an electric light/shaver/lawnmower*
electrical (=of electricity): *an electrical fault/storm*

classic (=memorable, great): *a classic mistake/performance*
classical (=of artistic styles, originally going back to the Greeks and Romans): *classical languages/literature/music*

1 Cover the box and for each blank supply an adjective formed from the word given in brackets.

1 My car's very ____. (*economy*)
2 He's a very ____ man. (*ambition*)
3 The plane was caught in an ____ storm. (*electricity*)
4 We visited a ____ house last weekend. (*history*)
5 He's an extremely ____ man. (*muscle*)
6 They've got some ____ bears there. (*pole*)
7 I haven't had a very ____ week. (*product*)
8 These birds have to be looked after because they come from a ____ country. (*tropic*)
9 There was a ____ opera on television last night. (*comedy*)
10 What I need for the garden is an ____ lawnmower. (*electricity*)

2 Game: *Make up a story* or *Mime it!* (See Teacher's Guide pp 31 and 42)

Discussion

In small groups, discuss and work out (as far as you can) the cost of the upkeep of a place that you know, for example, a flat or house, this school/college, a local sports stadium, etc. Discuss what is done or what has to be done regularly, giving examples of things that are being done now, were done in the past, or were being done when you were last there.

10

Exercises for homework

See if you can do these exercises in 60 minutes.

1 Use of English

Finish each of the following sentences in such a way that it means exactly the same as the sentence printed before it.

1 Someone is servicing my car today (at the garage).
My car ....
2 Someone stole my bicycle last week.
My bicycle ....
3 They were pulling down that old building when I passed last Monday.
That old building ....
4 Someone has to weigh all the young animals every day.
All the young animals ....
5 Someone cleans the windows of our flat once a month.
The windows ....
6 They had to put down that elephant because she was so old.
That elephant had ....
7 The keeper scrubs out the lions' cage twice a week.
The lions' cage ....
8 When we got there, someone was feeding the polar bears.
The polar bears ....
9 Security men check the bank every night.
The bank ....
10 The wind blew down those trees in the storm last night.
Those trees ....

2 Composition: Letter

Once a year, your own (or a nearby) town or village holds a special festival. Write a letter (about 150 words, not counting the address) to an English-speaking friend describing the preparations which are now being made a week or so before 'the great day'. If possible, describe what is usually done for the festival (and/or what was done last year) and what is being done this time. You should make the beginning and ending like those of an ordinary letter and use as much language from this and previous Units as you can.

10

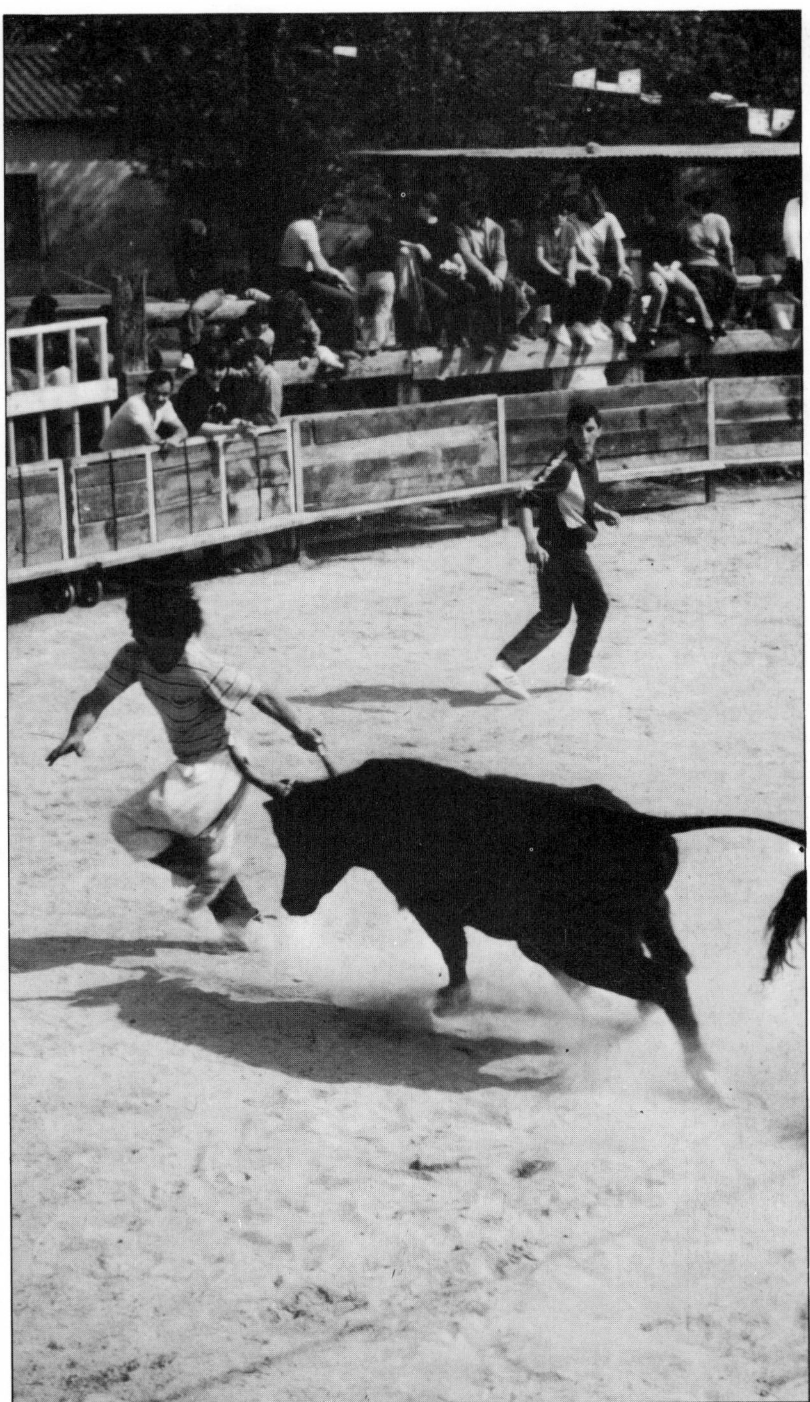

Oral Interview preparation

1 Situation for extended role play

You are on holiday in an English-speaking country and lose something important (your passport, your wallet or purse, watch, etc.). In fact you think the article has been stolen. So you go to the nearest police station to report the loss or theft.

In pairs, and using these notes, conduct the conversation between the policeman or policewoman and yourself. One student (as the policeman/policewoman) asks for, and the other student gives, the following information:

- full name (and spelling)
- address where staying, and for how long
- what has been lost or stolen + description
- where and when (you think) the article was lost or stolen

2 Look at this photograph and then answer these questions:

About the photograph

1 What part of the world do you think this photo was taken in? Why?
2 What's happening to the boy on the left?
3 How dangerous do you think the bull is?
4 What would happen if the bull injured or killed someone?
5 Do you think this might be part of an annual festival or something? Why?/Why not?

General

1 How are animals treated generally in your country?
2 Do you think animals should be kept in zoos or not? Why?
3 Animals are often used in experiments for scientific research. How do you feel about that? Why?

Unit 11

'Windsurfing chose me . . .'

EXAM FOCUS:
Reading Comprehension

Read and speak

Read this short passage, then do the exercises opposite.

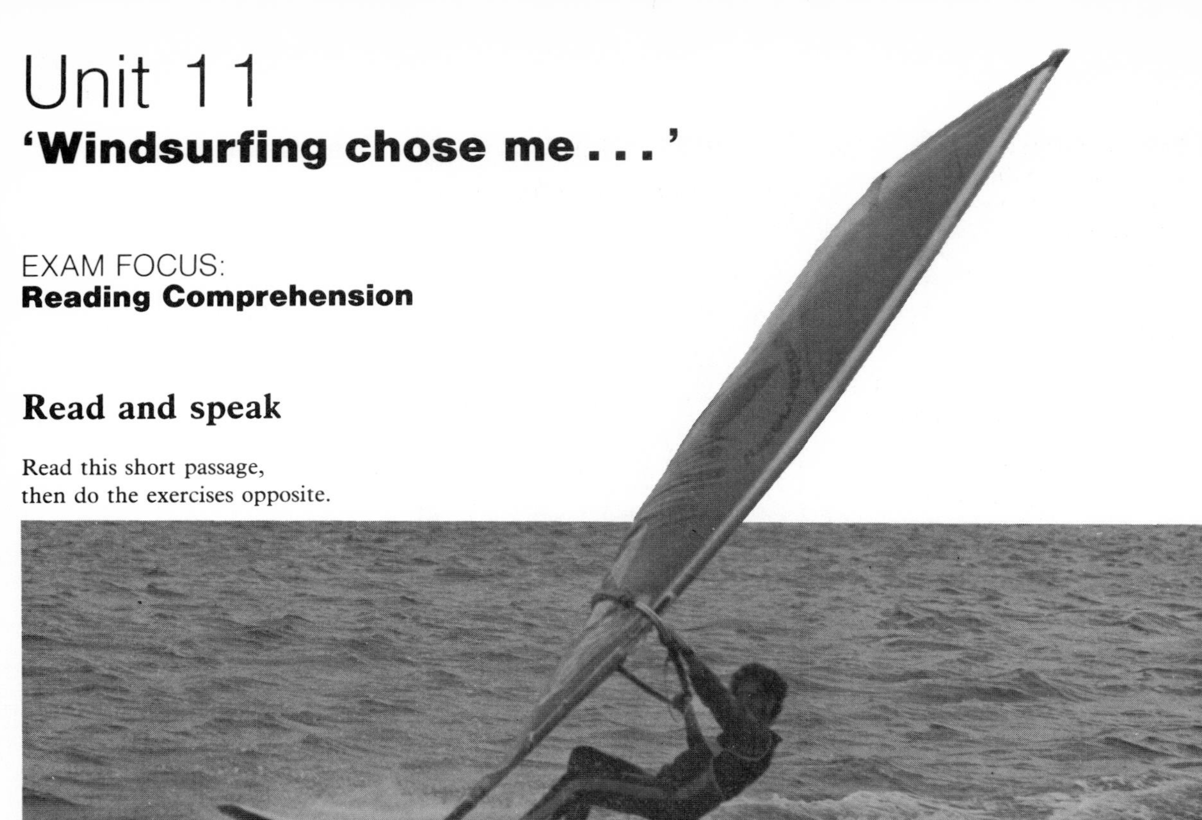

I'VE been windsurfing now for six years, and teaching others to do it for most of that time. I've taught in Corsica, North Wales, and now in Poole, where I run a windsurfer school and shop with my wife Jane.

I don't think *I* chose windsurfing as a hobby or profession: windsurfing chose me. Strangely enough, I had never even seen anyone windsurfing before I went to a sailing school back in the summer of 1975 in Propriano, on the island of Corsica. They had a school there, but no one was very proficient. After all, they had only had their boards a month when I arrived. However, as soon as I saw people enjoying the sport, I immediately decided to take it up. I had been sailing for at least ten years, and in some ways it seemed like another sailing-boat: at least it had a sail. And I saw it as a challenge. At the time, I had also just met Jane, who was teaching water-skiing there.

Probably because I have done so much windsurfing since then, I can't remember every detail of my first experience. What I do remember is that I spent most of the first day struggling with the board in the deep harbour water and trying to avoid all the boats that were moored there. At first I couldn't even stand up on the thing—after all, the board is only about 70 cm wide!—but after I had fallen off quite a few times, I soon caught on, and by the end of that first day, was doing quite well. I've never looked back.

For me, windsurfing is the most exhilarating sport there is. And it's not dangerous as long as you use your common sense and follow what you are taught. I've certainly never broken any bones: I've never even injured myself.

It wasn't until after I had come back to Britain that I came across proper courses for people who want to take up windsurfing. I admit I taught myself—I had to!—but if I'd gone to a proper school at the start, life would have been much easier.

James Ellis

1 From the information contained in the passage, are these statements true or false, or can't you tell? Give reasons.

1 James wrote the passage in 1979.
2 He hasn't always wanted to be a windsurfer.
3 The windsurfing school in Propriano had been in operation for ten years.
4 Before he took up windsurfing, James had taught water-skiing.
5 James met his future wife on the beach.
6 James can't really remember his first day windsurfing.
7 Propriano harbour was very busy.
8 Basically, James taught himself windsurfing.
9 At the beginning James found windsurfing very difficult.
10 James was glad he had been to the school in Corsica before he came back to Britain.

2 Discussion

In small groups, tell each other about a sport, hobby or some leisure activity you have been doing for some time. Say how long you've been doing it, how, why and when you started, what the first day was like, etc.

Grammar practice 1

Present Perfect Simple *has/have done* and Continuous *has/have been doing*

REVIEW

There are many different uses of the two aspects of the Present Perfect. Compare these two:

1 He has been running the shop for three years.

= He opened a shop three years ago. + He runs the same shop NOW.

2 He has run several (different, separate) shops since 1970.

= He ran one shop in 1970, another in 1974, etc. + He runs a shop NOW.

1970 1974 ? ? ?

Note how we sometimes use *has/have done* in place of *has/have been doing*, for example:

I've lived in this house for years.
She's worked for Mr James since 1975.

BUT we *cannot* use *has/have been doing* to replace the Simple Perfect when talking about a countable number of events or things. For example, we *must* say:

She's drunk three cups of tea.
(NOT She's been drinking three cups of tea.)

PRACTICE

In pairs, ask and tell each other

—how long
1 you've been learning English...
2 you've been living here...
3 you've been going to school/ going to work...
4 you've been riding a bicycle...

—and how many
books you've read in English.
houses or flats you've lived in.
schools you've been to/ jobs you've had.
bicycles you've had.

11

Grammar practice 2

Past Simple *did* and Past Continuous *was/were doing*

REVIEW

> I was working in Italy when I tried water-skiing for the first time.
>
> I tried water-skiing for the first time when/while I was working in Italy.

PRACTICE

Join these pairs of sentences using *when* or *while:*

1 He worked in London from 1970–1974. He met his wife in 1972.
2 I lived in America for a few years. I had my first flying lesson there.
3 She played tennis yesterday afternoon. Someone stole her money during the game.
4 He was in the middle of a fabulous dream. Then the teacher asked him a question and woke him up.
5 We went into the kitchen. She was using the coffee grinder.

Grammar practice 3

Past Simple *did* and Past Perfect Simple *had done*

REVIEW

> They had already left { when / before / by the time } I got there.
>
> = They left.
> Then I got there.
>
> It wasn't until I had read the letter that I believed it.
>
> = I read the letter (myself).
> Then I believed it.

PRACTICE

Join these pairs of sentences using *when, before, by the time* or *it wasn't until. . . .*

1 The film finished. Then we arrived.
2 She read the book. Then she saw the film.
3 I ground the coffee. Then I realised my mistake.
4 I broke one of their best wine glasses. Then they told me to be careful.
5 He spoke a few words to the audience. Then he froze.

Grammar practice 4

More irregular verbs

REVIEW

Study these irregular verbs, and then do the exercise.

break	broke	broken	steal	stole	stolen
choose	chose	chosen	(a)wake	(a)woke	(a)woken
freeze	froze	frozen	weave	wove	woven
speak	spoke	spoken			

fall	fell	fallen	find	found	found
fly	flew	flown	bind	bound	bound
give	gave	given	grind	ground	ground
see	saw	seen	wind	wound	wound

PRACTICE

Supply the correct form of the verbs (*did, was doing* or *had done*).

1 I (*already fly*) once before I (*fly*) to America last year.
2 When I (*see*) who was in the audience, I (*choose*) my words very carefully.
3 I (*just speak*) to her when she turned away, (*fall*) over and (*break*) her arm.
4 The alarm clock did not wake the children up, but they (*wake*) up the moment I (*speak*) to them.
5 I (*already grind*) the coffee after supper yesterday evening before I (*find*) out that no one wanted any!

Vocabulary

Phrasal verbs

answer back (=reply rudely)
back down (=admit you were wrong)
bear up (=show courage or strength)
break down (=lose control of one's feelings; fail (to work))
break off (=stop, e.g. a meeting, speech)
break out (=start suddenly, e.g. war)
break up (=come to an end)
carry on (=continue)
catch on (=understand; become popular, e.g. fashion, or a sport)
clear up (=improve, e.g. weather)
come about (=happen)
come to (= regain consciousness)
fall through (=fail to be completed)
find out (=discover)
get on (=make progress; agree with sby)
give in/up (=stop trying to do sthg)
hang about/around (=wait, doing nothing)
make out (=pretend, give the impression)
pull through (=recover, survive, e.g. an operation)
pull up (=stop, in a car)
ring off (=end a telephone conversation)
run out (=exhaust; have no more)
settle up (=pay a bill)
take off (=rise into the air, e.g. a plane)
take over (=assume responsibility)
turn out (=happen (to be) in the end)
turn up (=arrive)

These phrasal verbs (sometimes called 'Type 2') consist of a verb + adverb particle, like the others you have practised, but as used in this section, they have no object and cannot be used in the passive. Later, some of the verbs will be practised with an object, and can therefore also be used in the passive. The particle (*back, down, up,* etc.) is always stressed. Study the verbs and their meanings, then rephrase the sentences below using phrasal verbs.

1 My old car has *failed to work* again.
2 We *stopped* at 1 p.m. to have lunch.
3 The meeting *ended* in disorder.
4 Please don't stop: *continue.*
5 The plans have *failed to be completed.*
6 He *pretended* that he couldn't drive.
7 The car *stopped* outside my house.
8 After he had *paid the bill,* he left.
9 Our plane *left the airport* at mid-day.
10 When I *arrived,* everyone else had left.

Exercise for homework

Composition

See if you can write this composition in 40 minutes.

Write an account of an experience you had when everything seemed to go wrong (e.g. your first day in a new job, your first riding lesson, a birthday party, etc.). Your composition should be about 150 words in length. Plan it carefully before you start—think in terms of 'before the event', 'the event(s)' and 'after the event'—and try to include phrasal verbs from this and previous Units.

11

TEST: READING COMPREHENSION

Time: 30 minutes

Section A

Choose the word or phrase which best completes each sentence. Write your choice for each (A, B, C or D) on a separate piece of paper.

1 The boxer finally ________ ten minutes after he had been knocked out.
A came about B pulled through C turned out D came to

2 The boy had an accident because he didn't use his ________ sense.
A ordinary B usual C common D everyday

3 I ________ the man the money and left before I realised what I had done.
A already gave B was giving C have already given D had already given

4 The children are completely different in character, but they ________ very well.
A get on B settle up C catch on D carry on

5 It's not surprising she wasn't a very good dancer. ________, she'd only had one lesson.
A At first B However C Anyhow D After all

6 Strangely ________, although she's a famous actress, people rarely recognise her in the street.
A also B but C enough D so

7 When he heard the tragic news, he ________ and cried.
A broke up B broke down C broke off D broke out

8 That child's extremely ________. He's always answering people back.
A irresponsible B immoral C impolite D irrational

9 He'd better not do too much, ________ he won't get over his illness very quickly.
A so B unless C otherwise D if

10 She had ________ in a small village and so she couldn't get used to living in a city.
A brought up B got up C come up D grown up

Section B

Read this article carefully. Then choose which you think is the best suggested way of finishing the statement in each item below—A, B, C or D. Write your answers on a separate piece of paper.

ANOTHER FIREBOMB IN LARGE STORE

Newcastle, 16 June

Fire broke out in the early hours of yesterday morning in the large A & B Store in Newcastle. Fortunately the only casualty was the watchman, who was taken to hospital but was released this morning. There was extensive damage to the third floor of the building.

'From what we can gather at the moment,' the Fire Officer said, 'we don't think there was an electrical fault. In fact, we suspect the fire was started by an incendiary device which someone had set to go off at about 2 a.m., but are not *absolutely* certain yet.'

The only person in the store was Jim London, the 57-year-old night watchman. He was overcome by fumes and was taken to the General Hospital unconscious. When he came to, he told reporters, 'I had already done my third inspection of the store—I go round four or five times during the night—and was settling down to write my report when I noticed an odd smell and thought I heard something. I broke off and went to look into it. It wasn't until I'd made absolutely sure there was a fire and I couldn't do anything about it myself that I rang the fire brigade. And by that time, smoke was billowing everywhere so I didn't know how big it was.'

The manager told our reporter this morning, 'We have had a number of threats during the past few weeks, but the police have not been able to find out where they have come from. There was a minor fire in the store the same time last year and we had received a number of warnings before that one, too.'

He went on, 'When the Fire Prevention people inspected the store after that fire, they were slightly critical of our fire precautions, but since then we have installed a complete new fire prevention system.

'But for Mr London,' he added, 'it could have been much worse. We shall be showing our appreciation to him with a gift.'

11 Although the fire was quite serious,
- A only one floor was damaged.
- B no one was hurt.
- C only one fireman was overcome by fumes.
- D all of the store contents were saved.

12 The Fire Officer said that they
- A knew exactly how the fire started.
- B assumed it was set off by a firebomb.
- C thought some electrical wires melted.
- D were not quite sure how it started.

13 When Jim went to inspect the smell, he
- A was doing his third round.
- B had just sat down to write his report.
- C knew how bad the fire was.
- D had already heard the alarm bell.

14 It almost seemed as if this fire was connected with the one last year because
- A they both broke out on the same floor.
- B Jim London gave the alarm for both.
- C they had received threats both times.
- D both were started by a firebomb.

15 If Jim had not called the fire brigade,
- A the new 'system' would have put out the fire.
- B there would have been more damage.
- C 'A & B' were going to present him with something.
- D the store would have been inspected.

Unit 12

The Earth is being squeezed dry!

EXAM FOCUS:
Composition (Narrative)

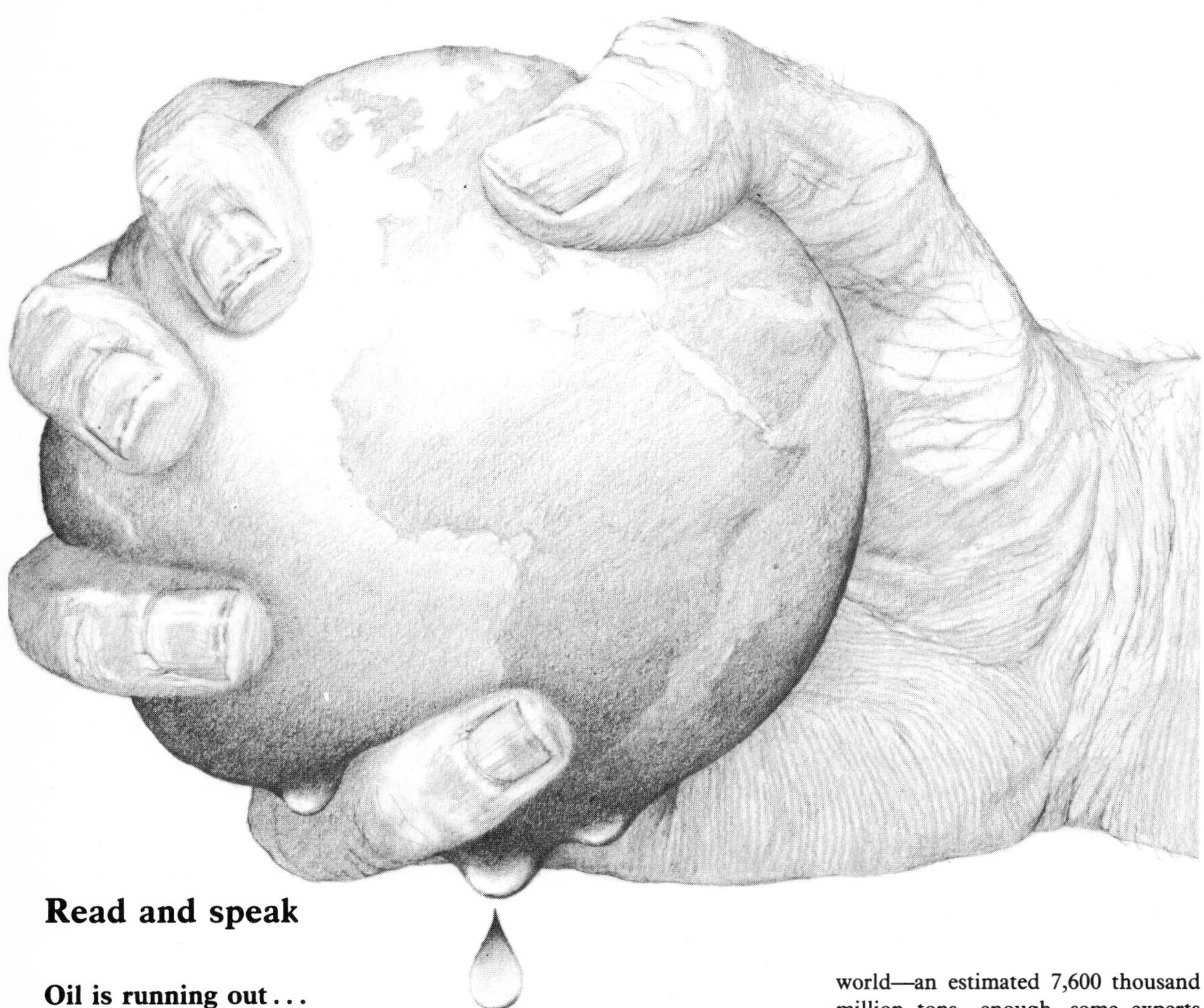

Read and speak

Oil is running out . . .

Electric light, gas cookers, petrol and oil—these are all things which a lot of us take for granted. But fossil fuels —oil, gas and coal—are not inexhaustible.

Oil is running out, but demand is not falling off. It was relatively cheap in the past, so the world, particularly modern industry and transport, has come to depend on it very heavily. World resources of oil are an estimated 500,000 million barrels, but the United States alone uses 24 million barrels *a day.*

Gas is running short. While 45% of power in the United States of America comes from oil, gas still accounts for 32%. And in Britain, gas and oil together make up a quarter of the power supply.

There is still plenty of **coal** in the world—an estimated 7,600 thousand million tons—enough, some experts say, for 250–300 years. But if coal replaced other fossil fuels completely, it would only last for about 50 years.

Some experts believe that by 1985 the USA will have to import about 50% of its oil as its own oilfields dry up. In Britain, North Sea oil and gas will keep disaster away for longer, but with an estimated output of 700 million barrels a year, it will only just keep up with demand.

It is true that there is still more

oil in the Middle East (an estimated 7,900 million barrels a year) than the world has used so far, but as other supplies run out and demand increases, even this will not be enough.

No one knows when the oil-wells of the world will dry up, but one thing is certain: before they do, alternative sources of energy must be developed.

So what is being done about energy from . . .

The atom? Very few countries are using nuclear power, and those that are, use comparatively little. About 10% of Britain's electricity now comes from atomic energy, for example. But there are problems: what about the danger of radiation, and what to do with radio-active waste?

The sea? Research was begun some years ago into the possibilities of tidal energy, and experiments are still being carried out. But progress in this particular area is still very slow.

The sun? Solar energy can be harnessed to provide us with heat and electricity. Experiments are being carried out all over the world. There is a large 'solar furnace' in the Pyrenees in France, for example, and solar heating panels are being installed in many homes in Britain and the USA.

The Earth? We have always known that there are vast sources of energy underground in the form of hot rocks, hot water and pressurised steam. And this 'geothermal' energy has been harnessed to provide electricity in Italy and the USA. But again, more research is needed.

---

1 Ask and tell each other, from the text, about our present world energy situation.

2 Referring again to the text, ask and tell each other what other sources of energy there are and how they are being developed.

3 Discussion

Are there any other sources of energy which are being or could be investigated and developed?

Grammar practice 1

Determiners indicating an indefinite quantity or number

REVIEW AND PRACTICE

1 Make statements (with certainty or conviction) about the world energy situation using these models:

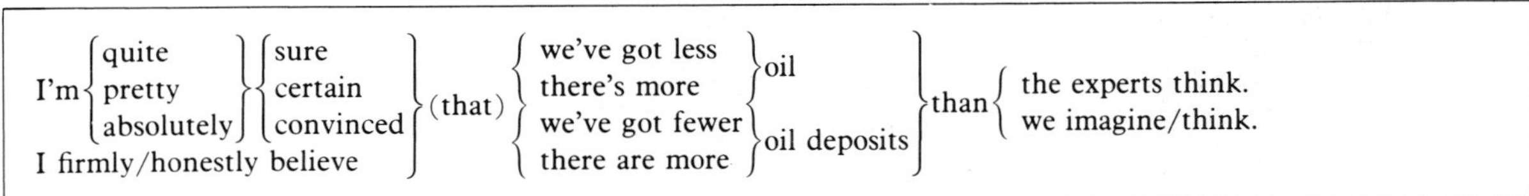

I'm {quite / pretty / absolutely} {sure / certain / convinced} I firmly/honestly believe	(that)	we've got less there's more	oil	than	the experts think. we imagine/think.
		we've got fewer there are more	oil deposits		

2 Make statements about the world energy situation using these models:

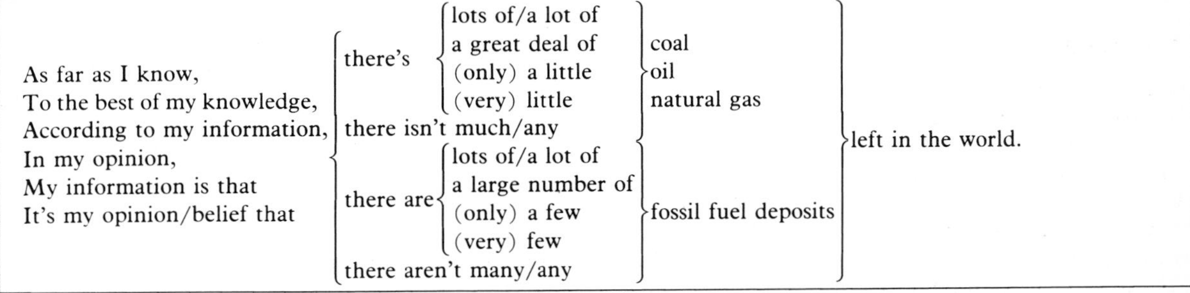

As far as I know, To the best of my knowledge, According to my information, In my opinion, My information is that It's my opinion/belief that	there's {lots of/a lot of / a great deal of / (only) a little / (very) little} there isn't much/any	coal oil natural gas	left in the world.
	there are {lots of/a lot of / a large number of / (only) a few / (very) few} there aren't many/any	fossil fuel deposits	

Note that we often use *plenty of* in place of *lots of, a lot of, a great deal of* or *a large number of.*

Note the superlatives *most, fewest* and *least* in, for example:

One of the countries with {the most/the least oil / the most/the fewest fossil fuel deposits} is . . .

12

Grammar practice 2 and 3

Uncountable nouns (*coal, weather, news,* etc.) and where *the* can be used.
Relative pronouns *which, that* and *who* as object to specify what we are talking about.
(Note that both grammar points are combined in the Review and Practice sections here.)

REVIEW

Study these lists of nouns and use them in sentences like those in the right-hand column.

1 These words usually occur in the singular and cannot be used with *a/an*:

coal, oil, gas, electricity, energy, fuel, money, safety, research

Coal is something (that/which) we take for granted.
The coal (that/which) we mine here is of a very high quality.
Oil is essential to industry.
The oil (that/which) we get from the North Sea is very good.

2 These words *always* occur in the singular and cannot be used with *a/an*:

weather, advice*, information*, progress, transport, health, luggage*, furniture*, knowledge, luck*, travel (= the general act of travelling), machinery*, junk*

*Note we can talk about *a piece of advice/information/luggage/furniture/luck/machinery/junk.*

We had terrible weather.
That's bad luck.
That's good advice/useful information.
(That's a useful piece of advice/information.)
Travel is something (which/that) I like.
Good health and knowledge are two things (which/that) young people need most.

3 These words always take a singular verb:

news, crossroads, means (= method), billiards, draughts (and other –s games), measles, mumps, diabetes (and other –s illnesses)

This is good news.
The news is bad today.
There's a crossroads ahead.
There is a means of solving the problem.
Billiards is a game (which/that) I enjoy.
Mumps is a very unpleasant disease.

Note that the object relative pronouns *who(m)* and *that* are used for people:

He's a man / They're people { (who(m) / that) } I admire very much.

That's the woman (that/who(m)) they mentioned in the news.
She's the girl (that/who(m)) I beat at draughts.
They're the men (that/who(m)) we met on the journey.

PRACTICE

Supply the word *the, who(m), which* or *that* where necessary.

1 ___ furniture ___ we ordered a month ago hasn't arrived yet.
2 Here's ___ information ___ you need.
3 ___ weather ___ we had was terrible.
4 She's a singer ___ I like very much.
5 ___ good health is something ___ we should all be thankful for.
6 That was ___ good advice ___ you gave me.
7 Can you pay me back ___ money ___ I lent you?
8 We must all try to save ___ energy.
9 ___ electricity is something ___ many of us couldn't do without.
10 ___ furniture ___ they have is very old.

Discussion

'Energy crisis? What energy crisis?'
'Oh, yes, I know there's an energy crisis—but we'll pull through somehow!'
'I'm not worried about it. It'll turn out all right in the end, won't it?'

What would you say to people who express opinions like this about the energy crisis? Why?

Exercises for homework

1 Use of English

See if you can do this exercise in 15 minutes.

Join each of the following pairs of sentences beginning with the word or phrase in brackets and keeping as close to the meaning of the original sentences as possible.

1 We can solve the problem. There is a means. (*There is . . .*)
2 Health is the thing. I value it most. (*Health . . .*)
3 We thought we had a lot of time. We had less. (*We had . . .*)
4 They mine coal here. It's of a very low quality. (*The coal . . .*)
5 We in Britain earn money from North Sea oil. It's essential now to our economy. (*The money . . .*)
6 There's plenty of coal left in the world. That's my information. (*My information . . .*)
7 A lot of homes could use solar energy. Then oil would last much longer. (*If a lot of homes . . .*)
8 The experts think there are lots of undiscovered oilfields. I'm pretty sure there are fewer. (*I'm pretty sure . . .*)
9 Medical research which uses animals is evil. That's my opinion. (*It's my opinion . . .*)
10 I want three things for my children. They are peace, health and luck. (*Peace, . . .*)

12

2 Study section: The narrative composition

The First Certificate Paper 2 nearly always contains a narrative composition. You might have to narrate an event or an experience, or be asked to write a short story. Whichever it is, it is advisable to tell the events in the order in which they happened. As with other composition types, make a rough plan, with a few ideas that you can use, and when writing this kind of composition, pay attention to the sequence of tenses in the past.
Study the subject, plan and ideas here and read the composition. Then plan and write your own composition on the same subject.

SUBJECT
'Write an account of a day you will never forget.'

Plan and ideas

Before the event
1 3 years ago—had always wanted to fly.
2 Booked trial lesson.

The event
3 'Historic day'—excited—airport—woman instructor.
4 She talked—I hardly took anything in.
5 Got in plane—took off.
6 Dual controls. After 10 mins 'You can take over'—froze.

After the event
7 Ground raced up to meet us. Embarrassing.
8 Nevertheless—went on flying. 3 years now.

That day in May three years ago could have put me off flying completely, but it didn't. I had always wanted to take up flying, but it wasn't until I had seen an advertisement for a cheap trial lesson that I decided to try it. I had very little money and no knowledge at all about flying, but I had a lot of courage—or at least I thought I did! So I rang up the flying club and booked a lesson.

I woke up very excited on the morning of the 'historic day' and cycled to the airport which was about ten miles away. When I turned up at the club, I paid and then met my instructor, who turned out to be a woman. Although she knew I had no experience at all, she took me straight out to the plane which was being tanked up with fuel. I should have listened to her from the moment we had shaken hands, because she was in fact giving me my own private lecture on the basics of flying. The trouble was that everything was so new and strange to me that I hardly heard anything she said.

We put on parachutes, got into the plane, which was about as big as a Mini inside, strapped ourselves in side by side, and took off. The instructor was still talking, giving me information and advice, but I couldn't take anything in. I wasn't frightened: I was just too interested in leaving the earth and in the view beneath us.

The instructor was flying the plane of course and I was just holding my dual controls. But we had only been up in the air for about ten minutes—and remember that this was the first time I had ever been in an aeroplane—when she said: 'Right. You can take over now. Good luck. Just keep her steady with the horizon.' And she took her hands off the controls.

I know that I froze for a moment or two, but I don't know exactly what I did after that. I obviously did something wrong because the next moment the ground seemed to be racing up to meet us. I thought we were going to crash, but with a calm 'I'll take over again now', my instructor took over the controls and we were soon flying straight again.

I honestly admit that the experience was more embarrassing than anything else. I have been flying regularly for three years now and can put a plane in and out of a dive, but friends won't let you forget things like that very easily, will they?

TEST: COMPOSITION

Time: 45 minutes

Write **one only** of the following composition exercises. Your answer must follow exactly the instructions given, and must be about 150 words in length.

Either

1 Write a story beginning like this:
'I thought our visit to the . . . was going to be boring. It turned out to be quite the opposite.'

Or

2 Someone has asked you to talk to a small group of people about one of your hobbies or interests. Write what you would say to them.

Or

3 'Private cars should be banned from the centres of large cities and towns.' What do you think? Give reasons.

(*Note:* For this Test you may refer back to Units in this coursebook to help you.)

Unit 13

'Successful' failures!

EXAM FOCUS:
Use of English

Read and speak

Read this and then do the exercises on the opposite page.

Western civilisation is obsessed with success, even though most of us have a genuine flair for the exact opposite. Several years ago, the writer Stephen Pile decided to do something about it: he formed the 'Not Terribly Good Club of Great Britain'. To get into the Club, you had to be not terribly good at something and preferably absolutely awful! Members addressed the Club on the things they did worst or couldn't do at all. Sometimes they gave displays and won standing ovations. Over the years they held appalling musical evenings, art exhibitions and so on until the membership grew from 20 to 200.

The official handbook of the Club which Stephen Pile produced in 1979 under the title *The Book of Heroic Failures* was described by critics at the time of its publication as 'irresistible', 'incredibly funny', 'almost unbelievable', and 'one of the most fascinating books I've ever read'.

Here are two extracts from that book.

The most incapable, least successful bank robber

Since he did not want to attract attention to himself, a bank robber at Portland, Oregon, in 1969 wrote all his instructions on a piece of paper rather than speak or shout.

'This is a hold-up and I've got a gun,' he wrote, and held the paper up for the cashier to read. Astonished, the cashier waited while the robber wrote out, 'Put all the money in a paper bag.'

The message was pushed through the grille. The cashier read it and then wrote on the bottom, 'I haven't got a paper bag,' and passed it back.

The bank robber fled.

The worst hijacker

We shall never know the identity of the man who in 1976 made the most remarkable and least successful hijack attempt of all time. On a flight across America, he rose from his seat, drew out a gun and took the stewardess hostage. Her alarm quickly changed to amused astonishment when he said,

'Take me to Detroit.'

'We're already going to Detroit,' she replied.

'Oh, . . . good,' he said, and sat down again.

1 In pairs, ask and say, about the introductory passage:

1 what the name of the Club was that Stephen Pile formed, and when.
2 how you could get into the Club.
3 what kinds of meetings and events the Club held.
4 how the 'official handbook' of the Club was described by critics.
5 if you believe the Club really exists or existed. (Why?)

2 In pairs, ask and tell each other about 'The Worst Hijacker' and 'The Most Incapable, Least Successful Bank Robber'.

3 About you

Tell each other about a book you have read or TV programme you have seen recently. Say what it was about and what you thought of it. (Was it boring? fascinating? terrible? incredible? frightening? etc. Did you find it interesting? unforgettable? etc.) Would you recommend it to someone else? Why?/Why not?

Grammar practice 1

Superlative adjectives

REVIEW

It's	the longest river in the world.
He's	the biggest person in our class.
It's	the nicest place under the sun.
It's	the busiest* city in the country.
She's	the cleverest* person in our family.
It's	the most boring book I've ever read.
She's	the least sensible person I know.
It's	the best dish on the menu here.
He's	the worst driver I've ever seen.

Remember that adjectives form their superlatives with (*adjective*)*-est* or *most/least* (+ *adjective*), or have irregular forms e.g. *best, worst,* etc.

*Note other two-syllable adjectives which form the superlative with *-est: common, stupid, narrow, quiet, polite, able, gentle, simple;* and all ending in *-y—tidy, pretty, healthy, silly,* etc.

ABOUT YOU

Finish these sentences in your own way.

1 The dirtiest city in the world must be . . .
2 (I'm not sure, but) I think the longest river in the world is . . .
3 The best film I've ever seen is . . .
4 The worst TV programme I've ever watched must be . . .
5 I think the most beautiful woman/the most handsome man in the world is . . .
6 The most sensible person I know is . . .
7 The silliest story I ever heard was . . .
8 In my opinion, the most impressive building in the world is . . .
9 The most interesting person I've ever met is/was . . .
10 The most unforgettable/embarrassing experience I've ever had was when . . .

13

Grammar practice 2

Superlative adverbs

REVIEW

> They all drive carefully,
> but John drives the most carefully.
>
> They all work well/badly,
> but Mary works the best/the worst.
>
> He works the fastest and the hardest.
> He drove the slowest.
> She shouts the loudest.
> We arrived the earliest.
> He has come the farthest.

Adverbs ending in *-ly* form their superlative with *the most* (+ *adverb*).

Note that in, for example, *John drives most carefully* (without *the*), *most = very.*
Adverbs with the same form as their adjective (i.e. *hard, soon, fast, near, late, early, long, near*) form their superlative with *-est.* Note *far—farthest.*

The common superlative adverb forms of *slowly, loudly* and *quickly* are *the slowest, the loudest, the quickest.*

PRACTICE

Complete each sentence with the superlative form of the adverb in brackets.

1 She writes the slowest, but reads ____. (*quick*)
2 I arrived at the party ____. (*late*)
3 Of all the girls, she writes ____. (*badly*)
4 ____ I can go in my old car is 50 miles per hour. (*fast*)
5 ____ we can stay is an hour. (*long*)
6 Jane dresses ____ of all the girls in the family. (*well*)
7 He works ____, but earns the least. (*hard*)
8 Look at the map. This is ____ you can drive. Then you have to walk. (*far*)
9 ____ she'll be ready is 8.30. (*early*)
10 'Which of you can shout ____?' (*loud*)

Vocabulary

More adjectives with suffixes

Study these adjectives with *-able, -ible, -ed* and *-ing.* Then do the exercises opposite.

	-able	*-ible*
People	(dis)agreeable	(ir)responsible
	(un)reliable	sensible
	(un)reasonable	terrible
	(un)sociable	horrible
	(in)capable	(im)possible
	dependable	(in)corrigible
Places/Events	(un)believable	horrible
	(un)forgettable	(in)credible
	memorable	terrible
	(un)remarkable	

Emotion: I was interested.
Place, event, etc: It was interesting.

Adjectives ending in *-ed* and *-ing* can be formed from these verbs:

-ed/-ing: alarm, annoy, astonish, disappoint, disturb, disgust, embarrass, frighten, interest, shock, thrill

-d/(e)-ing: amaze, amuse, bore, confuse, fascinate, excite, please, surprise

-(y) ied/-ying: satisfy, terrify, worry

Exercises for homework

See if you can do these exercises in 60 minutes.

1 Use of English

Make all the changes and additions necessary to produce, from the following sets of words and phrases, sentences which together form a paragraph from a letter.

1 Yesterday evening / John and I/ *go* / *see* / new Karl Frank film.
2 I / *think* / it / *be* / most fascinating film / I / *see* / years, / and probably / best / he / *ever produce.*
3 Not everybody / *like* / same thing, however, because John / *say* / it / *be* / worst, most boring thing / he / *ever see.*
4 There / *be* / few / actors / and / little / action / but / a lot / incredible scenery.
5 I / *know* / your taste / films / so I / *be* / absolute / convinced / you / enjoy / it / if you / *see* / it.

2 Composition: Description

Write a short description of a film you have particularly enjoyed, using the following questions as a guide. Your composition should be about 150 words in length.

Paragraph 1
What is/was the best, most interesting film you have seen? When and where did you see it? With whom?

Paragraph 2
Who were the main actors/actresses? Who was it produced by? What was the story? What did you think of the story? What was the acting like? What about the scenery, costumes and photography? What did you think of the film as a whole?

Paragraph 3
Why did you 'particularly' enjoy it? Why is/was it so unforgettable? Would you, or would you not, recommend it to someone else? Why?

1 Rephrase these sentences, for example:

I was amazed at the film.
→The film was amazing.

The book was boring (for her).
→She was bored by the book.

1 We were embarrassed by her behaviour.
2 The experience was exciting (for me).
3 I was fascinated by the scenery.
4 The lecture was disappointing (for her).
5 He was worried by the situation.

2 Make statements about people and places you know, films you have seen, books you have read or events you have been to. For example:

Bill's the most annoying, most irresponsible person I know.

Paris must be the most fascinating city I've ever been to.

(Use adjectives from the lists opposite.)

13

TEST: USE OF ENGLISH

Time: 40 minutes

Answer all the questions. Write your answers in ink on the paper provided by the teacher.

1 Finish each of the following sentences in such a way that it means exactly the same as the sentence printed before it.

1 I've never come across a more annoying person than James.
James is the...

2 They all found his behaviour shocking.
They were...

3 Tom and Mary both drive carefully, but Susan drives the most carefully (of the three).
Susan drives...

4 On the menu, pork is quite cheap, lamb is cheaper, and chicken is cheaper than both.
Chicken is...

5 I can't be there earlier than ten in the morning.
Ten in the morning...

6 I don't know a politer person than Ann.
Ann is...

7 There can't be a busier city in the world than Tokyo, I don't think.
I think Tokyo...

8 I haven't read a more alarming book recently than Alvin Toffler's *The Third Wave.*
The most...

9 The train left before I got to the station.
By the time I...

10 They didn't give me very much information about the place.
They gave...

2 For each of the numbered blanks in the following passage supply an appropriate word. Use only ONE word for each space.

I was reading a magazine in my dentist's waiting-room __(1)__ other day when I __(2)__ across an airline advertisement which immediately attracted my __(3)__. It invited me to fly with them to the largest wild game country __(4)__ the world, to climb the __(5)__ mountains __(6)__ their country, to lie on the __(7)__ magnificent pearl-white beaches on the continent and to enjoy the __(8)__ and most exciting shark-fishing in the Pacific. The whole thing sounded __(9)__! I have never __(10)__ anywhere so fascinating and immediately wanted to know __(11)__. I was just reading the prices when the person next __(12)__ me leaned over and said, 'Excuse me, but have you __(13)__ been there?' 'No,' I said, 'but I'd love __(14)__.' 'I wonder,' came the reply. 'I don't want to __(15)__ you, but I used to live there, and there's a lot that advertisements like that don't tell you.'

3 The word in capitals at the end of each of the following sentences can be used to form a word that fits suitably in the blank space. Supply the word for each blank in this way.

1 You can't trust her to do anything. She's extremely ________. RESPONSIBLE
2 The way Mary answered her father back yesterday was most ________. ASTONISH
3 The girl thought her parents were being very ________ when they refused to let her go to a dance. REASON
4 How can you drink that stuff? It looks ________! DISGUST
5 For most people, flying for the first time is an ________ experience. FORGET
6 He's always playing tricks on people. You'll never change him. He's ________. CORRECT
7 You know, Susan works the ________ of all the girls in the office HARD
8 . . . but she's paid the ________. BAD
9 He's very unpleasant. In fact, I think he's the most ________ person I know. AGREE
10 I was ________ informed a few days ago that they're going to build a new town hall. RELY
11 The girl they wanted for the job had to speak English and one other foreign language, ________ Spanish. PREFER
12 The ________ thing that happened to us on holiday was when we got lost in the back streets of the city. FUNNY
13 To the best of my ________, there isn't another bus into town until 10 o'clock. KNOW
14 That fisherman is the ________ 60-year-old I've ever met. HEALTH
15 A film which is perhaps amusing for adults can be ________ for children. TERRIFY

Unit 14
How good's your memory?

EXAM FOCUS:
Listening Comprehension

Look, listen and speak

Listen to the talk (on cassette or read by the teacher) and look at the lists below. Then do the exercises on the opposite page.

Grand National Winners*

Year	*Winner*
1971	Specify
1972	Well To Do
1973	Red Rum
1974	Red Rum
1975	L'Escargot
1976	Rag Trade
1977	Red Rum
1978	Lucius
1979	Rubstic
1980	Ben Nevis

fond of	responsible for
keen on	sorry for
interested in	tired of
ashamed of	good at
hopeless at	sick of
proud of	useless at
brilliant at	

*The Grand National: a horserace held annually in March at Aintree, Liverpool, over a 4½-mile course with 30 jumps.

1 Ask and tell each other:

1 if you find it easy or difficult to remember things.
2 if there's a simple way to improve your memory.
3 what the speaker suggested you should practise doing.
4 what the speaker said to the friend who always made notes.
5 why you should avoid making notes.
6 how you *could* memorise the list of Grand National winners.
7 the story the speaker told to help memorise the Grand National winners (as far as you can).
8 what you have to remember in order to recall the names of the Grand National winners.
9 what suggestions the speaker made for remembering the adjectives.
10 which list you think is easiest to memorise, and why.

2 Cover p 79. Then in pairs, test each other on how many of the Grand National winners and adjectives and prepositions you can remember.

Grammar practice 1

Adjectives + prepositions + gerund (*keep on swimming*) and adjectives + to-infinitive (*keen to help*)

REVIEW

<table>
<tr><td rowspan="4">He's</td><td>brilliant excellent
expert very good
poor no good
very slow useless
hopeless terrible</td><td>at</td><td rowspan="4">(doing) maths.
(learning) history.
swimming.
(playing) tennis.
sailing.
playing the piano.
learning English.</td></tr>
<tr><td colspan="2">interested in</td></tr>
<tr><td colspan="2">keen on</td></tr>
<tr><td>fond sick
tired (in)capable</td><td>of</td></tr>
</table>

Compare these pairs of sentences:

I'm afraid of forgetting something.
I'm afraid to say this, but you're wrong.

He's proud of winning/having won the race.
He's proud to be here.

She's ashamed of letting the side down.
She's ashamed to admit it, but she was wrong.

He's very keen on riding.
He's always keen to help other people.

ABOUT YOU

1 In pairs, discuss people you know using the adjectives above, and this model:
A: What's John like at sport?
B: Oh, he's brilliant at swimming, but I'm sorry/afraid to say he's useless at running.

2 Make statements about your own abilities like this:
I'm afraid/sorry to say I'm useless at geography.
I'm pleased/proud to say I'm quite good at sailing.

14

Grammar practice 2

Some verbs always followed by the gerund (for an action)

REVIEW

He avoided telling her the truth.

I'm considering going to London soon.

Practise remembering things without writing down notes for yourself.

I just can't imagine living in a big city.

I've finished reading this book.

I resent filling in forms.

She didn't feel like going to work, so she stayed home instead.

Here are some common verbs which are usually followed by another verb in the gerund:

admit anticipate appreciate avoid
delay feel like finish imagine involve
keep (on) mind miss pardon postpone
prevent practise put off resent resist
risk suggest

Remember also the verbs practised in Unit 4, p 20 (*detest*, *enjoy*, etc.).

PRACTICE

1 Join these pairs of sentences.

Example: He told lies. *He admitted* it. ⟶ He admitted telling lies.

1 Please open the window. *Do you mind?*
2 'Let's go out.' That's what *he suggested.*
3 Flying to the moon! *Just imagine* it!
4 Stay at home? *I don't feel like* it.
5 We might have to sell the factory. At least, *we anticipate* it.
6 He was writing a letter. *Has he finished?*
7 I can't go away now. *I daren't risk* it.
8 We won't pay that bill. *We'll delay* it.
9 I went to meet them. *They appreciated* it.
10 He didn't see his children. *He missed* that.

2 Game: *True or false?* (See Teacher's Guide p 51)

Grammar practice 3

The verbs *stop, forget, remember, try, mean, need* and *help* with the gerund or infinitive

REVIEW

I have stopped writing things down.

I shall never forget visiting Paris.

I shall always remember going to India.

Try wearing that hat the other way round (to see what it will look like).

If you want to go to college, it will mean (=involve you in) studying hard.

The car needs cleaning (=needs to be cleaned).

She couldn't help (=stop herself from) crying.

I stopped to take a photograph.

I forgot to post these letters.

I must remember to ring him tomorrow.

You must try (=make an effort) to remember things without writing them down.

I really mean (=intend) to pass this examination.

We need to (=must) get to the airport by seven o'clock.

Can I help you (to) do that job?

PRACTICE

Join these sentences, beginning with the words in italics.

1 He's going to be a millionaire one day. *He means* it.
2 You must be more helpful. *You must try.*
3 I used to smoke. *I stopped* six months ago.
4 *She stopped.* Then she spoke to an old man.
5 I feel that this is wrong. *I can't help* it.
6 How about opening it with a knife? *Why don't you try* that?
7 I didn't get any vegetables. *I forgot.*
8 She once flew in Concorde. *She'll never forget* it.
9 I turned out all the cupboards. *John helped me.*
10 *These papers* have to be sorted out. They *need* it.

ABOUT YOU

In pairs or small groups, tell each other about things you will always remember/never forget doing.

Vocabulary

Adjectives with suffixes (and nouns with *-ness*)

Here are more adjectives formed with suffixes. Study them carefully, and then do the exercises below.

-ful	useful, careful, hopeful, restful, harmful, merciful, successful, forgetful, pitiful, delightful, dreadful, grateful
-ly	manly, worldly, friendly, brotherly, sisterly, cowardly, daily, weekly, fortnightly, monthly, yearly
-y	creamy, meaty, sandy, hairy, silky, crunchy
-less	useless, careless, hopeless, restless, harmless, merciless, pointless, aimless, blameless, speechless
-ish	childish, foolish, selfish, girlish
-like	childlike, lifelike, workmanlike, statesmanlike

Note that nouns can be formed from these adjectives by adding the suffix *-ness* (except with *-like* adjectives and *daily, weekly, monthly,* etc.) for example: *usefulness, friendliness, meatiness, carelessness, foolishness.*

Now cover the box and complete the following with words from it:

1 A person who shows no mercy is ____.
2 Something which can cause harm is ____.
3 A statue which looks as if it is alive is ____.
4 Something which feels like silk is ____.
5 A person who can never remember things is ____.
6 Someone who acts like a fool is ____.
7 Someone who only thinks of himself or herself is ____.
8 An action which has no point or reason is ____.
9 A magazine produced every four weeks is a ____ magazine.
10 Someone who can't settle down or rest is ____.

Make up more definitions like this for other students to complete.

14

Exercises for homework

See if you can do these exercises in 60 minutes.

1 Use of English

Join the following pairs of sentences, beginning with the word or words in italics.

1 She can't iron shirts. *She's useless.*
2 He stole that money. *He's ashamed* of it.
3 I really want to win that race. *I'm very keen.*
4 'Let's go out for a meal.' That's what *he suggested.*
5 'Write that report. *Finish* it today if you can.'
6 I didn't go and see the manager. *I completely forgot.*
7 She doesn't sing in the choir now. *She misses* it.
8 I think I'll have a winter holiday next year. At least, *I'm considering* it.
9 I don't want to live here any more. *I'm tired* of it.
10 She can always solve other people's problems. *She's expert* at it.

2 Use of English

A shop was broken into during the night. A policeman is now interviewing the girl assistant whose responsibility it was to lock up last night and open up this morning. Read the dialogue and complete the sentences numbered (1) to (5).

POLICEMAN: (1) Do you remember ....this morning?
ASSISTANT: Yes, I unlocked the door. I'm sure I did. I remember it, yes.
POLICEMAN: But Mr James the manager says you're a little forgetful.
(2) Tell me, ...?
ASSISTANT: Forget to lock up when I left last night? No, I didn't.
POLICEMAN: Are you absolutely sure?
ASSISTANT: (3) Yes, quite sure, because ....
POLICEMAN: So you locked the door, put the key in your handbag, then checked the door again to make sure it was really locked properly.
ASSISTANT: Yes.
POLICEMAN: (4) Well, now, ...?
ASSISTANT: Oh, I got here about nine o'clock—a little later than usual.
POLICEMAN: Why was that?
ASSISTANT: (5) My shoes ....
POLICEMAN: You stopped on the way to take them to the shoe repairer's.
ASSISTANT: Yes.

3 Composition: Narrative

Write a story which ends with this sentence: 'In spite of everything that had happened, however, I just couldn't help smiling to myself.' Refer back to the Study section on p 71 and plan and write a composition of about 150 words. Wherever possible, use language you have practised in this and recent Units.

TEST: LISTENING COMPREHENSION

Time: approx. 20 minutes

You will hear two extracts of spoken English (each twice on cassette or read by the teacher), and you will be given time to choose your answers to the questions. Before you listen to each extract, read the questions (and suggested answers) or statements carefully. Read again as you listen and before the second recording and choose A, B, C or D, or tick *True, False* or *Don't know.* Check your answers while you are listening for the second time.

---

1 She knows that he
A will stick to his decision.
B has never tried to stop before.
C is hopeless at making decisions.
D probably won't be able to give up.

2 He intends to succeed this time
A in order to save money.
B even though he has failed before.
C because he wants to get fit.
D so that he doesn't disappoint his friends.

3 He means to
A write to all his friends about it.
B eat a lot more regularly.
C avoid places where smoking is allowed.
D anticipate problems from now on.

4 Another smoker would describe him as
A hardly a 'smoker' at all.
B a light smoker.
C a heavy smoker.
D a very heavy smoker.

From what you hear, are these statements true, false, or don't you know?

	True	False	Don't know
5 The family remember the holiday so well because nearly everything went wrong.			
6 They often oversleep.			
7 They started out later than they had planned.			
8 Even though they arrived late, they were given a delightful corner of the campsite.			
9 The speaker is quite expert at putting up a tent.			
10 There were no instructions with the new tent that they had bought.			
11 None of the rest of the family knew anything about putting up a tent.			
12 It had started raining the moment they left home.			
13 They had a meal before they went to bed.			
14 They had a very restful first night.			
15 They are going away in a caravan next year.			

Unit 15
It wouldn't have happened if . . .

EXAM FOCUS:
Oral Interview

Read and speak

Read this article and look at the photo. Then do the exercises below and on the opposite page.

1 In pairs, ask and say:

1 where and when the accident happened.
2 how the accident happened.
3 how many people were injured or killed.
4 how the tanker driver is now.
5 why a fireman also went to hospital.
6 what happened to the tanker container.
7 what happened to the petrol.
8 how the petrol caught fire.
9 if the car belonged to the driver (of the car).
10 who took the photograph, and when.

2 Role play

In pairs, role-play an interview between a policeman/policewoman and a witness of the accident. Begin like this:

POLICEMAN/ POLICEWOMAN: Where were you and what were you doing when the accident happened?

'Inferno' follows fatal accident

Police diverted traffic after a serious accident and tanker fire in Hightown yesterday afternoon.

A large petrol tanker was travelling along London Road when a car shot out of the junction with West Way and smashed into the side of it. The driver of the car died instantly. The passenger in the car and the tanker driver were both severely injured and taken to Hightown Hospital where the car passenger is said to be recovering. The tanker driver has still not come to after being knocked out. A further casualty, a fireman who was overcome by fumes, was discharged from hospital after treatment.

3 Look at the photo and refer to the article again, and make statements about what would or wouldn't have happened if . . .. Here are two examples:

If the car hadn't shot out of West Way, it wouldn't have hit the tanker.
The police wouldn't have diverted the traffic if there hadn't been a serious accident.

4 About you

Say what you would have done if you had been nearby and had witnessed the accident yesterday afternoon.

Carelessness caused fire

Both were lucky to escape with their lives because shortly after they had been taken to hospital, the junction became, in the words of a police spokesman, 'a raging inferno'. He explained, 'What happened was that the tanker container split, petrol started leaking out, and spread all over the road. Then, before we could cordon off the area, some careless passer-by stopped to light a cigarette and threw the match down in the road. You can imagine what happened. It was a miracle no one else was injured.'

Stolen car

The police have since discovered that the car involved in the accident had been stolen minutes before from a garage in Market Street.

(Our photo was taken by a resident in a nearby house immediately after the accident happened.)

15

Grammar practice 1

Past conditional *would/wouldn't have done . . . if had/hadn't done* or *if had/hadn't been doing;* and *would/wouldn't do/be now . . . if had/hadn't done,* for regret, criticism and comments on past actions

REVIEW

She criticises . . .

You wouldn't have had an accident if you'd walked to work.

You would have avoided that lorry
if you hadn't been looking at a girl!

You wouldn't be here now
You'd be safe at home now } if you'd walked to work.

He regrets . . .

If I'd walked to work, I wouldn't have had an accident.

I wouldn't have hit that lorry if I'd been watching the road.

If I'd been watching the road, I wouldn't be here now.

'The bus ride was terrible. If you hadn't crashed the car, I would have driven here to see you!'

Note the forms and abbreviated forms in past conditional sentences:

I would I'd I wouldn't	have done that if	I had I'd I hadn't	known. been thinking.

Make more sentences like those in the box above that *she* might have said to him (criticism) or that *he* might have said (regret).

PRACTICE

Comment on or criticise the actions of these people.
What would or wouldn't have happened if . . .?

1 War broke out because one soldier fired a shot across the border.
2 The police arrested the man for stealing a car from the garage.
3 They weren't listening, so they didn't take in what the lecturer said.
4 He's out of work now because in his last job he was late every day.
5 The girl wasn't looking where she was going, so she fell down and broke her arm.

ABOUT YOU

Express regret about things you have done in the past, like this:

I lost my passport when I was on holiday last year.
I wouldn't have lost it if I hadn't been so careless.

Grammar practice 2

More irregular verbs

REVIEW

Study these verbs, and then do the exercise below:

get	got	got	beat	beat	beaten	sit	sat	sat
lose	lost	lost	hear	heard	heard	spit	spat	spat
shine	shone	shone	light	lit	lit	stand	stood	stood
shoot	shot	shot	make	made	made	lay	laid	laid
			say	said	said	pay	paid	paid

PRACTICE

Put in the correct form of the verbs (*would have done* or *had done*).

1 If you had made the child eat it, he (*spit*) it out.
2 They (*hear*) everything that was being said if they had sat still.
3 He would have beaten his opponent if he (*not lose*) his concentration.
4 She (*not pay*) so much if she had got a ticket earlier.
5 If he (*shine*) his torch in the right direction, it would have lit up the whole room.

Exercises for homework

See if you can do these exercises in 60 minutes.

1 Use of English

Finish each of the following sentences in such a way that it means exactly the same as the sentence printed before it.

1 They criticised me because I made a simple mistake.
If I hadn't ....
2 The lion was attacking the man, so he shot it.
The man wouldn't ....
3 He was making so much noise that he didn't hear the telephone.
If he hadn't...
4 He's a millionaire now because he worked so hard when he was younger.
He wouldn't...
5 She lost all her money in the business because she wasn't careful.
If she had ....

2 Composition: Narrative in a letter

Write a letter to an English-speaking friend telling him or her about what happened to delay you while you were recently on your way to an important appointment. Tell him/her what you did to get to the appointment and to inform the people you were going to meet that you would be late. Your letter should be about 150 words (not counting the address).

15

Oral Interview preparation

1 Look at this photograph and then answer the questions on the opposite page.

2 Reading aloud

Part of the First Certificate Oral Interview involves reading aloud a short passage, as here. Practise reading this passage aloud, noting the following:

- the pronunciation (and main stress) of long or apparently difficult words e.g. *pho'tographer, de'tached, te'rrific ex'plosion, 'miracle, 'injured,* etc.
- the general 'flow' of phrases and sentences. Commas and full stops indicate the best places to pause.
- the intonation of sentences, especially questions and tag-questions where they occur.
- the clarity and pace of your reading. Do not read too slowly or too quickly.

Hey, listen to this from the paper!

'Mr Ray Patrick, a local photographer, had the narrowest escape of his life yesterday evening. He had just left his detached house in Market Road, where he lives alone, when a terrific explosion rocked the house. The front door was blown out and glass from the windows was thrown all over the road and garden.

"It was a miracle," Ray told our reporter. "If a friend hadn't rung up ten minutes before and asked me to go out, I would have been sitting watching television. I'm sure I would have been killed or badly injured."

A fire service spokesman said: "We believe the explosion was caused by escaping gas. It's amazing there were no casualties."'

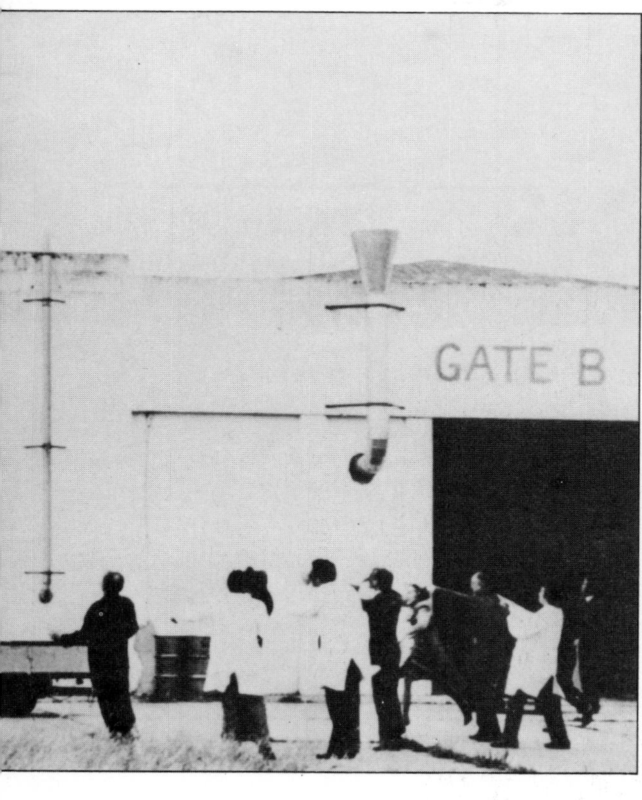

About the photograph

1 Where was this photo taken, and at what time of day, do you think? Why?
2 What are most of the people doing? Why?
3 What do you think you would have done if you had been there?
4 What do you think would have happened if the motorcyclist had misjudged his jump?
5 Can you think of any reason why the motorcyclist did this stunt?

General

1 Would you risk doing a stunt like this? Why?/Why not?
2 How do you feel about stunts like this? Do you think they are admirable, pointless, harmless, childish? Why?
3 What's the most thrilling/frightening feat or stunt you've ever seen, and where was it? Would you have done it? Why?/Why not?

3 Situation for extended role play

You arrive at an airport in an English-speaking country only to find that your luggage has not arrived with you! You go to the airport official who deals with missing luggage. In pairs, conduct the conversation between the official and yourself. Ask for and/or give the following information:

- your name and what flight you arrived on
- where your luggage could be
- what you would have done if you had known this was going to happen
- what luggage you had + description
- what the airline company is going to do
- address you will be staying at

4 Game: *Just a minute* (See Teacher's Guide, p 56)

Unit 16
The Tour of the Century

EXAM FOCUS:
Reading Comprehension

Read and speak

Read this extract from a travel brochure for the year 2083 AD. Then do the exercises below.

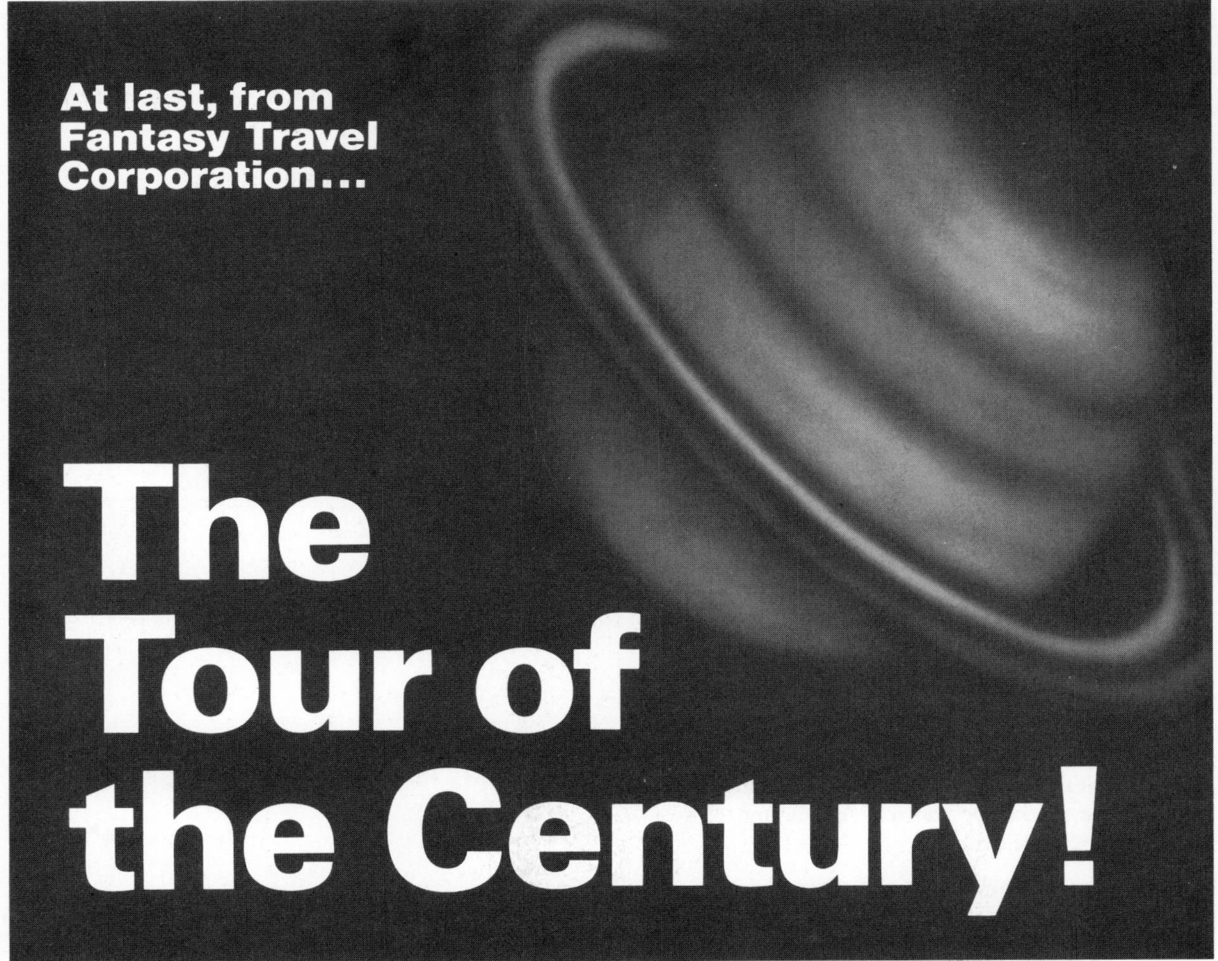
At last, from
Fantasy Travel
Corporation...
The
Tour of
the Century!

1 In pairs, ask and say:

1 how long the tour will last.
2 how you get to Luna Sat Base.
3 what speed you will be travelling at.
4 how long you spend on the Moon.
5 how far Mars is from the Sun and Earth.
6 what you do on the journey to Mars.
7 what you will visit on Mars.
8 how long it will take to get to Jupiter.
9 why Saturn is an incredible sight.
10 how you return from Saturn.

. . . to the Moon, Mars, Jupiter and Saturn ! ! !

What are you doing for the next two years?
What about that *special* holiday you've been promising yourself?

Fantasy Travel Corporation, famous throughout the solar system for fantastic journeys for over half an Earth century, invite you now to book your seat on The Tour of the Century.

Stage 1: You blast off from Terra Base on 15th of the (Earth) month in one of our luxury shuttle ferries to the Moon, and land on Luna Sat Base 72.5 hours later. On the way you will be travelling at more than 5,000 kph, but you will feel nothing unusual. You will see Mother Earth from space for the very first time with your own eyes. The view is breath-taking, unbelievable, unforgettable . . .!
You transfer down to Luna City by shuttle and spend two days on the Moon before you take off for Mars.

Stage 2: From Luna City we join Luna Sat where you board the major transport ship 'Fantasy Voyager', your ship and home for the journey to Mars, Jupiter and Saturn. We reach Mars, 228 million km from the Sun and the same distance from Earth, in two months under deep hibernation: to you, it will be a single night of sleep. On Mars, you will visit the deep ravines, the dry ice polar caps, giant volcanoes and steep mountains. You spend two weeks on Mars where the planetary shuttle is available for your pleasure.

Stage 3: Blasting off again in 'Fantasy Voyager', we head out towards the giant world of Jupiter, first of the outer planets, with its 16 moons. It is 778 million km from the Sun. This will take four months, but to you (in deep hibernation) it will pass like three nights' sleep. You will spend two weeks orbiting this massive planet, with time to visit one of the larger moons.

Stage 4: On out to Saturn, the highlight of the tour at 1,427 million km from the Sun. You will not be disappointed. Saturn, second largest planet in the solar system, is an incredible sight with more than twenty moons and its spectacular ring system. You will visit Titan and make a fantastic trip through the outer rings, surely the most memorable experience known to mankind.

Stage 5: And from Saturn, planet of dreams, we return through hyper-space-time to Luna Sat Base where you will be revived from deep hibernation and given automatic illness therapy. After 5 days' acclimatisation at the Base you will transfer to a luxury shuttle ferry for the descent to Earth. You land 20 months after you left.

Don't miss this ***chance of a lifetime!***

For price in Convertible Currency Units, details and bookings, contact:
Komputer Bureau, Fantasy Travel Corporation, 1481 Neptune Drive, Sol City

2 Role play

In pairs, role-play the conversation between a travel agent for Fantasy Travel Corporation and a person who wants to book a seat. Check all the information, travel details and times.

3 Discussion

Do you think people will be taking this kind of holiday in a hundred years' time? Will everyone be able to go? Why?/Why not? Would *you* want to go? Why?/Why not? Or perhaps such holidays will never be possible? What do you think?

16

. . . and now, back on Earth, and back to *Now* . . .

Grammar practice

Expressing the future with Present Simple, Present Continuous, *will do* and *will be doing*

REVIEW

The coach leaves at 9.00 tomorrow morning.	Present Simple for 'timetable' future.
We're spending next Thursday night in Scarborough.	Present Continuous for definite future arrangements.
We'll be in Grasmere next Tuesday.	*will* for plain statements (or promises).
We'll be coming back through London.	*will be doing* for something fixed or decided for the future.

PRACTICE

Read this travel brochure itinerary for a seven-day coach tour in Britain. Then do the exercises on p 94.

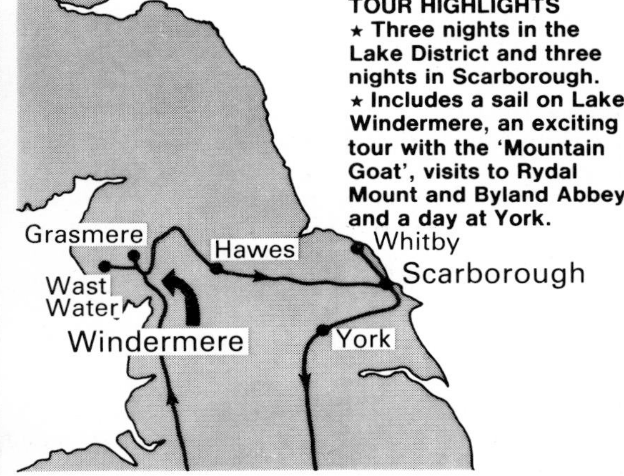

TOUR HIGHLIGHTS
★ Three nights in the Lake District and three nights in Scarborough.
★ Includes a sail on Lake Windermere, an exciting tour with the 'Mountain Goat', visits to Rydal Mount and Byland Abbey, and a day at York.
Grasmere
Hawes
Whitby
Scarborough
Wast Water
Windermere
York

Monday – We travel to the beautiful Lake District to spend three nights at the ***Storrs Hall Hotel,*** formerly an imposing country mansion, and delightfully situated in woodland gardens on the shore of Lake Windermere.
Tuesday – A visit to the nearby resort of Bowness, a busy touring centre, full of quaint climbing streets and charming craft and souvenir shops. From here we take a cruise on Lake Windermere to Ambleside, then visit Rydal Mount nearby, Wordsworth's home from 1813 to 1850. Finally we have time for sightseeing in the delightful village of Grasmere.
Wednesday – An exciting full day excursion by the famous 'Mountain Goat' minibuses, climbing over spectacular countryside to reach peaceful Eskdale, then on to Wast Water beneath mighty Scafell. Unforgettable!
Thursday – Leaving Lake Windermere we travel through Wensleydale and Thirsk to visit Byland Abbey, the remains of a church and monastic buildings dating from the 12th century. On to Scarborough where we spend three nights at the friendly and comfortable ***Alton Hotel.***
Friday – Morning at leisure in Scarborough. In the afternoon we cross the North Yorkshire Moors to visit picturesque Whitby.
Saturday – A full day excursion to the historic city of York with its famous Minster and narrow medieval streets.
Sunday – We leave Scarborough and Yorkshire to return home.
Accommodation & Meals – 6 nights dinner, bed, breakfast & lunch.

HOLIDAY 566

Departure Day – Monday
Return Day – Sunday

July 13	**£169**
Aug 10	**£163**
Sept 7	**£158**

Departure arrangements

Bournemouth	0900
Oxford	1235
Portsmouth	0900
Salisbury	1035
Southampton	1000
Swindon	1115

1 You are going on the seven-day coach tour and will be joining it at Oxford next Monday. In pairs, ask and tell each other about the tour. Ask questions like this:

When does the coach leave (on Monday)?
Where do we stay the first night?
What will we be doing on Tuesday morning?
When are we coming back?
etc.

2 In groups, and taking the itinerary on p 93 as a model, choose a country and discuss and plan a seven-day coach tour in that country for a group of English-speaking tourists. As you discuss the itinerary, write it out as if for the information of the tourists.

```
Coach tour of/to: ....................
......................................
from: ............ to: ..............
Duration: ............................
Dates: Departure: ....................
       Return: .......................
Highlights of the tour: ..............
......................................
......................................
......................................
Itinerary: ...........................
......................................
......................................
......................................
......................................
......................................
......................................
......................................
......................................
......................................
Notes (requirements for the tour,
special clothes, sports equipment,etc)
......................................
......................................
Accommodation and meals: .............
......................................
Cost (and insurance): ................
......................................
```

Exercises for homework

See if you can do these exercises in 90 minutes.

1 Use of English: Directed writing

Taking your information from 'The Tour of the Century' itinerary on pp 91–92, write three paragraphs, as if in a letter to a friend, telling him or her about your forthcoming fantastic trip. Continue each of the three paragraphs below. Use no more than 50 words for each paragraph.

I've decided to spend all my life's savings and go on a fantastic space tour . . . .

After we've spent 48 hours on the Moon, ...

For me, Saturn will be . . . .

2 Composition

Plan and write *one* of these compositions.

1 Write a letter to an English-speaking friend describing your most recent holiday away or a trip you have been on recently. You should make the beginning and ending as for an ordinary letter, but the address is not to be counted in the number of words, which should be between 120 and 180.

2 You have been asked to organise a two-week coach tour through two or three countries. Write a detailed itinerary, including days and times, stopping places, requirements for the journey and any other information you think the travellers will need. Write it in the form of a hand-out to be sent to members of the party before the tour. You should write between 120 and 180 words.

16

TEST: READING COMPREHENSION

Time: 35 minutes

Section A

Choose the word or phrase which best completes each sentence.
Write your choice (A, B, C or D) on a separate piece of paper.

1 The instructor on the course was hopeless ____ explaining things.
A in B of C at D to

2 She never told anyone because she was ____ of what she had done.
A incapable B selfish C useless D ashamed

3 I'd ____ your coming to the meeting if you can make it.
A like B appreciate C anticipate D look forward

4 The club has ____ meeting, held every other Wednesday.
A a weekly B an annual C a monthly D a fortnightly

5 If we want to catch the early train, it'll ____ getting up at six.
A need B mean C imagine D suggest

6 Because of the fog, all incoming aircraft were ____ to another airport.
A diverted B put off C postponed D driven

7 She ____ here now if she hadn't done so well in her interview.
A wouldn't work B wouldn't have worked C wouldn't be working D didn't work

8 Don't lay that bottle on its side: the top might start ____.
A spilling B leaking C falling D spreading

9 It's a ____ he's alive after being in a crash like that.
A spectacle B fantasy C miracle D chance

10 The press couldn't speak to the firemen: they had to wait for a statement from a Fire Department ____.
A speaker B messenger C reporter D spokesman

11 We're going to ____ a cruise on the river next weekend.
A take B go C travel D sail

12 If I had been thinking, I ____ that silly mistake.
A didn't make B wouldn't make C wouldn't be making D wouldn't have made

13 I know it's a boring journey, but the time will ____ quite quickly if you read something.
A pass B spend C take D return

14 The space probe will be ____ the planet for a week.
A surrounding B orbiting C blasting off D travelling

15 We leave London ____ Brighton at 7.30 tomorrow morning.
A to B towards C on D for

Section B

Read this passage carefully. Then choose which you think is the best suggested answer or way of finishing the statement in each item below—A, B, C or D. Write your answers on a separate piece of paper.

'We leave at dawn and head out overland by jeep towards Base One. We'll get as far as we can before proceeding on foot,' Mark explained.

The others sat and listened. Sarah, particularly, as a "casualty of events", wouldn't have known what to say or suggest even if she'd been asked. But Harry had a lot to say.

'We'll never make it,' he protested. 'We'll still be crossing the desert when they catch up with us. They'll know where we're heading for and they'll simply follow us and kill us out there in the desert with no one to see. They seem to know every move we make or are going to make.'

Mark said nothing, but spread his hands out as if to say "Well, what do we do then?"

'We wouldn't be in this mess now,' Harry went on, almost ignoring Mark's gesture, 'if we hadn't stopped to rescue Sarah.' (He glanced at her briefly.) 'But since we did, we must get on—but not across the desert. There's the sand, and deep ravines which are almost invisible until you're right on them—and then the heat. You have to be acclimatised to go out there, and none of us is. This is no "morning at leisure" on some pleasant coaching holiday, you know! If we went north instead and made for the river, . . .'

He broke off and looked around at the others, feeling somehow that his argument was pointless. No one said anything.

'Good,' said Mark, looking around with authority, and returned to checking their stores.

A spectacular sunrise was about to burst over the horizon as the jeep headed out towards Base One.

16 It seems clear from the passage that the group of people
   A were on an expedition.
   B were being hunted.
   C were on an African safari.
   D were holidaying in a hot country.

17 Mark's plan was that they should
   A drive across the desert.
   B make for the river on foot.
   C set off before dawn and leave Sarah.
   D drive so far, then walk.

18 Harry felt certain that
   A they would be followed.
   B someone in the group was a traitor.
   C their situation was all Sarah's fault.
   D they could hide in ravines in the desert.

19 Why did Harry think that they should make for the river?
   A The journey would be more pleasant.
   B A river cruise would be safer.
   C The desert heat would kill them.
   D He knew the road leading north.

20 They kept to Mark's plan because
   A no one liked Harry.
   B Mark was clearly the leader.
   C they wanted to see the sunrise.
   D there were no other alternatives.

Unit 17

When Mount St Helens finally erupted . . .

EXAM FOCUS:
Composition (Dialogue)

Disasters are usually unexpected. For once, this was one which everyone had expected. Even so, when Mount St Helens actually exploded in Washington State on Sunday, 18th May 1980, it did so suddenly and dramatically—and left some 100 people dead.

Geologist David Johnston was keeping watch at the Coldwater Two observation post five miles north of the summit of Mount St Helens. For seven weeks the 2,949-metre snow-covered mountain had been giving out signs of imminent eruption. Johnston was at one of a number of observation points from which geologists were keeping up with the state of the mountain and reporting back to the US Geological Survey base 40 miles south of the summit at Vancouver, Washington State.

At 8.32 a.m. that Sunday, Johnston got on to the base and shouted over the radio: 'Vancouver, Vancouver. This is it. The mountain's going!' They were the 30-year-old geologist's last words. He died instantly as the volcano exploded with a force 500 times greater than the atomic bomb dropped on Hiroshima, taking 400 metres off the top. Any attempts to get through to Johnston again were useless.

People heard the noise 200 miles away. But the mud and ash quickly caught up with Bert Delfonso, a logger, only 25 miles away. He said it was 'like the end of the world. Heavy, thick clouds boiled up, white and blue, lightning flashes crackled through the mountains. It rained mud balls. And after that the ash came down. It just got black, and I mean pitch black'.

Another witness said: 'I broke out in a cold sweat, and ran.'

Within seconds the volcano had put on a terrible display. The north wall collapsed and gas, ash and rock blasted up into the air, some up to 16 miles into the stratosphere. Snow melted instantly and avalanches of mud and rock hurtled down the sides of the volcano at 100 mph, sweeping away homes, cabins, bridges and millions of fir trees. One flow of debris blocked the outlet of Spirit Lake. When the ash fell, it fell on the state fish farm at Green River killing 10,000,000 salmon, and on the wheat fields and orchards to the east.

Until 1980 the volcano had been inactive since 1857. In 1975 geologists had predicted that it might erupt 'perhaps before the end of the century'. And then seven weeks before the disaster, the experts came up with a more exact prediction. They said an eruption was imminent and that an evacuation programme should begin. They declared two zones around the mountain (a red zone and a blue zone) and set up blockades to stop people going in. But in the weeks that led up to that Sunday, tourists, loggers, property-owners, newsmen and

Shopping after the dustfall

mountain climbers had entered the 'forbidden' zones. Some of these people paid with their lives. Later, it was found that ash and molten mud had caught up with many: falling trees had killed others.

David Johnston had always known that the mountain would blow fast when the time came. He thought they would have about two hours' warning. In the event, he had hardly any warning at all. Searchers found only a four-foot-high pile of black ash where Johnston's trailer had stood.

Read and speak

Read the article opposite carefully and then do the exercises below.

1 General questions

1 What is Mount St Helens and where is it?
2 What happened on 18th May, 1980?
3 When was the last time it did that?
4 Had people expected this to happen? Why?
5 Was it a large eruption, or only a small one?
6 How much damage was done?
7 How many people were killed?
8 Why didn't David Johnston escape?

2 In pairs, ask and tell each other:

1 what David Johnston's job was.
2 where he was and what he was doing that Sunday morning.
3 how long the volcano had been giving out warning signs.
4 what the geologists were doing at the different observation points.
5 when Johnston got on to the base.
6 what he actually said.
7 why it was useless to try to get through to Johnston again.
8 where Bert Delfonso was when the mud and ash caught up with him.
9 how Bert described what happened.
10 what another witness said.

Continue to ask and answer more questions.

3 Discussion

When the dust and ash had finally settled, what kinds of problems do you think people in nearby towns and cities had to face up to?

17

Grammar practice 1

Temporal conjunctions *when, while, (just) as, before, after, as soon as, the moment (that)* and *hardly/scarcely . . . when* in accounts of past events

REVIEW

David was contacting the base when the volcano erupted.

While David was contacting the base, the volcano erupted.

David Johnston died instantly when/as the volcano erupted.

David gave a warning (just) before the volcano erupted.

When/After the dust had finally settled, people began to clear up.

He got on to the base {as soon as / the moment (that)} he thought the mountain was going to erupt.

He had hardly/scarcely started speaking when the volcano erupted.

Note the use of the *-ing* form after *before, after* and *on.*

The volcano gave out warning signs before erupting.
(= before it erupted)

He died shortly after getting through to the base.
(= after he had got through . . .)

On hearing the explosion, the man broke out in a cold sweat.
(= When he heard . . .)

PRACTICE

Join these sentences using the words in brackets.

1 The ash came down. It got pitch black. (*As soon as . . .*)
2 Bert heard the explosion. Mud and ash caught up with him. (*. . . hardly . . . when . . .*)
3 Some people were killed by falling trees. They were camping in the red zone. (*. . . while . . .*)
4 Experts knew an eruption was imminent. They evacuated the area. (*The moment . . .*)
5 People could clean up. The ash had stopped falling. (*. . . only after . . .*)

Now refer to the text again on pp 97 and 98 and make more statements like these using *when, as soon as, hardly . . . when, after,* etc.

Grammar practice 2

More irregular verbs

REVIEW

Study these irregular verbs, and then do the exercise.

bend	bent	bent	send	sent	sent
build	built	built	spend	spent	spent
lend	lent	lent			

bleed	bled	bled	hold	held	held
breed	bred	bred	lead	led	led
feed	fed	fed	read	read	read
flee	fled	fled	/ri:d/	/red/	/red/

PRACTICE

Supply the correct form of the verbs in this paragraph:

When I was young, my father [1](*breed*) Afghan hounds. We had a lot of ground behind our house, and he had [2](*spend*) a lot of money and [3](*build*) kennels and large runs. Of course, I [4](*feed*) the dogs quite often. I remember one day my father had [5](*send*) me down to feed them before I went off to school. As I [6](*bend*) over to pick up a dog bowl, one of the older Afghans bit me on my arm and [7](*hold*) on so tightly that it started to bleed. I would have torn myself away and [8](*flee*), but it [9](*bleed*) so much that I passed out . . . Sad to say, the incident [10](*lead*) to the dog being put down.

Vocabulary

Phrasal-prepositional verbs

These phrasal verbs (sometimes called 'Type 4' or phrasal-prepositional verbs) consist of a verb + adverb particle (stressed) + preposition (unstressed), for example: *look 'forward to, come 'up with, run 'out of, put 'up with.* The particle and preposition are not usually separated or transposed:

What are you looking 'forward to?
I'm looking 'forward to the party.
I'm looking 'forward to it.

Study the verbs in these sentences. Then play the game below.

I *broke out in* a rash after eating crab.

They left earlier than I did, but I soon *caught up with* them in my fast car.

I've *come up against* a terrible problem.

They *came up with* some very good ideas.

They've *done away with* the old theatre.

Teenagers have to learn to *face up to* their responsibilities.

He *fell in with* the suggestion I made.

I *got on to* the insurance company yesterday about the claim on my car.

I couldn't *get through to* the manager when I rang.

He *went along with* everything I suggested.

Mary *went down with* flu last week.

His father wanted him to *go in for* politics when he left university.

He *went on about* that broken cup for ages.

Slow down! I can't *keep up with* you.

It all *led up to* a massive explosion.

I'm *looking forward to* seeing them.

Nothing can *make up for* his rudeness.

They had to *put up with* a lot of hardship during the war.

After the meeting, he *reported back to* his boss.

We've *run out of* envelopes. I'll get some.

He respected people who *stood up to* him.

Game: *Make up a story* (see Teacher's Guide p 31)

17

Exercise for homework

Study section: Dialogue writing

If you had to write a dialogue, how should you tackle it? Read this example:

'Two friends had agreed to meet outside the local theatre last Saturday evening, but one of them did not turn up. Write the conversation that takes place between them when they meet on the Monday morning and in which one apologises to the other. Write the conversation in dialogue form, giving only the name of each speaker followed by the words spoken.'

As with other types of Composition that you have practised, there are certain things that you must bear in mind. Read the notes on the right and the sample below. Then do the exercise below the dialogue.

MARIA: Helen! Whatever happened to you on Saturday?

HELEN: Hello, Maria. Yes, I'm very sorry . . .

MARIA: I hung around for ages, and when you didn't turn up, I finally went home.

HELEN: Yes, I said I'm sorry. I've been trying to get through to you since late Saturday afternoon, but your phone seems to be permanently engaged.

MARIA: There must be something wrong with it then, because no one else has phoned, either. Anyway, what happened?

HELEN: Well, on Saturday John went down with flu or something, and I didn't want to leave him, so I went out to a callbox to ring you. When I couldn't get through, I decided to drive over and see you to cancel our arrangement.

MARIA: Well, I was in all afternoon.

HELEN: Perhaps you were, but I'd only gone about two miles when I ran out of petrol. Still, by the time I'd gone for petrol and then got the car going again, you had certainly left home. So I went home, too.

MARIA: Oh, well, let's forget it. But next time, you can call for me. Then if you can't make it, at least I'll be at home.

Now write, in dialogue form, the conversation between yourself and an old friend whom you meet while you are hurrying to get somewhere and whom you haven't seen for a very long time.

Notes

When writing a dialogue, think in terms of three things: content, form and language.

1 *Content:*
The situation (above, for example) is usually carefully defined. Try to think yourself into the situation: decide what you would say in that situation and how you think the other person would react, and therefore what he or she would say. Make sure, too, that the conversation deals only with the subject set.

2 *Form:*
The layout should be as in this example, and because you are writing speech, take extra care with punctuation.

3 *Language:*
This should be natural and appropriate to the situation and the people who are talking. Short forms will nearly always be used—*isn't, wouldn't, can't,* etc.

TEST: COMPOSITION

Time: 90 minutes

Write **two only** of the following composition exercises. Your answers must follow exactly the instructions given, and must be of between 120 and 180 words each.

1 You are at the airport an hour before your plane is due to take off when you realise that you have left something important in the flat you share with an English-speaking friend. Telephone the friend, explain the situation, and give him or her details of where to find what you have left. Then ask him or her to bring it to the airport in time for you to catch the plane. Write the conversation in dialogue form, giving only the name of each speaker followed by the words spoken.

2 Write a story which ends like this:
'. . . by the time I reached the end of the garden, the house behind me was a raging inferno.'

3 You have just returned from a holiday during which you had a memorable experience. Write a letter to an English-speaking friend telling him or her all about it. You should make the beginning and ending like those of an ordinary letter, but the address is not to be counted in the number of words.

(*Note:* For this Test you may refer back to Units in this coursebook to help you.)

Unit 18

You can't believe your eyes

EXAM FOCUS·
Use of English

Read, look and speak

This is a self-portrait drawn by Maurits Cornelius Escher, the famous Dutch graphic artist who died in 1972 at the age of 73. At school he was no good at maths, but his drawings nearly all show an understanding of mathematical principles and perspective. Indeed, mathematicians are fascinated by his drawings, in particular his 'impossible' buildings. He once wrote: 'Although I am absolutely without training or knowledge in the exact sciences, I often seem to have more in common with mathematicians than with my fellow artists.'

The woodcut below, entitled *Day and Night* (1938), is typical of Escher's drawings. Study it carefully and then complete the unfinished sentences.

If you look to the left of the picture, it looks as if the birds are flying towards the left and the ships seem to be sailing up the right side of the river. And if you look to the right of the picture, . . .
But it's not quite a mirror image because . . .

18

Belvedere

This drawing is called *Belvedere.* Study it carefully and read the short paragraphs about it. Then complete the unfinished sentences yourself.

Belvedere is typical of many of Escher's drawings which bring you up against strange ideas. How does he get away with it? He certainly hasn't done away with perspective. What he has done is to twist it. The pillars on the first floor seem to do the impossible: those at the front seem to be supporting the back of the upper floor, and those at the back . . .

And there's that ladder! The man at the top looks as if he's standing on the ladder outside the building, but the man at the bottom seems . . .

And what about the man sitting on the bench by the steps? He seems to be holding . . .

And now look at the picture as a whole. The building is an impossibility! The first floor extends from left to right, while the top floor seems to . . .

Strange, isn't it?

Discussion

Are these pictures 'art' or 'technical drawing'? What do you think? Why?

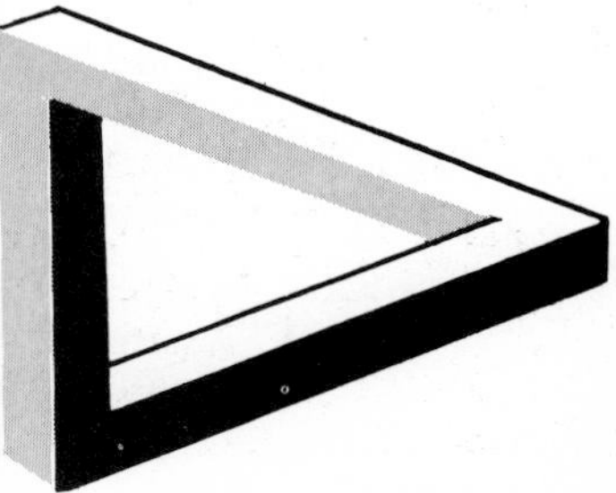

18

Grammar practice 1

'Stative' verbs *seem, appear* and *look,* and modal verbs *must, may, might* and *could* to express an assumption, deduction or possibility regarding actions going on now

REVIEW

Assumption/ Deduction	He looks as if/as though he's waiting for someone.
	He {seems / appears} to be waiting for someone.
	(I think) he must be waiting for someone.
Possibility	He {may / might / could} be waiting for someone, but I don't really know

PRACTICE
What must the people above be doing? What might they be doing? Give reasons.

Grammar practice 2

***seem, appear* and *look,* and *must, may, might* and *could* (+simple and continuous verb forms) to express an assumption, deduction or possibility regarding past actions**

REVIEW

Assumption/Deduction

NOW
He looks {as if / as though} he {ate too much (at the party). / has eaten and drunk too much.}
He seems to have drunk too much.
(I think) he must have had a good time.

IN THE PAST
When I saw him, {
he looked {as if / as though} he was having a good time.
he {appeared / seemed} to be enjoying himself.
he must have been drinking champagne. }

Possibility

When I saw him, he	may might could	have been drinking tonic water, but I don't really know.

He left the party early, so he may/might/could have been ill.

PRACTICE

1 Cover the four pictures in the middle of p 105 and make statements about them like this:

I thought the man in the first picture must have been riding something.
The man in the first picture looked as if he was riding something.
The man in the first picture seemed to be riding or driving something.

2 Speculate about these different people with *must have done, may have done,* etc.

You saw a friend who . . .

1 was walking with a limp.
2 came out of a restaurant looking ill.
3 was reading a letter and smiling.
4 had just put down the phone and was crying.
5 came out of a bank looking worried.

Vocabulary

Phrasal-prepositional verbs (cont.)

Here are some more phrasal-prepositional verbs. Refer back to p 100 and revise the verbs there. Then study these verbs and their meanings and rephrase the sentences using phrasal-prepositional verbs.

be fed up with (=have had enough of)
bring sby up against (=make sby face)
bring sby in on (—usually=ask sby to join e.g. a discussion about sthg)
catch up on (=bring or get up to date)
cut down on (=reduce consumption of)
fall back on (=use when there is a failure or lack of other means)
get away with (=succeed in a deceit)
get away [with] (=escape [with e.g. stolen money] without being caught)
get (a)round to (=find time to do)
get rid of (=get free from, by selling, giving away, killing, etc.)
look down on (=have a low opinion of)
look up to (=have a high opinion of)
run away with (=win a game/competition easily)

1 Escher would *easily win* any prize for originality.
2 I really must *reduce my consumption of* cigarettes.
3 He must have *found time to write* those letters after I left.
4 The moment I have time, I may *get up to date with* some reading.
5 He seems to *have had enough of* doing the same job all the time.
6 The thief might have *escaped with* the jewels if that old lady hadn't hit him!
7 Who's that man over there? Someone must have *asked him to join* the meeting.
8 This job has *made us face* all sorts of new problems.
9 If things get bad, we've got some money in the bank to *use if necessary.*
10 I can't find my old gardening boots. Someone must have *given them away or something.*

18

Exercises for homework

See if you can do these exercises in 80 minutes.

1 Use of English

Finish the sentences with the correct form of the words in brackets.

1 I don't think they've gone to the cinema. They might . . . (*go to the theatre*).
2 He doesn't look bored. He seems . . . (*have a good time*).
3 The thief didn't have the money on him when he was arrested. He must . . . (*get rid of it*).
4 She was limping badly in the second half of the game. I think she may . . . (*hurt her leg earlier*).
5 As far as I can see, the children appear . . . (*enjoy the film*). None of them has started yawning or shuffling in their chairs yet!
6 John looked ill when I visited him. He didn't say so, but from the expression on his face, I think he must . . . (*suffer badly*).
7 I think she might . . . (*tell me yesterday*), but I can't remember.
8 I can't see very well from this distance, but he looks . . . (*crawl around*) on the ground looking for something.
9 It's unusual for Ann to be late. She could . . . (*stop for a meal*), I suppose.
10 You must . . . (*read about that accident yesterday*). It was in all the papers.

2 Use of English

Supply the following sentences with the correct particle and preposition. (They are all phrases with the verb *get*.)

1 He's one of those lucky people who seem to get ______ everything!
2 'Miss Jones, can you get ______ Mr Smith today and ask if I can see him tomorrow morning?'
3 After putting it off for ages, Jim finally got ______ putting a roof on his garage.
4 I would have got ______ the car if I'd known how much trouble it was going to give me.
5 Because of the dreadful weather, it took the rescuers three days to get ______ the climbers on the mountain.

3 Composition: Dialogue

A friend of yours has been offered a new job, but doesn't know whether to take it or not. Write the conversation between the friend and yourself in which you try to persuade him or her to accept it. Write the conversation in dialogue form, giving only the name of each speaker followed by the words spoken. Begin like this:

FRIEND: You know I'm fed up with the job I'm doing now . . .
SELF: Yes, you said you were looking for something different.
FRIEND: Well, . . .

TEST: USE OF ENGLISH

Time: 45 minutes

Answer all the questions. Write your answers in ink on the paper provided by the teacher.

1 Finish each of the following sentences in such a way that it means exactly the same as the sentence printed before it.

1 They did away with the old cinema because they wanted to build a block of flats.
If they hadn't wanted to build..........

2 He left the house just before the explosion occurred.
He had hardly..........

3 I think he's broken his leg, but I'm not sure.
I think he may..........

4 On hearing the news, I immediately telephoned my uncle.
The moment..........

5 We visit the castle first, and then we come back here.
We'll be coming..........

6 I'm pretty sure he was driving far too fast.
He must..........

7 She forgot to post the letters because she was in such a hurry.
If she..........

8 I went to the butcher's and then I went to the baker's.
After..........

9 He's useless at maths now because he didn't pay enough attention at school.
He wouldn't..........

10 I'm pretty sure they're catching up with us.
They must..........

2 On the next page is a transcript of the discussion among the organising committee for the end-of-term 'party' at an International College. Using the information given in the discussion, continue each of the three paragraphs given after it as if for an article to be published in the College magazine. Use no more than 50 words for each paragraph and write your article on the paper provided by the teacher.

PLEASE TURN OVER

USE OF ENGLISH TEST

continued

MARK: Well, before getting round to other matters on the agenda, let's talk about the end-of-term party. We know it'll have to be on Tuesday, 5th August, a week later than last year, to fall in with the new exam timetable.

JANET: All right, the date's definite. But does it have to be a 'party'? I thought we wanted to do away with the party idea this year.

RAY: I know you've been going on about 'something different this year', but can you suggest anything?

JANET: Well, no, not right at this minute, but . . .

MARK: Quite honestly, if we can't come up with any workable new ideas, then we'll have to fall back on the party. We haven't got much time.

JANET: All right, I'll go along with it.

RAY: So will I. Besides, everyone seems to have enjoyed it last year.

JANET: All right. Let's remind ourselves. What exactly was the programme last year?

RAY: Well, the disco started at eight, didn't it?

JANET: Yes, and people had hardly started dancing when we had that balloon-blowing competition. It was fun, but I think that if we do the same, the competition should be much later—say, ten o'clock.

MARK: Yes, I agree. But when should we serve the barbecue food then? Last year we had the food at about half past nine.

RAY: I think it would be better if we had it half an hour earlier.

JANET: Good idea. And don't forget that before we began the disco, a lot of people had been swimming in the pool. I thought that we might have started later, but I suggest we stick to that.

MARK: All right. Swimming from seven on.

RAY: By the way, what about a 'theme'? You know, last year it was an 'angels and devils' party with everyone dressed up in costumes. It seems to have been successful. But what about this year?

JANET: I've been thinking about that. What about 'artists and paintings'?

MARK: Yes, I like that. People could dress up as famous artists or characters in paintings.

RAY: I like the idea, too. Let's do that. And to go back to something earlier, let's go on with the disco after the competition till midnight.

MARK: Of course. It looks as if it could be a good evening. Just one thing—I know we did it last year, but let's not run away with the idea that it's going to be easy this year. It'll mean working just as hard, so we'll need lots of help.

Following the success of last summer's end-of-term party, we are proposing to hold another similar event this year. It . . .

As last year, . . .

But unlike last year, . . .

So come along and support us. You'll have a great time!

Unit 19

Murderer caught 'by wireless'

EXAM FOCUS:
Listening Comprehension

Look, listen and speak

Listen to this part of a radio programme on famous murder cases and look at the wireless message. Then do the exercises on the following page.

The captain: Henry Kendall

His quarry: Dr Crippen

First message, July 22, 1910: Captain Kendall has a strong suspicion

This was the first message to be sent by Wireless
H Kendall

Form No. 1. 100. 19.10.07. Sent date.

The MARCONI INTERNATIONAL MARINE COMMUNICATION COMPANY, Ltd.
WATERGATE HOUSE, YORK BUILDINGS, ADELPHI, LONDON, W.C.

No. 1 OFFICE 190

Prefix Code Words

Office of Origin S
Service Instructions: Sent to Crookhaven 3.30 p.m July 22nd

CHARGES TO PAY.		
Marconi Charge ...		
Other Line Charge...		
Delivery Charge ...		
Total . . .		

Office sent to	Time sent	By whom sent
	m.	

READ THE CONDITIONS PRINTED ON THE BACK OF THE FORM.

To: Pers Liverpool
3 PM GMT Friday 130 miles West Lizard have strong suspicions that Crippen London cellar murderer and accomplice are amongst saloon passengers moustache taken off growing beard accomplice dressed as boy voice manner and build undoubtedly a girl both travelling as Mr and Master Robinson Kendall

PLEASE ASK FOR OFFICIAL RECEIPT.

19

1 From what you heard, are these statements true or false?

1 Ethel had helped Crippen to bury his wife.
2 Kendall first suspected Crippen because the doctor acted strangely.
3 Crippen and Le Neve both wore grey hats.
4 The clothes Le Neve had bought for her disguise were too big for her.
5 Chief Inspector Dew arrested Crippen and Le Neve in Canada.

2 In pairs, ask for and give a reported version of the first message sent by Captain Kendall (on p 110).
Begin like this:

A: What did Kendall say in his first message?
B: He said that he had a strong suspicion . . .

3 Now do the same with the second message which you heard in the programme.
Begin like this:

A: And what did he say in his second message?
B: He said that he was more . . .

Grammar practice 1

Passive *He's said to be* etc. to express generally held opinions

REVIEW

Note how the active *People say (etc.) that he is . . .* is often turned into the passive *It's said (etc.) that he is . . .* or *He's said to be . . .*
to be doing . . .
to have been/to have done

People	say think believe know	that	he's an honest man. he's living in Canada. he was/has been in trouble in the past.

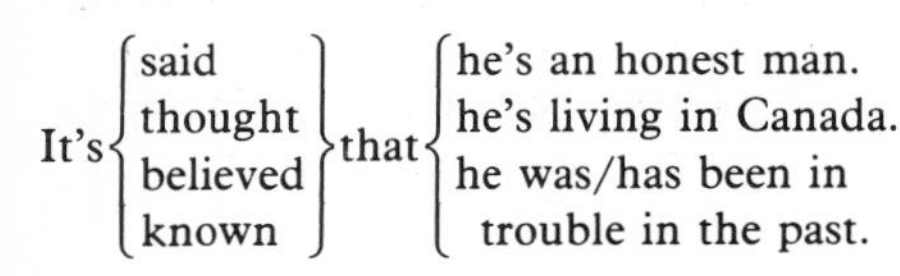

It's	said thought believed known	that	he's an honest man. he's living in Canada. he was/has been in trouble in the past.

He's	said thought believed known supposed	to be an honest man. to be living in Canada. to have lived in South America at one time. to have been in trouble.

PRACTICE

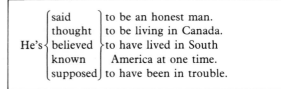

An English-speaking couple have come to live near you. Using the prompts (right), adapt this conversation to ask and tell each other about them. Ask what they do, where they come from, what they're like as people, etc:

A Do you know what he does for a living?
B: Well, he's said/supposed/thought to be an artist, but I don't know if it's true or not.

People say/believe/think/know that
'. . . he's an artist.'
'. . . she's looking for work.'
'. . . they came here from America.'
'. . . they're easy to get on with.'
'. . . he's held exhibitions all over the world.'
'. . . she was once a famous ballet dancer.'
'. . . he's written some books on art.'
'. . . they have three grown-up children.'

Grammar practice 2

Reporting what people asked and said in the past

REVIEW

'Is the man really Crippen?'
'What are the two doing?'
'How long have you suspected them?'
'When did you first realise it was Crippen?'
'Has the man been talking to the other passengers?'
'What was the "boy" doing that made you suspicious?'

→

The Chief Inspector	asked the captain / wanted to know	if the man was really Crippen. what the two were doing. how long he had suspected them. when he had first realised it was Crippen. if the man had been talking to the other passengers. what the "boy" was doing/had been doing that made/had made him suspicious.

'I'm a doctor.'
'I'm going to Canada.'
'I've left England for good!'
'I was married ten years ago.'
'I've been hoping to avoid being recognised.'
'I was already growing a beard when the captain realised who I was.'

↓

When he was questioned	he told the court / he said	that	he was a doctor. he was going to Canada. he had left England for good. he was/had been married ten years ago. he had been hoping to avoid being recognised. he was/had been growing a beard when the captain realised who he was.

PRACTICE

Refer back to p 110 (and listen to the recording again if possible), and say what Captain Kendall told the Chief Inspector about Dr Crippen and his accomplice in his wireless messages.
Then say what the Chief Inspector might have asked the Captain in messages to the ship, beginning:
He probably wanted to know . . .

Vocabulary

Phrasal-prepositional verbs (cont.)

Study the verbs in these sentences, and then play the game below.

The police said they were *checking up on* his story.
It's rude to *break in on* private conversations.
I don't *get on with* her very well.
Don't trust him. He's known to have *gone back on* his word more than once.
He'd already done half the job when he said he didn't want to *go through with* it.
He wanted to know if I had *grown out of* playing with toy trains!

It's said that she *held/hung on to* all her jewellery even when she had no money.
The men are said to be *holding out for* higher wages.
He said he'd *look out for* her in town.
The men have just *put in for* a 25% pay rise.
The assistant said she was *standing in for* someone else who was ill.
He's known to be a man who *stands up for* his rights.
That man *walked out on* his wife and family.

Game: *You mean . . .?* (see Teacher's Guide, p 36)

19

Exercises for homework

See if you can do these exercises in 40 minutes.

1 Use of English

Finish each of the following sentences in such a way that it means exactly the same as the sentence printed before it.

1 People know that he lived in South America at one time.
He is ....
2 'We've been holding out for better conditions,' the spokesman said.
The spokesman said that..
3 'Why are you leaving your present position?' she asked Mary.
She asked Mary why ....
4 It's thought that the criminal is making for a port or an airport.
The criminal ....
5 'They look as if they're waiting for someone,' John said.
John told me that...

2 Reading Comprehension

Choose the phrase which best completes each sentence.
Write your choice for each on a separate piece of paper.

1 Half the people in the office have ________ a strange illness.
A gone in for B gone along with C gone through with D gone down with

2 The police are going to ________ him very carefully.
A check up on B catch up on C hold out for D run away with

3 She ________ someone who knew a lot more about the subject than she did.
A cut down on B ran out of C came up against D put in for

4 We've almost ________ coffee. We'll have to get some more tomorrow.
A run away with B done away with C cut down on D run out of

5 I'm sorry I can't help you. I'm only ________ someone who's at lunch.
A standing up to B standing in for C putting in for D standing up for

3 Use of English

Read this part of a newspaper report and then rewrite it as a dialogue with the words as they were actually spoken.

The man told the court that he had never gone back on his word to anyone in his life, and that once he had agreed to take part in the robbery, he had to go through with it. When asked by the magistrate what he had been doing since the robbery, he said that he had gone to London and that he had been staying with friends. When asked further who these 'friends' were, he told the court that he didn't want to say. He said that he knew *he* had done wrong and that the law had caught up with him, but he didn't want to be involved in the others being caught.

TEST: LISTENING COMPREHENSION

Time: approx. 20 minutes

You will hear four short extracts of spoken English (each twice on cassette or read by the teacher), and you will be given time to choose your answers to the questions. Before you listen to each extract, read the questions (and suggested answers) carefully. Read or look again as you listen and before the second recording and choose A, B, C or D, complete the statements, choose the right order, or whatever you are asked to do. Check your answers while you are listening for the second time.

1 The waiter wrote down one of these orders. Which?

A *Tomato juice*
Steak (rare)
Peas
Potatoes

B *Steak (medium rare)*
Mushrooms
Peas

C *Soup*
Steak (medium)
Side salad

D *Tomato juice*
Steak (medium rare)
Mushrooms

2 What did the man do?

A He escaped from a police van near Birmingham.
B He stole money and stamps worth £900.
C He put on a false moustache before going into the post office.
D He held up a bank.

3 A police spokesman said that the man

A could be making for a police station.
B was believed to live near Birmingham.
C might be carrying a gun.
D was known to be very dangerous.

4 From what the man said, it was clear that he

A had no idea what to do.
B only wanted to save himself.
C wasn't regarded very highly by others.
D couldn't face up to the situation.

5 What did the woman want to do?

A Persuade him to save the people.
B Stay there with him.
C Walk out on him and join the villagers.
D Go and ask the people to help.

6 Complete these statements.

A Someone with this ticket should ______
______
______
______

British Skyways
Cairo
632

B A person with this ticket should ______
______
______
______

British Skyways
Athens
165

C A passenger with this ticket should ______
______
______
______

British Skyways
Rome
345

Unit 20

'Here is the news . . .'

EXAM FOCUS:
Oral interview

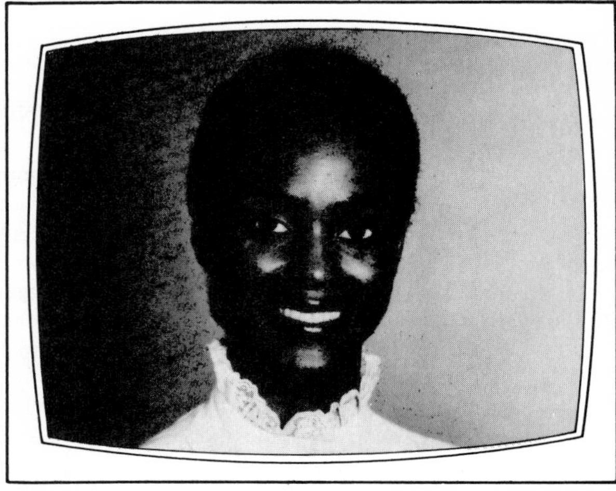

Look, listen and speak

Listen to each news item. Then ask and answer the questions on the opposite page.

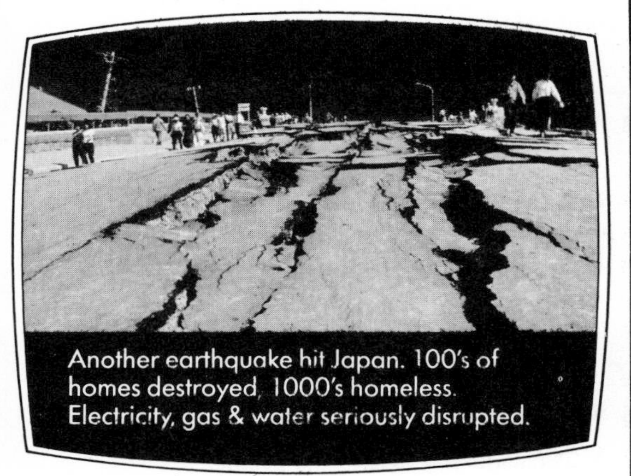

Another earthquake hit Japan. 100's of homes destroyed, 1000's homeless. Electricity, gas & water seriously disrupted.

Workmen have uncovered an ancient boat preserved in mud. It will be taken to a London museum.

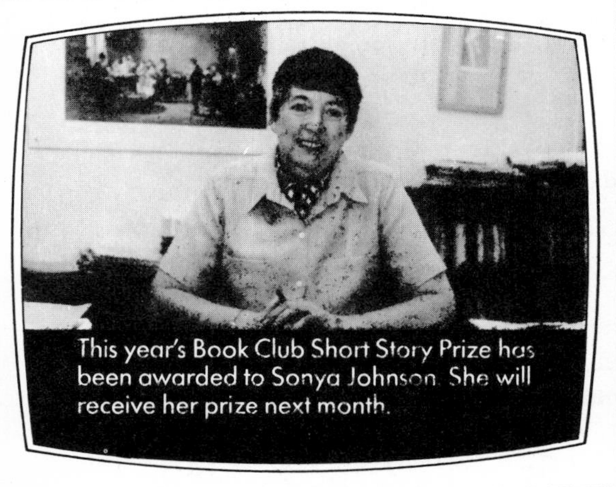

This year's Book Club Short Story Prize has been awarded to Sonya Johnson. She will receive her prize next month.

The ten British hostages have been released. They are being taken to a hospital in Edinburgh.

After each news item, ask and answer these and similar questions:

1 What happened to Japan last night?
How much damage has been done? (homes/people/electricity/gas/water)
What do experts believe?

2 What has been uncovered?
Where?
By whom? And what were they doing?
How old is it thought to be?
What do archaeologists say about it?
What will happen to it now?

3 What does Mrs Susan James do?
What's her pen-name?
How has she been honoured?
When and where will she be presented with her prize?

4 Who have just been released?
Where have they been held? By whom, and for how long?
Where are they being taken?
What will happen to them there?

Grammar practice 1

Present Perfect Passive *has/have been done*

REVIEW

Someone has uncovered an ancient boat.	→	An ancient boat has been uncovered.
Someone has already examined it.	→	It has already been examined.
Someone has just released the hostages.	→	The hostages have just been released.
No one has taken the boat away yet.	→	The boat hasn't been taken away yet.
Something has preserved the boat in mud for 2,500 years.	→	The boat has been preserved in mud for 2,500 years.
Gunmen have held the men hostage since November.	→	The men have been held hostage (by gunmen) since November.

Note that the passive *has/have been done* is used like the active *has/have done* to talk about past actions (with no time mentioned) and with *just, already, not . . . yet, since* and *for.* (Compare with *was/were done* in Unit 10.)
Note also the use of the preposition *by* with the agent (if known).

ABOUT YOU

In pairs or small groups, tell each other about the following, using *has/have been done*:

1 recent events in the news (national and international), for example:
(I've just heard that) the murderer they were looking for has been caught.

2 things that have been done in your own village, town or city, for example:
The new library has just been opened.
(I hear that) the old cinema's been closed down.

20

Grammar practice 2

Present Perfect Passive with verbs which have two objects: *bring, give, grant, hand, offer, owe, promise, read, send, show, take, teach, tell, write*

REVIEW

Someone has given me a present.	< I've/I have been given a present. A present has been given to me.
Someone has sent her an invitation.	< She's/She has been sent an invitation. An invitation has been sent to her.
Someone has just told them a joke.	< They've/They have just been told a joke. A joke has just been told to them.

Note that the same transformation would also occur in other tenses, for example: *Someone handed me a note.→I was handed a note.* or *A note was handed to me.*

PRACTICE

Rephrase these sentences, beginning with the word or words in brackets.

1 Someone has just shown me the new timetable (*I . . .*)
2 Someone has offered her a job. (*She . . .*)
3 They haven't granted us permission to build the factory yet. (*We . . .*)
4 Someone has written a letter to the government about the problem. (*A letter . . .*)
5 Someone has given the Club £100. (*£100 . . .*)
6 Someone has promised John a part in the new school play. (*John . . .*)

Grammar practice 3

Future Passive *will be done* and *is going to be done*

REVIEW

Someone will take the boat to a museum.	→ The boat will be taken to a museum.
More earthquakes will hit the country.	→ The country will be hit by more earthquakes.
A team of doctors is going to examine them.	→ They are going to be examined by a team of doctors.
Someone will present Mrs James with an award.	→ An award will be presented to Mrs James. or: Mrs James will be presented with an award.

ABOUT YOU

In pairs or small groups, tell each other about things which are going to be done or will (soon) be done in your own village, town or city, for example: *(I hear that) the new road will be opened soon.*

Vocabulary

Verbs with prefixes *un-*, *de-*, *dis-*, *mis-* and *mal-*

The prefixes *un-*, *de-* and *dis-* mean 'reverse the action of' or 'get rid of', and the prefixes *mis-* and *mal-* are pejorative, meaning 'bad(ly)' or 'wrong(ly)'. Study the verbs carefully and then do the exercise below.

un-	undo, uncover, unpack, unbutton, unwrap, unlock, untie, unscrew
de- /di/	decode, defrost, defuse
dis-	disapprove, disconnect, dislike, disobey
mis-	miscalculate, misinform, mislead, mislay
mal-	maltreat

Supply the appropriate verb from those above:

1 We don't know what the message means. It hasn't been ____ yet.
2 He ____ the safe and took out the money.
3 The area won't be safe until the bomb has been ____.
4 My shoelaces are so wet I can't ____ them.
5 The moment we arrived at the hotel, we all ____ our cases.
6 The boy was told to stay home, but he ____ his father and went out.
7 You've been ____, I'm afraid. The number 64 stops around the corner.
8 We must ____ the fridge. It hasn't been done for two months.
9 ____ the parcel and let's see what's inside.
10 Our telephone was ____ once when we didn't pay the bill.

Exercise for homework

See if you can write this composition in 45 minutes.

Composition: Narrative

Imagine that you have been asked to supply three news items for inclusion in an English-language radio broadcast in your own country. Choose three events or 'stories' of national or international interest from this past week, and write a paragraph of 40–60 words for each using the kind of language you have heard and practised in this Unit. You should write a total of between 120 and 180 words.

20

Oral Interview preparation

1 Look at this photograph and then answer the questions below.

About the photograph

1 What's happened to the flat?
  And what's happened to the woman, do you think?
2 How do the two people at the door feel? How do you know?
3 How would you feel if you saw a scene like this?
  What would you do?
4 When the police arrive, what do you think will be done to
  a) the room, and b) the woman?
5 What will happen to the person who committed this crime
  when he or she is caught?

General

1 What kinds of people have to deal with scenes like this in real life?
2 Would you do a job which involved dealing with scenes like this?
  Why?/Why not?
3 In many countries, crime is increasing year by year.
  Why, do you think?

2 Reading aloud

Imagine you have been asked to stand in for a radio newsreader on an English-language broadcast in your own country. Practise reading these news items aloud.

> 'A major new archaeological discovery has been made in South America, it was reported yesterday. The remains of an enormous temple have recently been uncovered. The remains are in such a good state of preservation that it is already thought that the temple will be rebuilt at some time in the future.
>
> 'The east coast of the United States has been hit for the third time in two weeks by a hurricane. In one small town, fifty homes have been flattened and hundreds have been made homeless. The total cost of the damage caused by the hurricanes to date has not been calculated, but it is believed that the bill will be about ten million dollars.'

3 Situation for extended role play

You are spending your holiday in a hotel in an English-speaking country. You asked the hotel to do some laundry for you and were told it would be ready today. When you ask, you are told it *isn't* ready. In pairs, conduct the conversation between the hotel receptionist and yourself. Ask and/or say:

- who you are and what room you're in
- why your laundry isn't ready yet
- when it will be ready, etc.

4 Topics for individual talks

As part of the Oral Interview, you may be asked to give a very short talk on a topic of general interest. Below are examples of such topics. Choose one, write brief notes on the subject, and then give a short talk to the class. You should try to talk for 15–30 seconds. When you have finished, the class may ask questions.

- Keeping animals in zoos and circuses.
- Should children be brought up strictly, or given a lot of freedom?
- The importance of saving energy.

Unit 21

Daydreaming: 'This time tomorrow...'

Read and speak

Read this, then do the exercises on the opposite page.

EXAM FOCUS:
Reading comprehension

This time tomorrow I shall be lying on a sun-soaked beach on a tropical island sunbathing and sipping a long cool drink. The last thing I'll be worrying about is work - and as for the children, the housework, shopping, and all that, well . . . I shall have left it all behind! I'll just be doing what I've always wanted to do - what everybody wants to do: get away from it all!

Who am I kidding?! Tomorrow's Friday, and just like every Friday I shall be working away in the office here the same as everybody else!

In fact, by this time next year I shall have been working here for ten years. Ten years?! How did it happen? Surely no one plans to stay in one job that long!

I remember when I left school at 16, a Careers Officer asked me what I intended to do. I had to think about that, I remember, because I wasn't planning to do anything in particular. With my education, I wasn't likely to become a brilliant scientist or a university professor overnight! On the other hand, if I didn't pick something fairly quickly, I was liable to become a professional unemployed person and go on the dole for the rest of my life - or at least until I got married.

It's not that the job 'stinks': that's what some of the others say. The job's all right. It's me. I haven't pushed enough when I've been due for promotion. And I've been trodden on a couple of times, I know . . .

By the time I'm 32, I shall have been sitting at this desk for nearly half my life: that's a depressing thought!

Ah, well, back to the accounts . . .

1 From what you read, are these statements true or false, or can't you say?

1 She's a working mother.
2 She intends to leave her family soon.
3 She will have got a new job by next week.
4 She won't really be lying on the beach on a tropical island tomorrow.
5 It's likely that she works in a Careers Information Office.
6 She's been working in the office for nine years.
7 When she was younger, she had no special career plans.
8 She wasn't worried about not getting a job.
9 She's probably a very quiet person who is not very ambitious.
10 She is now 19 years old.

2 In small groups, discuss and make a list of some of the things the girl will be doing in the office tomorrow.
Then tell each other what she will have done by the time she leaves the office at 5.30 tomorrow evening.

3 Discussion

Do you understand how the girl feels? Do you ever feel like that yourself?
If she asked you for advice, what would you say to her?

Grammar practice 1

Future Continuous *will be doing*

REVIEW

> This time tomorrow I shall be working away in the office.
>
> If you ring me up this evening at 7, I'll (still) be having supper.
>
> Don't come to see John before 9. He'll be watching his favourite programme from 8 to 9.

Note that we use the Continuous *will be doing* to describe something that will be going on at a point in the future—a sort of 'background' future (very much like the 'background' Past Continuous *was/were doing*). Compare this with the use of *will be doing* to describe an action fixed or arranged for the future (see Unit 16, p 93).

ABOUT YOU

Tell each other what you will (probably) be doing
- at 7 a.m., mid-day, 5.30 p.m., 9 p.m. and at this time tomorrow.
- this time next week.
- from 2 to 4 on Saturday afternoon.
- from 9 to 12 on Sunday morning.

21

Grammar practice 2

Future Perfect Simple *will have done* for single (and countable) actions and Continuous *will have been doing*

REVIEW

I {shall / will} have {typed fifteen letters / written two letters / dealt with all the post / had two meetings} {by six o'clock this evening. / by the time I leave work this evening.}

By this time next year I {shall / will} have been {studying English for five years. / living in this town for ten years. / working at Smiths for three years. / driving (a car) for two years.}

Note the use of the preposition *by* (with *will have done* and *will have been doing*) to indicate a time limit in the future.
Note also the addition of a prepositional phrase with *for* to show how long someone *will have been doing* something by the time limit given.

ABOUT YOU

In pairs, tell each other
1 what you will have done by ten o'clock this evening.
2 what you will have done (this week) by Sunday morning.
3 how long you will have been learning English, going to this school, living in your present house/flat, working in your present job, etc. by this time next month.

Grammar practice 3

Verbs + *to*-infinitive to express intentions, plans etc. for the future and unfulfilled intentions, plans, etc. in the past

REVIEW

I {intend / mean / want} to stay home tomorrow evening.

I {intended / meant / wanted} to stay home yesterday evening, but some friends came and took me to the cinema.

I'm {planning / arranging / preparing} to go to London next week.

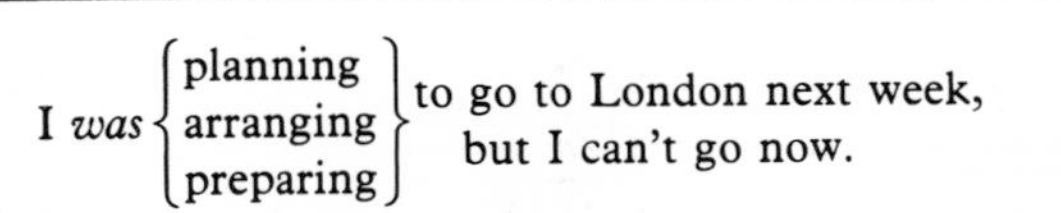

I *was* {planning / arranging / preparing} to go to London next week, but I can't go now.

ABOUT YOU

1 Tell each other about things you or friends, or members of your family intend, mean or want to do, or are planning, arranging or preparing to do in the future.
2 Tell each other about things in the past that you, friends or members of your family intended etc. to do or were planning etc. to do, but which went wrong. Say what happened.

Grammar practice 4

Adjective + *to*-infinitive structures in place of modals

REVIEW

Note that the following adjectives (+ *to*-infinitive) are sometimes used in place of a modal verb.

Example	*Structure with corresponding modal verb*
I'm likely to be here for ages. (It's likely that I'll be here for ages.)	likely to . . . = may (possibility)
That dog's {liable / apt} to be temperamental.	{liable / apt} to . . . = can be; tends to be
I am {obliged / bound} to go to the meeting tonight.	{obliged / bound} to . . . = have to, must (obligation)
He's bound to be at the meeting.	bound to . . . = will certainly (do)
The plane's {(just) about to take off. / going to take off soon. / due to take off at 10.00.}	{(just) about to . . . / going to . . . / due to . . .} = will do (with degrees of future nearness)
I was just {about / going} to phone you when I got your letter.	was (just) {about to . . . / going to . . .} = was on the point of . . .
You're {free / allowed} to do whatever you like.	{free to . . . / allowed to . . .} = can, may (permission)

PRACTICE

Rephrase these sentences using an adjective + *to*-infinitive in place of the word or words in italics. Make any other changes necessary.

1 The new shop *will* open on 1st January.
2 They *may* keep talking until late tonight.
3 She was *on the point of* picking up the phone when it rang.
4 The students here *can* come and go as they please.
5 She *will certainly* be in town on Saturday: that's when she goes shopping.
6 That boy *tends to* be moody.
7 The train *will* leave *any second now.*
8 If you don't ask him to leave, he *may* stay for ever.
9 Our computer *tends to* go wrong from time to time.
10 We were *on the point of* getting on the train when we heard the news.

21

Exercises for homework

See if you can do these exercises in 60 minutes.

1 Use of English

Finish each of the following sentences in such a way that it means exactly the same as the sentence printed before it.

1 It's possible that he'll be late again.
He's likely ....
2 You can look at anything you like.
You're free ....
3 If he drives like that all the time, he *must* have an accident soon.
He's bound...
4 I had every intention of going to see him, but I forgot.
I meant...
5 I've been living in this flat for nine years, and next year will make it ten.
By next year...
6 It was quite possible that she would lose her job, but she didn't worry.
Although she was liable...
7 Come round at eight because I'm planning to have finished supper by then.
I shall...
8 He's already written two reports, and will write another before he leaves.
He will have...
9 Someone has just offered John a university scholarship.
John ....
10 'How long have you been studying English?' he asked her.
He asked her how ....

2 Use of English

Complete this table:

NOUN (subject, etc.)	ADJECTIVE	NOUN (person)
(1)	mathematical	a mathematician
accident	(2)	—
music	(3)	(4)
(5)	political	(6)
the Tropics	(7)	—
archaeology	(8)	(9)
(10)	electric(al)	(11)
(12)	(13)	a technician
(14)	(15)	a magician

3 Composition: Narrative

Write a story of between 120 and 180 words which begins like this:
'By this time next week I shall have been living in this cave for a month. It all started . . .'

TEST: READING COMPREHENSION

Time: 45 minutes

Section A

Choose the word or phrase which best completes each sentence.
Write your choice for each (A, B, C or D) on a separate piece of paper.

1 According to this timetable, the plane's ____ to land at 2.30 tomorrow evening.
A liable B bound C likely D due

2 By the time the tour ends, the football team ____ twenty matches in five countries.
A will play B will have played C will be playing D will have been playing

3 When he came in out of the snow, he ____ his coat, took it off and shook it.
A defrosted B wrapped up C unbuttoned D mislaid

4 He didn't lie because he knew the police were bound to ____ his story.
A go back on B check up on C get away with D look up to

5 'What do you ____ to do when you grow up?' he asked the girl.
A prepare B going C decide D intend

6 When asked what she wanted to do, she said she didn't want to do anything ____.
A in particular B in fact C indeed D in general

7 You're ____ to be at the meeting. That means you *have to* be there.
A apt B liable C likely D obliged

8 This time tomorrow, with any luck, we ____ through France enjoying the first day of our holidays.
A drive B shall drive C shall have driven D shall be driving

9 You never quite know where you are with John: he ____ to be very moody.
A means B likes C acts D tends

10 Archaeologists are examining the ____ of a Roman temple near our village.
A rest B remains C leftovers D debris

11 The girl who rescued the boy from the river has been ____ with an award for bravery.
A awarded B offered C promised D presented

12 They ____ us if we enjoyed learning English.
A enquired B said C asked D told

13 You looked ____ you were having a good time when I saw you last night.
A while B as C how D as though

14 ____ reading the news, I immediately rang to see if I could help.
A When B On C As soon as D The moment

15 One thing is certain. He is ____ to have robbed one bank. He may have robbed more.
A known B believed C said D thought

Section B

In this section you will find after each of the passages a number of questions or unfinished statements about the passage, each with four suggested answers or ways of finishing. You must choose the one which you think best fits—A, B, C or D. Write your answers on a separate piece of paper.

First passage

(This is part of a report by the Chairman of the Charities Committee of a Club.)

1 By March this year, we shall have raised enough money, we hope, to buy the equipment for the Youth Club. When we have raised the money, we are planning to go back to the Youth Club leaders in order to discover exactly what is needed most. Plans have been made for the Book Sale which will be held on 15th February. This means that many of us will be spending the first two weeks of February collecting books. The event is likely to be held in the Town Hall. If there are problems here, however, we hope that other Club members might come up with some alternative suggestions.

2 As we are proposing to sponsor a student from Africa on a three-month language course in this country, we also intend to hold a Charity Dance in the spring. Such events are apt to be difficult to organise, so all members of the Club must feel free to contribute or help in any way they can.

3 The moment I was asked if we could possibly help in some way with the new Club for the Disabled, I said yes. As Chairman, I am bound to say that this is the sort of social work many Club members would like to do - other than simply raising money. We are therefore planning to ask members if they can perhaps help out on one Saturday every month (on a rota basis).

Finally, by January next year the Club will have been going for twenty years, and the Committee intends to mark this anniversary with some kind of dinner, a dance or a party. We have already been offered (unofficially) the use of the dance hall at 'The Forest Hotel'. However, we shall be devoting one of our meetings in the near future to a full discussion on the form of the event, etc. Any suggestions will be welcome.

16 The Committee will be going back to the Youth Club leaders
A to ask for money in March.
B to tell them about the equipment.
C to find out what the Club needs.
D to collect old books from them.

17 The Committee does not yet know
A when books will be collected.
B when the Book Sale will be held.
C how to get the books to the Town Hall.
D where the Book Sale will take place.

18 Every Club member has been asked
A to help with the Charity Dance.
B to sponsor a foreign student.
C to write to an African student.
D to organise something for the Dance.

19 In order to help the new Club for the Disabled, members will be asked
A to raise some money.
B to make a contribution.
C if they can plan a Club programme.
D to help at the Club once a month.

20 There will be an event next January
A because the Club has been offered 'The Forest Hotel'.
B to celebrate the Club's twentieth birthday.
C to raise money for a student from Africa.
D which will take the form of a discussion evening.

Second passage

(This is an extract from a short story.)

'You will meet a man in the theatre foyer,' K. explained. 'He will have left before the play ends and will be waiting for you. He'll be wearing a dark suit and carrying a theatre programme upside down, although I doubt if you could miss him. There shouldn't be many people waiting in the foyer at that time of night. Whatever he asks you to do, whatever instructions you're given, co-operate. Understood?'

I shrugged, but gave a curt 'Yes, sir,' while thinking that this was all too melodramatic to be true. I knew of course that we were planning to have discussions with 'the other side' and that we intended to buy back one of our own men, but all this seemed a bit ridiculous. I had been told at the training school that I would be likely to get some simple but rather strange assignments to begin with. They had been right.

The curtain had hardly come down on the last act of the play when I was out of my seat and walking from the dark of the theatre into the bright lights of the foyer. He was there. But the moment I saw him, I had the feeling that something unpleasant was about to happen. He seemed to be staring at a spot on the floor, and looked as if he was just about to pick something up when there was a single gun shot and he was thrown against the wall. The warning signs had obviously got to me before I realised consciously what was going to happen, because I had broken out in a cold sweat on seeing the expression on his face. The moment the shot rang out, I automatically fell back on my training and threw myself to the ground.

When no more shots followed, I looked up and was just in time to see two masked men dragging my 'contact' out of the front door of the theatre. I didn't know whether he was dead or badly injured, but I intended to find out. I got up slowly and carefully and made for the door.

21 The man that the writer had to meet
- A would be waiting outside the theatre.
- B would not have been inside the theatre.
- C would be holding a theatre programme.
- D would expect some instructions.

22 The writer thought that
- A he would have to act.
- B his training had been ridiculous.
- C the man intended to kill him.
- D this job was very strange.

23 The man was shot
- A as he was coming out into the foyer.
- B before the play finished.
- C while he was standing in the foyer.
- D after he had picked something up.

24 The writer threw himself to the ground
- A as soon as he heard the shot.
- B when he started to sweat.
- C the moment he saw the man.
- D when the man gave him a warning.

25 The two masked men
- A carried the dead man out of the theatre.
- B attacked the writer on their way out.
- C wanted to know who the injured man was.
- D did not seem to worry about the writer.

Unit 22

Are we heading for a nuclear holocaust?

EXAM FOCUS:
Composition (Argument)

Read and speak

Read this text carefully and then do the exercises opposite.

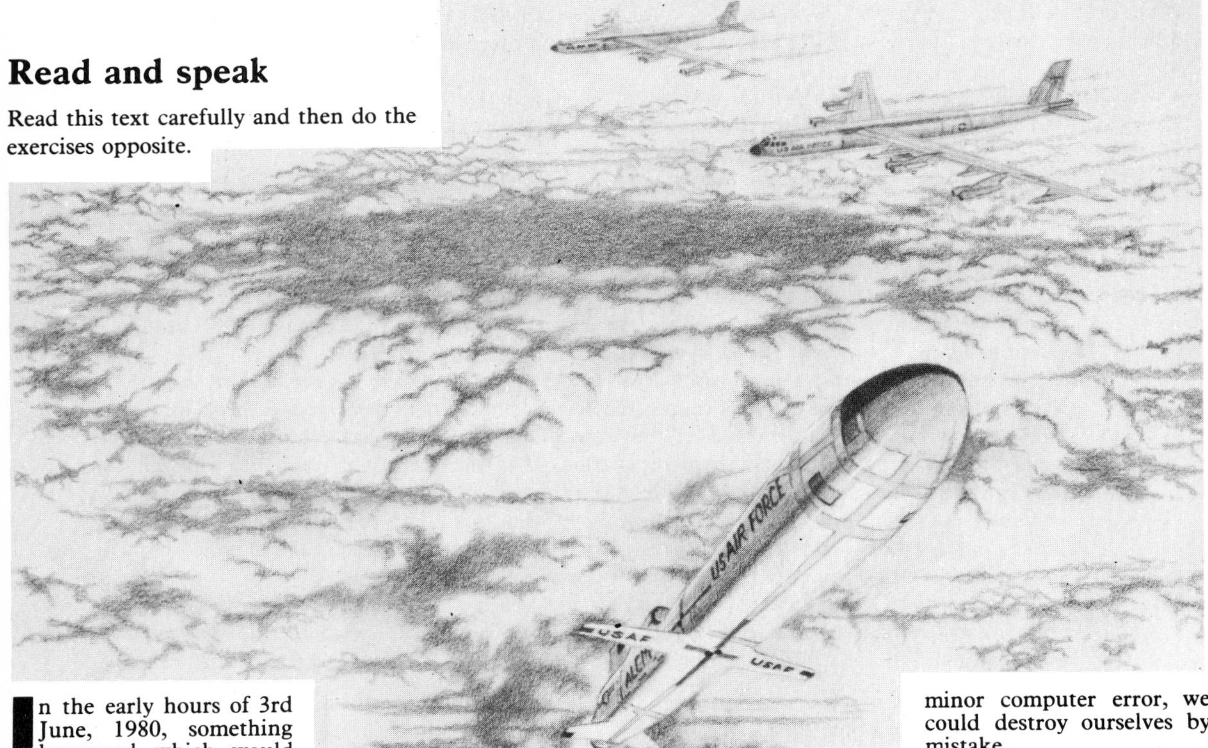

Will we have destroyed the world and ourselves by the year 2000?

In the early hours of 3rd June, 1980, something happened which would have terrified most people if they had known about it. A small electric circuit, no bigger than your thumbnail, went wrong, and for three minutes the world slid towards the brink of catastrophe.

The circuit was part of America's early-warning system in Colorado Springs, which suddenly announced (by accident) that the United States was being attacked by missiles.

In the three minutes that it took to verify that this was in fact a computer error, one American Air Force control aircraft took off from Hawaii, crews of B52 nuclear bombers and commanders of nuclear submarines were alerted, and missile controllers were ordered to have their launch keys ready.

It was one of the three major false alarms that year.

For most people, a nuclear holocaust is totally unthinkable—so they don't think about it. (Or perhaps they tell themselves there is nothing they can possibly do . . .) But developments are taking place in the world that make nuclear war not only thinkable, but more likely than ever before.

Firstly, there is an alarming spread of nuclear weapons. It is rarely publicised, but it is thought that about thirty countries could possess nuclear weapons by the mid-1980s. There are already more than 50,000 nuclear weapons in the world, and even if the Russians and Americans agree to limit their production of nuclear arms, that number is bound to increase. (And if the gap between East and West widens, what then?)

Secondly, there is the risk of accident. Because of a minor computer error, we could destroy ourselves by mistake.

Thirdly, nuclear weapons are becoming more accurate. They will have become so accurate in a few years' time that they will be able to pick out the enemy's missile sites with deadly accuracy. So there is likely to be a temptation on both sides to 'strike first'—to launch your own missiles from their 'hidden' sites before they can be hit. And since there is or will be so little time to retaliate, this in turn leads to the development of what are called 'launch on warning' systems. With such systems, the chances of an accidental catastrophe are dramatically increased.

Of course, these arguments simplify the situation. But is it possible to justify the continuation of the arms race and the production of nuclear weapons?

1 In pairs, ask and tell each other

1 why the world slid towards the brink of catastrophe on 3rd June, 1980.
2 what the early-warning system announced.
3 how long it took to verify that this was a computer error.
4 what happened during that time.
5 if this was the only false alarm that year.

2 Refer to the rest of the text and take turns to explain to each other why, according to the writer, nuclear war is now more likely than ever before.

3 Discussion

In groups (or as a class debate), discuss the statement: 'Nuclear weapons are now necessary'. During the discussion, take notes—you will need them later in the Unit. State the arguments:

● IN FAVOUR OF the statement
1 Major countries *must* keep nuclear weapons to prevent smaller countries from threatening the peace of the world. etc.

● AGAINST the statement
1 Nuclear weapons will spread: all countries will (want to) have them soon.
2 The risk is too great: we could blow ourselves up by accident. etc.

Grammar practice 1

The words *some, most, all, both, none, every,* etc.

REVIEW

Study this and then do the exercise.

COUNTABLE	
some / most } (of the) countries / people / students	both ([of] the) men
half / all } (of) the people	none / every one / each (one) / (n)either (one) } of the people/countries

UNCOUNTABLE	
some / most } (of the)	nuclear waste / natural gas / information / furniture
all (of) the / half (of) the / none of the	

Note that all of these modifiers use *of* when followed by a personal pronoun, for example:
both of them, all of us, none of you, most of us, each of them, etc.

ABOUT YOU: A SURVEY

'What are the biggest problems the world is faced with at the moment?'
In pairs or small groups, devise a short questionnaire of four or five (or more) questions to find out what other students think. The 'questionnaire' (on the right) provides some ideas. Go round and ask other students to answer the questions, and then report what you find with sentences like this:
Most of the students I spoke to said . . .
Every one of the students I interviewed thought . . .
None of the students I asked thought . . .

A QUESTIONNAIRE

	Yes	No
Do you think there is a threat of nuclear war?		
Is there a problem with world population and food?		
Is there really still an energy crisis?		

22

Grammar practice 2

Reflexive pronouns *myself, yourself, himself, herself,* etc.

REVIEW

Emphatic	I meant to do the job myself. I spoke to the girl herself—no one else.	
Reflexive verbs	We could easily blow ourselves up. Most young children talk to themselves. I pinched myself to make sure I wasn't dreaming. She could have kicked herself for making such a silly mistake.	
Indirect object	They made/built themselves a shelter. He got/ordered himself a new suit. She made herself a cup of coffee.	= a shelter for themselves = a new suit for himself = a cup of coffee for herself

Note these other common reflexive verbs in English:
cut oneself
enjoy oneself
hurt oneself
look at oneself
burn oneself

Note also the expression *(all) by himself,* etc. = alone, without company or help.

PRACTICE

Put in the correct reflexive pronoun in these sentences.

1 He cut ______ while he was shaving.
2 I shall have to do the job ______.
3 Most of the people enjoyed ______.
4 You look dreadful. Just look at ______.
5 While we were waiting, we got ______ a meal.
6 You two should look after ______ better.
7 In the end she did the job ______.
8 I must make ______ some bookshelves.
9 Take him to the doctor. He's hurt ______.
10 All the people at the camp kept ______ to ______.

Vocabulary

Verb suffixes *-ify, -en* and *-ise/-ize*

Here are some English verbs which end in *-ify, -en* and *-ise/-ize*. Study them carefully and then do the exercise below.

-ify:	terrify, simplify, justify, electrify, identify, certify, satisfy, amplify, verify
-en:	deafen, sadden, ripen, quicken, tighten, loosen, widen, shorten, broaden, lengthen, heighten, strengthen, threaten, frighten
-ise/-ize:	organise, publicise, modernise, realise, criticise, legalise, symbolise, rationalise

The word in capitals at the end of each of these sentences can be used to form a word that fits in the blank space. Supply the correct form of the word.

1 It's impossible to ________ the use of nuclear weapons. JUST
2 She had to ________ the dress she bought: it was too long. SHORT
3 The music at the disco was ________. I couldn't hear myself think! DEAF
4 Instead of building a new hospital, they're going to ________ the old one. MODERN
5 The big nations are always trying to ________ their position in the world. STRONG
6 We're waiting for the apples to ________ before we pick them. RIPE
7 I ate so much that I had to ________ my belt! LOOSE
8 Every one of that man's children has turned against him. You see, he's always ________ them: he's never praised them. CRITIC
9 The men have ________ to go on strike if they don't get more money. THREAT
10 I read a ________ version of that book. It was very good. SIMPLE

Exercises for homework

1 Use of English: Directed writing

See if you can do this exercise in 30 minutes.

Taking your information from the text on p 129 and from notes you made before or during the Discussion (p 130), continue the two paragraphs below. Do not use more than 100 words for each paragraph.

Those who are in favour of nuclear weapons justify their argument by saying . . .

Many others, however, criticise the production and use of nuclear weapons on the grounds that . . .

2 Study section: The 'argument' composition

One of the Composition subjects in the First Certificate (Paper 2) is an 'argument'. Sometimes you are asked to argue for or against an idea; sometimes to try to solve a problem, or suggest alternative solutions to a problem; or you might have to present both sides of a discussion point. Whatever you are asked, decide on your own attitude or viewpoint, then present your ideas in a logical order to discuss the subject. As with other Composition types, there are certain things you must bear in mind. Read the notes and the sample below. Then do the exercise.

Many countries in the world are faced with the appalling connected problems of increasing population and a shortage of food. It has been estimated that by the year 2000 the world's population will have risen to about ten thousand million. It therefore seems that more countries could find themselves in this situation in the future.

There are a number of possible solutions to the problem, but none of them is easy. Firstly, the governments in such countries could discourage people from having large families. Why not just have one or two children, instead of six or seven, which is common in some countries?

Secondly, one of the problems in countries which cannot produce enough food for their own people is that farming methods are very simple and often inefficient. If the people bought new agricultural machinery, modernised their farming methods and developed more land, they might soon produce enough food to satisfy the needs of the people.

Thirdly, of course, many countries have natural resources which other countries would like to buy. If countries with a food shortage exported their oil, wood, iron or whatever, they could import at least some of the food they need from other countries.

All of these possible solutions (and there are of course many more) simplify the problem. But they show that, if people mean to solve the problems of increasing population and food shortages, there are means of doing so.

Notes

However complicated the discussion point may be, always try to keep your sentences clear and simple. Avoid 'I' wherever you can, and always use language that you know and have practised. Plan the composition carefully. Study the subject, plan and ideas here and read the composition (left). Then do the exercise below.

SUBJECT
In some countries there is hardly enough food for the growing population. Suggest some ways in which this problem might be solved.

Plan and ideas

Introduction
1 Problem of population & food—future rise in world population.

Development
Possible solutions:
2 Discourage large families.
3 Modernise farming & develop land to produce more food.
4 Export resources to import food.

Conclusion
5 Spread world resources better—especially food. Keep increase in population as low as possible.

Now plan and write this composition:
'Many countries have thousands/millions of unemployed. How do you think the problem of mass unemployment might be solved?'

TEST: COMPOSITION

Time: 90 minutes

Write **two only** of the following composition exercises. Your answers must follow exactly the instructions given, and must be of between 120 and 180 words each.

1 Write a letter to an English-speaking pen-friend telling him or her about a holiday you will be going on in the near future or about your general plans for the next three months. You should include the beginning and ending as for an ordinary letter, but the address is not to be counted in the number of words.

2 Write a conversation between a student who is looking for accommodation in an English-speaking country and a person who has a room or a flat to let, including the questions each may want to ask and any information each may want to give. Write in dialogue form, giving only the name of each speaker followed by the words spoken.

3 'All countries of the world must stop producing nuclear weapons now.' What do you think?

(*Note:* For this Test you may refer back to Units in this coursebook to help you, but do *not* copy out whole sentences or paragraphs from texts.)

Unit 23
Two points of view

EXAM FOCUS:
Use of English

Read and speak

Read this extract from a magazine article about a monkey which has been trained to look after a young American who is severely handicapped. Then read the two letters opposite carefully and do the exercises.

Robert Foster is 24 and cannot feed himself. He is paralysed from the shoulders down, the result of a car accident. Hellion is four, a Capuchin monkey who has been trained to act as Robert's arms and legs. When Robert makes clicking sounds with his tongue, or gives verbal commands, Hellion feeds him. She also fetches and carries his food, opens the refrigerator (far right), takes out prepared meals and clears the dishes afterwards. The white stickers in the refrigerator indicate areas which the monkey recognises as 'forbidden'.

Each morning Hellion tidies Robert's hair (right) with a soft-bristled hair brush. He rewards her with banana pellets which are dispensed from a device attached to his wheelchair.

This is the result of a long training programme which did not always go so well. Early on, Hellion stuck her tongue out and threatened her trainers and Robert. She had to have all her teeth taken out to make sure she did not give anyone a dangerous bite. Even without teeth, when she bit the photographer who took these photos, it was unpleasant enough. Once, Hellion unscrewed a fuse in the electric motor on Robert's wheelchair, and she expressed her disapproval in many other ways.

She has adapted now and actually seems to enjoy looking after Robert: and he would now be lost without her.

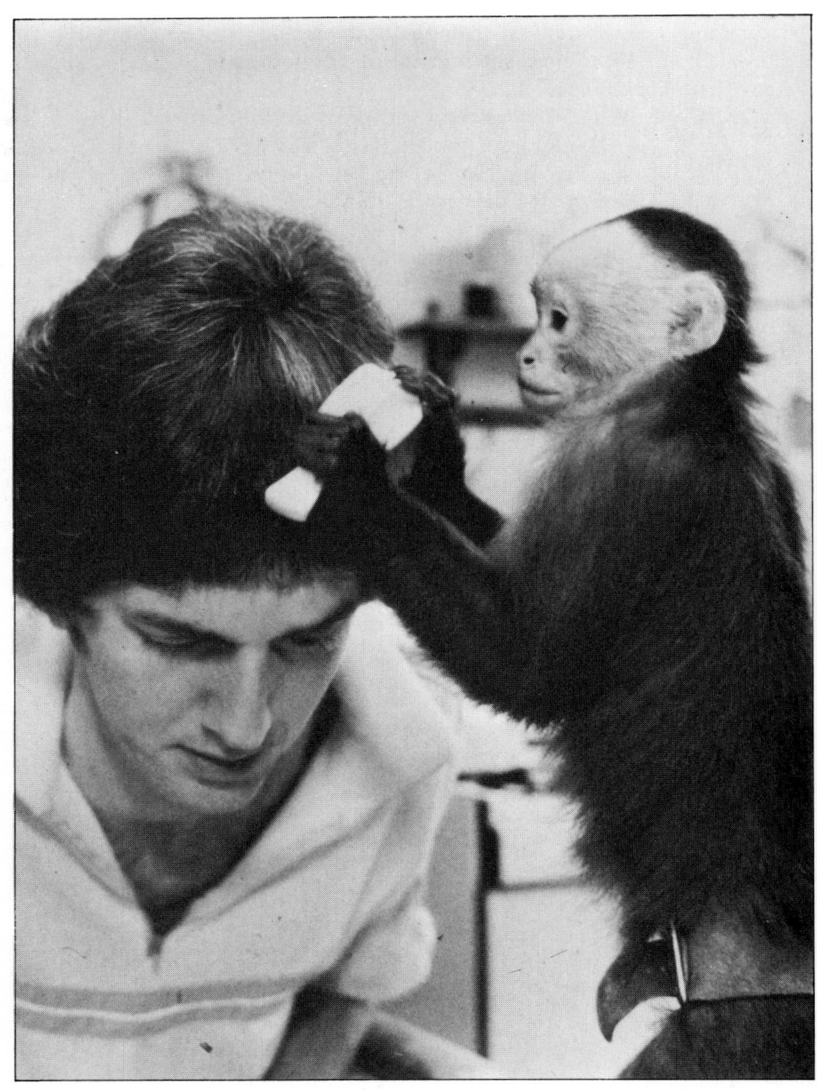

Sir,

I am sometimes horrified and saddened at the depths we humans will sink to in order to avoid looking after our own disabled ourselves. (I refer to your article 'This little monkey is nursemaid to a man'.)

Not only is this yet another example of scientists' cruelty to the weak and helpless (that is, dumb animals), it is also a sad reinforcement of the fact that our 'caring society' is not caring enough.

The scientists who trained the monkey in this experiment seemed surprised at the monkey's early reactions. If I had received such treatment, I feel sure I would have done the same!

But there is another aspect of this 'experiment' which requires comment. If I were disabled, I would personally shrink from the thought of being looked after by a monkey. And I would be quite nauseated, for instance, by the thought of an animal actually feeding me.

I remain,
Yours faithfully,
Edna B.

Sir,

I am full of admiration for the scientists who trained Hellion, the monkey, to do so much to make Robert's life bearable when his nurse is not there. If other animals could be trained in the same way to look after the disabled, the elderly, and perhaps the very young and the sick, it would be absolutely marvellous! After all, we already train guide dogs for the blind, don't we? So surely it's not such a revolutionary idea as it might seem at first.

We all know that it is becoming much more difficult to get helpers (paid or voluntary) to look after the disabled and the sick. So think of the benefits if animals could be trained to do many of those small tasks which sick or disabled people find difficult, such as undoing buttons, picking up things they've dropped, and so on.

And those who think that animal-training is cruel have been sadly misinformed. Such animals are often treated rather better than many human patients in hospital.

Yours faithfully,
Brian J.

1 In pairs, ask and tell each other:

(*referring to Edna's letter*)

1 how Edna felt about the experiment.
2 what she said it was an example of.
3 what the monkey's reactions were to the experiment and the training.
4 if Edna would mind being looked after by a monkey, and why/why not.

(*referring to Brian's letter*)

5 how Brian felt about the experiment.
6 why he referred to guide dogs for the blind.
7 what trained animals could do for the sick or the disabled.
8 what he said about animal-training.

2 Discussion

In small groups, discuss the pros and cons of training animals to help look after the sick and disabled. Take points from the letters and add your own ideas.

23

Grammar practice 1

Intensifiers *much, rather, such, quite, pretty* and *fairly* with adjectives

REVIEW

	SINGULAR COUNTABLE	PLURAL COUNTABLE	UNCOUNTABLE
much (+comparative)	He's a much better player than I thought.	These are much more interesting books than those.	We had much better weather than we had expected.
rather (+comparative)	She's a rather better typist than I thought.	They're rather more expensive flowers than I wanted.	This is rather thinner paper than I usually use.
such	He's such a nice man.	They're such nice people.	I've never heard such nonsense/rubbish!
quite	He's quite a good tennis player.	They're quite good tennis players.	He gave us some quite useful information.
pretty/fairly/ rather	She's a pretty/fairly/rather good singer.	They're pretty/fairly/rather good singers.	This is pretty/fairly/rather good coffee.

PRACTICE

Add the words in brackets to these sentences:

1 She's a good girl! (*such*)
2 They received dreadful treatment. (*quite*)
3 Most of us were given comfortable accommodation. (*fairly*)
4 They've been here for some time. (*quite*)
5 The monkey underwent a long training programme. (*pretty*)
6 This is a more difficult problem than we had foreseen. (*rather*)
7 We had awful weather! (*such*)
8 It was a more fascinating programme than we had expected. (*much*)
9 She's got sharp teeth. (*rather*)
10 These are nicer cakes than those. (*much*)

Grammar practice 2

Definite article + adjective to describe groups of people

REVIEW

> The disabled need as much help as we can give them.
>
> Braille is the system used in books for the blind.
>
> The elderly often find it difficult to look after themselves.

Note that *the disabled* means 'all disabled people' or 'the disabled people' (NOT 'a/the disabled person'), and takes a plural verb.

Only certain adjectives can be used in this way. Here are some of them:
rich, poor, deaf, dumb, blind, dead, living, young, old, elderly, unemployed, guilty, innocent, wise, weak, helpless, sick, disabled, homeless

ABOUT YOU

Tell each other what is done, what is being done, or perhaps what is going to be done in future in your country for these people:
the elderly, the poor, the disabled, the deaf, the blind, the unemployed, the homeless

Grammar practice 3

More irregular verbs

REVIEW

Here are more irregular verbs, some of which have occurred in the last three Units. Study them and then do the exercise below.

bite	bit	bitten	sink	sank	sunk
hide	hid	hidden	swim	swam	swum
slide	slid	slid	shrink	shrank	shrunk
speed	sped	sped	spring	sprang	sprung
stride	strode	(stridden)	stink	stank	stunk
tread	trod	trodden			

PRACTICE

Complete each sentence with the correct form of the verb given:

1 Ouch! I've just been ______! (*bite*)
2 He ______ on the cat as he left. (*tread*)
3 Haven't you ever ______ in the sea? (*swim*)
4 The car ______ round the corner so fast that he couldn't avoid an accident. (*speed*)
5 The cheese ______ so much yesterday that we had to throw it out. (*stink*)
6 Where have you ______ my newspaper? (*hide*)
7 He ______ into the office as if he owned the place. (*stride*)
8 This shirt has ______! (*shrink*)
9 The ship ______ so quickly that no one escaped. (*sink*)
10 When the teacher walked in, the students ______ to their feet. (*spring*)

Exercise for homework

See if you can do this exercise in 30 minutes.

Use of English: Directed writing

Using the information given on pp 135–136, continue the paragraphs below.
Use no more than 50 words for each paragraph.

Edna strongly disapproves of the idea of animals looking after people. . . .

Brian, on the other hand, thinks that it is a very good idea. . . .

TEST: USE OF ENGLISH

Time: 1 hour 20 minutes

Answer all the questions. Write your answers in ink on the paper provided by the teacher.

Section A

1 Finish each of the following sentences in such a way that it means exactly the same as the sentence printed before it.

1 This food is much tastier than we normally get.
This is..........

2 I last swam in the sea when I was ten years old.
I haven't..........

3 Something's just bitten me!
I've..........

4 Of the people at the meeting, half were for the idea and half were against.
Half..........

5 He's been working for us for nineteen years, and next year will make it twenty.
By next year..........

6 It's likely that she'll be late.
She's..........

7 No one has identified the man yet.
The man..........

8 Someone told me a very funny joke the other day.
I was..........

9 'I'm standing in for someone else,' the (girl) assistant said.
The assistant told me that..........

10 People think that he trod on a few colleagues to get to the top.
He's..........

2 The word in capitals at the end of each of the following sentences can be used to form a word that fits suitably in the blank space. Supply the correct form of the word.

1 I'm very sorry. I must have ________. I'll add it up again.	CALCULATE
2 He was badly ________ in an accident and can't walk now.	ABLE
3 The boy's mother had to ________ his trousers as he grew older.	LONG
4 It would have taken a ________ to solve that particular problem.	MATHEMATICS
5 I wonder how many people dream of living on a ________ island?	TROPICS
6 This disease has spread ________ in the past few years.	ALARM
7 The view from the top of the mountain is ________.	SPECTACLE
8 As soon as he was arrested, the man made a ________ to the police.	STATE
9 This magazine only comes out ________.	FORTNIGHT
10 He's terribly ________. He doesn't remember anything you tell him.	FORGET

3 Make all the changes and additions necessary to produce, from the following five sets of words and phrases, five sentences which together make a paragraph from a letter. Note carefully from the example what kinds of alterations need to be made, especially to the words underlined. Write your paragraph on a separate piece of paper.

Example: By this time / next year / I / work / Smiths / six years.
You write: By this time next year I shall have been working at Smiths for six years.

1 I / be / just about / call / you yesterday / tell you / our holiday / when / I / receive / your letter.

2 I / keep / mean / send / you / a card / but we / have / such / relaxing holiday / I / never seem / get round to it.

3 We / always stay / in / quite / good hotel / in / past / but we / book / into / much / cheaper hotel / this time / save money.

4 We / have / such / good service / and / other guests / be / so / pleasant / we / be / almost bound / go back / there again.

5 And if we / go / same town / again / next year / we / spend / five holidays / there.

PLEASE TURN OVER

Section B

4 Below are the covers and brief descriptions of four books (as found in a catalogue). Imagine you want to buy two of the books for a thirteen-year-old boy who is learning English and who is interested in most sports and enjoys watching adventure and science fiction films on television. Using the information given, continue in about 50 words each of the four paragraphs at the bottom of the page, giving your reasons.

The Kraken Wakes
John Wyndham

An exciting and frightening story of a world threatened by some unidentifiable form of life in the oceans.

Girl Against the Jungle
Monica Vincent

A plane crashes in the Andes; only a teenage girl survives, but can she survive the fearful dangers of the Amazon jungle to reach safety? A remarkable true story. Includes photographs from the film.

The Energy Crisis

Based on a BBC television series, this is an analysis of our present sources of energy, how we can conserve them, and what a future involving nuclear power will mean to us.

Pele, King of Football
Noel Machin

The magic of Pele the footballer is world famous, but few people know about his early life as a poor boy in Brazil. Told in full-colour, comic-strip style.

My first choice for him would be . . .

My second choice would be . . .

I don't think I would buy him . . .

And I'm pretty sure he wouldn't enjoy . . .

Unit 24
'Forbidden!'

EXAM FOCUS:
Listening Comprehension

Look, listen and speak

Listen to the radio extract and look at the pictures. Then do the exercise below.

In pairs, and referring to the pictures, ask and tell each other why or how the different people are breaking the law. (At the same time, suggest why the different laws might have been made.)

24

Grammar practice 1

The verbs *allow, forbid, permit* and *prohibit; make* and *let*

REVIEW

The law { doesn't { allow / permit } / forbids } you to park here.

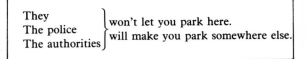

They / The police / The authorities } won't let you park here. / will make you park somewhere else.

You are { not allowed / not permitted / forbidden } to park here (by law).

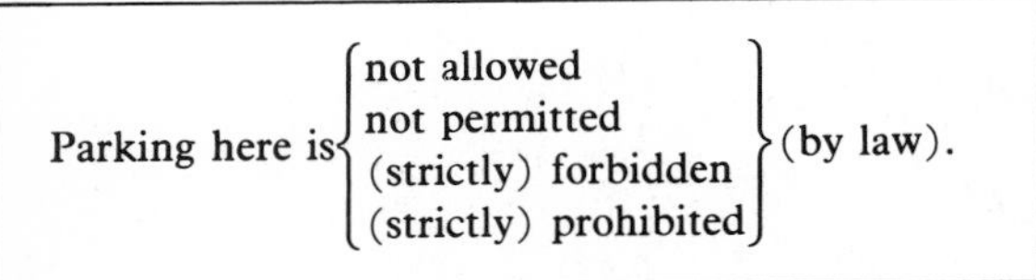

Parking here is { not allowed / not permitted / (strictly) forbidden / (strictly) prohibited } (by law).

ABOUT YOU

Imagine you are telling an English-speaking visitor to your country about things he or she is not allowed to do. Think of as many things as you can connected with driving, shopping, visiting churches, mosques or other places of interest, having a meal with a family, etc., and tell each other like this:

If you have a meal with a family, you're not allowed to start eating before the father does.

In my/this country, you're forbidden to drink alcohol.

If you go into a church in my country, they'll make you wear a headdress/ they won't let you wear shoes.

Grammar practice 2

More irregular verbs

REVIEW

Study these verbs and revise those on p 138, then play the game.

draw	drew	drawn
forbid	forbade	forbidden

forget	forgot	forgotten
forgive	forgave	forgiven

Game: *Mime it!* (see Teacher's Guide, p 79)

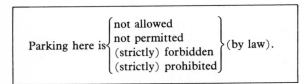

Grammar practice 3

Verb + object + preposition + gerund (e.g. *stop someone from doing*)

REVIEW

Study the verbs in these sentences. Then do the exercises below.

for	Everyone *admired* him *for* saving the man's life. I must *apologise* (to you) *for* being so late/*for* not coming earlier. He was *arrested for* stealing some money. They *blamed* the woman *for* causing the accident. *Excuse* me *for* asking, but are you allowed to smoke here? We often have to *forgive* foreigners *for* not knowing the law. *Pardon* me *for* butting in, but I must speak to you. It's important. The woman *praised* the man *for* acting so quickly. The two boys were *prosecuted for* shoplifting. She *punished* her son *for* telling lies. *Thank* you *for* giving me all that information.
from	His accident *prevented* him *from* riding a bike for a year. She was a good swimmer, so she managed to *save* her friend *from* drowning. They *stopped* her *from* doing what she wanted to do.
of	They *accused* him *of* breaking the law.
on	The teacher *congratulated* all the students *on* passing the exam.

PRACTICE

1 Join these pairs of sentences.

Example: The boy was just about to burn himself. His mother prevented him.

You say: The boy's mother prevented him from burning himself.

1 Someone stole £500 from the shop. The police accused Harry.
2 He does such a thankless job. Most people admire him.
3 I did such a stupid thing. I must apologise.
4 Mary got much better marks than expected. Her teacher congratulated her.
5 I trod on his glasses by accident. He finally forgave me.
6 The old lady was about to step off the pavement in front of a bus. I stopped her.
7 She was very brave. They all praised her.
8 The children came home very late. They were punished.
9 That woman has stolen a sweater. She will be prosecuted.
10 I did so much for them on their holiday. They said they wanted to thank me.

2 Refer back to p 142 and look at the pictures again. What could the different people be arrested or prosecuted for?

24

Exercises for homework

See if you can do these exercises in 60 minutes.

1 Reading Comprehension

Choose the word or phrase which best completes each sentence. Write your choice for each (A, B, C, D or E) on a separate piece of paper.

1 He's never ________ his father for making him go out to work when he was fourteen.
A forgotten B accused C forgiven D disapproved E forbidden

2 It's ________ a long time since I've ridden a bicycle.
A much B quite C fairly D pretty E so

3 You're not allowed ________ in this lake: it's protected.
A fish B to fish C fishing D for fishing E by fishing

4 We're raising money to buy a guide dog for ________ blind.
A a B the C most D some E all

5 Smoking is ________ forbidden in cinemas in that country.
A legally B strongly C hardly D strictly E kindly

2 Use of English

In the following conversation, some sentences have been left incomplete. Complete them suitably. Write out the whole dialogue on a separate piece of paper.

Sue: Hello, Mary.
Mary: Hello, Sue. Come in.
Sue: (1) Excuse...
Mary: You're not disturbing me at all. What can I do for you?
Sue: (2) Well, I wanted to ....
Mary: It's good of you to apologise, but I don't know what you mean. You did bring my book back—last week.
Sue: Really? How stupid of me! (3) I honestly don't.....................................
Mary: Well, *I* remember. You gave it to me last Wednesday. (4) I thanked you...
Sue: Oh, I am glad. (5) People are always accusing me.................................
Mary: Well, you are a little forgetful sometimes, you must admit.

3 Composition: Letter

When you got home after staying with some English-speaking friends recently, you unpacked to find that you had picked up one of their towels by mistake. Write a short letter (about 150 words) thanking them for their hospitality and apologising for taking the towel. (Don't forget to ask if they would like you to send it back or to give it back to them on your next visit.)

TEST: LISTENING COMPREHENSION

Time: approx. 20 minutes

You will hear four short extracts of spoken English (each twice on cassette or read by the teacher), and you will be given time to choose your answers to the questions below. Before you listen to each extract, read the questions and choices carefully. Read them again as you listen and before the second recording and choose A, B, C or D, re-order the items, or whatever you are asked to do. Check your answers while you are listening for the second time. Write your answers on the paper provided by the teacher.

1 Which message is completely correct?

A
John Brown called. Tel: 3773 4289. He sent his apologies for not coming today and wanted to know if he could explain everything tomorrow afternoon.

B
John Brown called by. Tel: 3737 4298. He was sorry about today and wants to come at 12 tomorrow. If it's inconvenient, perhaps we could call him.

C
John Brown rang. Tel: 3737 2948. He couldn't see you because something came up, but he'll be seeing you the day after tomorrow.

D
John Brown rang up. Tel: 3737 4298. He apologised for missing today's appointment. Will it be all right for him to call by at ten a.m. tomorrow?

2 Which is the correct order in which these are mentioned?

A

B

C

D

3 Although she thinks that other callers have made some good points, the woman

A doesn't agree with any of them.
B criticises half of them.
C disagrees with all of them.
D wants to make another point.

4 Who does the woman think should be blamed most for the present state of education?

A The government.
B Parents.
C Teachers.
D Schools.

5 Only one of these rules applies in the College. Which?

A
NO SMOKING DURING BREAKS BETWEEN LECTURES

B
STUDENTS MUST BE PUNCTUAL FOR ALL LECTURES

C
STUDENTS' CARS, MOTORCYCLES AND BICYCLES MUST BE LEFT BEHIND THE COLLEGE

D
ALL COLLEGE FEES MUST BE PAID BY THE SECOND WEEK OF TERM

Unit 25
I wish . . .

EXAM FOCUS:
Oral Interview

Look and speak

Look at these photos and do the exercises.

1 Add a caption

What do you think these people are saying or thinking? Think of as many as you can using—

I wish . . .
It's about/high time . . .
If . . .

For example:
I wish I could lose weight.
It's about time someone asked me to dance.
If I had put my car away in the garage, this might not have happened.

2 In pairs, ask and answer questions about each photo, for example:
What's the woman doing?
Why is she standing on one foot?
How heavy do you think she is?

3 Discussion

In small groups, discuss
1 ways of losing weight.
2 old people's homes—what old people do/don't like—what kinds of entertainment old people do/don't enjoy, etc.
3 experiences that you have had which you would rather forget.

25

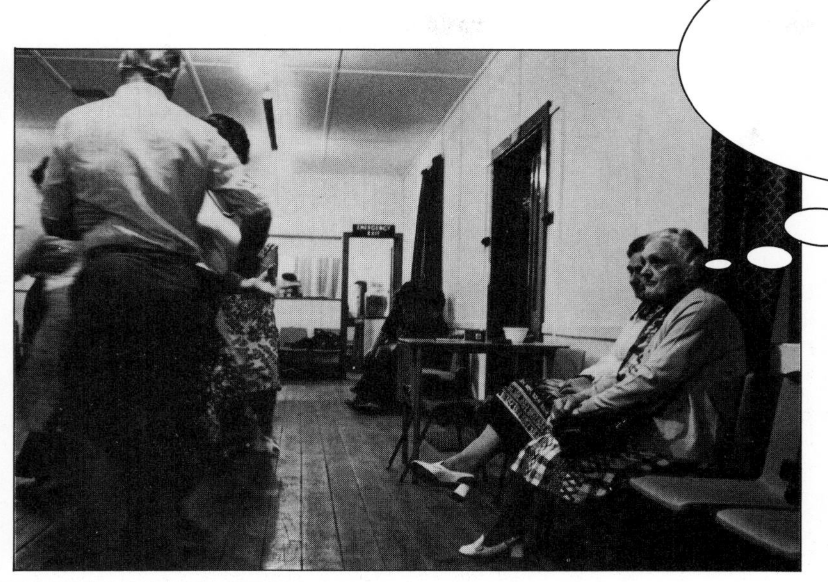

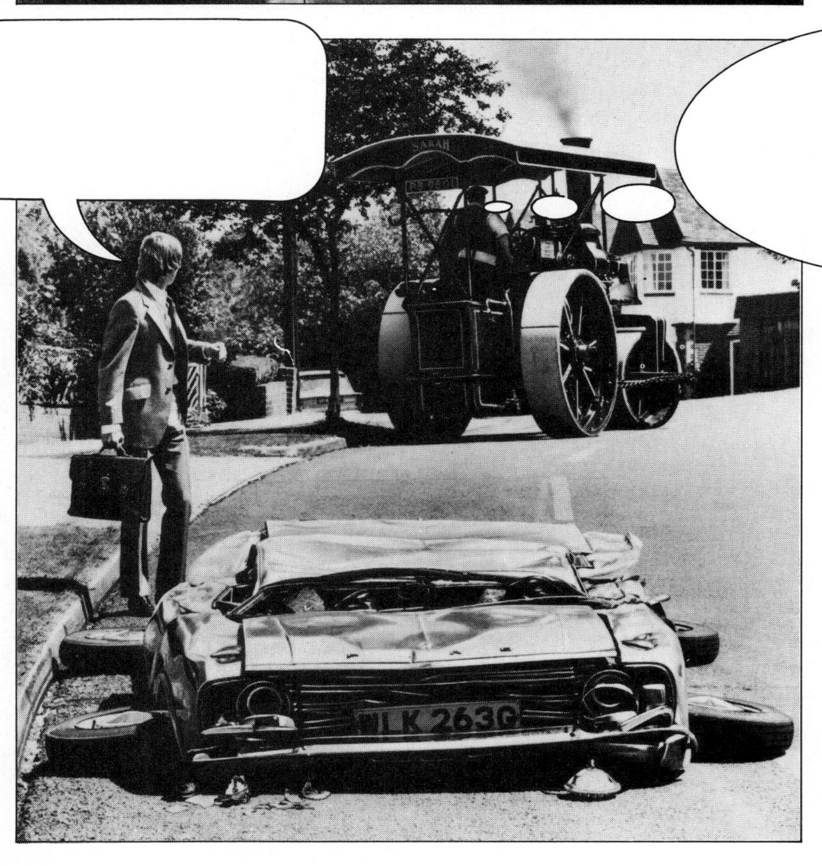

25

Grammar practice 1

Expressing regret with *I wish . . .*, advice with *It's (about/high) time . . .*, and preference for other people's actions with *I'd rather . . .*

REVIEW

Study this, then do the exercises below.

Situation	**Response to situation**
	Regret
I'm not on holiday. I haven't got a job. I can't swim. They won't help me. I burnt some old letters. I didn't mow the lawn.	I wish { I were on holiday (now). I had a job (now). I could swim. they would help me. I hadn't burnt those old letters (yesterday). I had mown the lawn (last week).
	Advice
You haven't done any work. She hasn't lost any weight. He hasn't learnt to spell.	(I think) it's { high / about } time { you did some work. she lost some weight. he learnt to spell.
	Preference for someone else's activity (now)
You're doing something. He's sawing some wood. She's doing her homework.	{ I would / I'd } { rather / sooner } { you didn't do that. he mowed the lawn (instead). she sewed her dress up (instead).

PRACTICE

What would you say in or about these situations?
Begin with the words in brackets.

1 Your brother can't get a job. (*I wish . . .*)
2 They haven't allowed people to park in the Town Centre for years. (*It's about time . . .*)
3 John broke Paul's bike. He won't apologise. (*I wish . . .*)
4 We do very little for the disabled in this country. (*I think it's high time . . .*)
5 A friend wants to help you in your garden, and wants to know whether to mow the lawn or saw some wood first. (*I'd rather . . .*)
6 You think a friend should get herself a new dress. (*It's about time . . .*)
7 You hid a present for a friend and can't find it now. (*I wish . . .*)
8 You went out for a meal and ate too much. Now you feel ill. (*I wish . . .*)
9 A friend of yours looks as if he/she needs a holiday. (*I think it's about time . . .*)
10 Some musicians are playing a tune, but you'd like them to play something else. (*I'd sooner they . . .*)

ABOUT YOU

1 Express regrets about your own life, for example:
I wish we didn't (always) have so much homework.
I wish I had done more work last year.
etc.

2 Express advice for other people, for example:
It's about time John had a haircut.
I think it's time Helen bought a new bike.
etc.

Grammar practice 2

More irregular verbs

REVIEW

Study these verbs and then do the exercises below.

burn	burned/burnt	burned/burnt
kneel	kneeled/knelt	kneeled/knelt
learn	learned/learnt	learned/learnt
smell	smelled/smelt	smelled/smelt
spell	spelled/spelt	spelled/spelt
spill	spilled/spilt	spilled/spilt
spoil	spoiled/spoilt	spoiled/spoilt

deal	dealt	dealt
mow	mowed	mown/mowed
saw	sawed	sawn/sawed
sew	sewed	sewn/sewed
show	showed	shown/showed
sow	sowed	sown/sowed
swell	swelled	swollen/swelled

PRACTICE

1 What would you say, using *I wish . . .*, in these situations?

1 You didn't learn to ride a horse when you were younger.
2 You can't spell very well.
3 You spoilt your chances of promotion by insulting the boss.
4 You regret not sowing some vegetable seeds last year.
5 You burnt some cakes yesterday.

2 What would you say, using *It's about time you . . .* or *Isn't it about time you . . .?*, to these people?

1 Someone who hasn't dealt with a letter from the bank manager yet.
2 Someone who should have mown his lawn a long time ago.
3 Someone who hasn't learnt to spell yet.
4 Someone who has had a rip in her skirt for a long time.
5 Someone who hasn't shown anyone else what he/she had for his/her birthday.

"I'D RATHER YOU DIDN'T LOOK, MRS. PRENDERGAST. JUST CALL THE POLICE."

25

Oral Interview preparation

1 Look at this cartoon carefully and then answer the questions.

About the cartoon

1 Who do you think is saying 'I wish we'd never come to live in the green belt*?' Why do you think that?
2 How do you think the other person feels about living there?
3 If they were friends of yours, what advice would you give them? (Use *I think it's about time*... or *I think you should*....)
4 What do you think the inside of the cottage is like?
5 Where do you think this couple used to live before? Why?

General

1 Where do you live?—in the country? or a town or city?
2 Do you like living there? Or would you rather move?
3 Assuming you had enough money, where would you most like to live, and why?
4 And what kind of a house or flat would you like? Why?
5 Do you have 'green belts' (or anything like them) in your country? If so, do you think they are a good idea? Why?/Why not?
If not, do you think you will have (or need) them one day?

" I WISH WE'D NEVER COME TO LIVE IN THE GREEN BELT. "

**green belt*—a stretch of land, round a town, where no new building is allowed, so that fields, woods, old cottages, etc. remain

2 Reading aloud

You come across this letter in an English newspaper and read it out to a friend over the telephone. Practise reading it aloud.

Dear Sir,

Were the authorities really justified in prosecuting Mr Smith for allowing his house and garden to become completely overgrown with trees, shrubs and creepers? (I refer to your report on 20th January.) I know he lives in the town and that there are certain laws which forbid a houseowner to do certain things with the property. But if he wanted 'a house in a jungle', what was there to prevent him? I do think it's about time the authorities stopped wasting their time persecuting people like Mr Smith, and spent a lot more time looking after people in our society who need their help—people like the elderly, the unemployed, the poor and the sick.

Yours faithfully,
I.R. Jones

3 Situation for extended role play

You are touring an English-speaking country in your car with your family or some friends, and stop at a hotel where you would like to stay for two or three days. You have not booked. In pairs, conduct the conversation between the hotel receptionist and yourself. Ask and/or say:

- if there are any rooms free
- how many rooms/beds you would like, and for how long
- whether you want bed and breakfast or full board, and the cost
- name(s) (+ spelling), nationality and home address (+ spelling), etc.

4 Topics for individual talks

Choose one of these topics below, write brief notes, and then give a short talk to the class. You should try to talk for 30–45 seconds. When you have finished, the class may ask questions.

- If you had three wishes, what would they be?
- The advantages and disadvantages of living in a city or in the country.
- What I would do if I ruled the world.
- What could be done in your own country to help the unemployed?
- Nuclear weapons.

Unit 26
Strange visitors

EXAM FOCUS:
Reading Comprehension

Read and speak

This passage is adapted from *Pawley's Peepholes,* a short science fiction story by John Wyndham. The story is about some unwanted visitors—time-travellers from the future—who, because they are in a different dimension, can walk through people and objects. Read the passage carefully and then do the exercises.

The trouble seemed to come thickest in the district that Jimmy had originally marked out. You *could* meet them in other places, but in that area you couldn't help meeting gangs of them, the men in coloured shirts, the girls with their amazing hair-do's and even more amazing decorations on their shirts, sauntering arm-in-arm out of walls, and wandering indifferently through cars and people alike. They'd pause anywhere to point things out to one another and go off into helpless roars of silent laughter. What amused them most was when people got angry with them. They'd make signs and faces at the more old-fashioned sort until they got them hopping mad—and the madder, the funnier. They ambled as the spirit took them, through shops and banks, and offices, and homes, without a care for the raging occupants. Everybody started putting up 'Keep Out' signs; that amused them a lot, too.

It didn't seem as if you could be free of them anywhere in the central area, though they appeared to be operating on levels that weren't always the same as ours. In some places they did look as if they were walking on the ground or floor, but in other places they'd be inches above it, and then in some places you would meet them moving along as though they were wading through the solid surface. It was very soon clear that they could no more hear us than we could hear them, so that it was no use appealing to them or threatening them in any way, and none of the notices that people put up seemed to do anything but arouse their curiosity.

After three days of it there was chaos. In the worst affected parts there just wasn't any privacy any more. At the most intimate moments they were liable to wander through, visibly sniggering or laughing out loud. It was all very well for the police to announce that there was no danger, that the 'visitors' appeared unable actually to *do* anything, so the best way was to ignore them. There are times and places when giggling bunches of young people demand more 'ignore-power' than the average person has got.

The news had begun to get about, and that didn't help, either. News collectors of all kinds came streaming in. They overflowed the place. The streets were snaked with leads to movie cameras, television cameras and microphones, while the press-photographers were having the time of their lives, and, being solid, they were almost as much of a nuisance as the 'visitors' themselves.

1 From your reading of the passage, are the following statements true or false, or don't you know?

1 The 'visitors' tended to appear in one geographical area.
2 All the 'visitors' were young people.
3 The town's residents wished the 'visitors' would go away.
4 The 'Keep Out' signs worked for a while.
5 The people who sent the 'visitors' from the future put them exactly where they wanted to be.
6 Town residents and 'visitors' could see and hear one another, but couldn't touch one another.
7 The 'visitors' would avoid wandering into bedrooms or bathrooms.
8 Everyone followed the advice given by the police.
9 When the news got out, the town was invaded by reporters.
10 The 'visitors' enjoyed being photographed and filmed.

2 In pairs, ask and tell each other

1 how the 'visitors' dressed.
2 how they acted.
3 what they did which annoyed the residents.
4 why they didn't always walk on the ground.
5 why the residents were helpless to do anything.

3 Discussion

If you could travel in time, which period or periods in the past would you visit and why? Or would you rather visit the future? Why?/Why not?

26

26

Grammar practice 1

would do, used to do* and *be/get used to doing

REVIEW

When I was very young,
- my grandfather {would / used to} tell me stories.
- I {would (often) / (often) used to} go for walks by myself.
- my brother {would (always) / (always) used to} help me if I was in trouble.

Note that *would do* and *used to do* are used to talk about past habits. For states, however, we can only use *used to.* In sentences like 'She used to be fat' or 'She used to have black hair: now it's grey', 'would be' and 'would have' would be impossible.

I used to have a very light breakfast, but now I'm getting used to eating a large breakfast.

Since I've been here, I've got used to riding a bicycle.

Don't worry about me. I'm used to looking after myself.

Note that *be/get used to doing* = *be/get accustomed to doing.*

ABOUT YOU

Tell each other about things that you, friends or relatives would do or used to do when you were very young, and if possible compare those with things that you have got or are used to doing now, for example:

I would always sleep with a light on when I was younger, but I've been used to sleeping in a dark room now for years.

Grammar practice 2

***it's no use, it's (not) worth* and *there's no point in* + gerund**

REVIEW

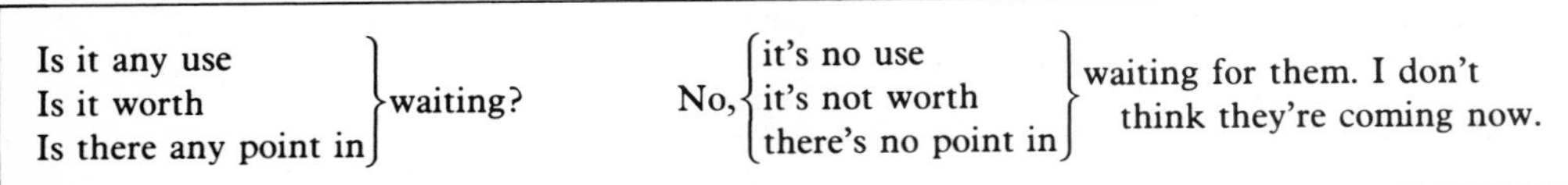

{Is it any use / Is it worth / Is there any point in} waiting?

No, {it's no use / it's not worth / there's no point in} waiting for them. I don't think they're coming now.

Note that *worth* can be used with a noun/pronoun subject, for example:
That film's (well) worth seeing./He's not worth worrying about.

PRACTICE

Join these pairs of sentences.
Begin with the words in italics.

1 Don't ask him for an explanation.
There's no point.
2 Don't wish you were someone else.
It's no use.
3 Shall I mow the lawn today?
It is worth it?
4 Do I need to learn these verbs?
Is there any point in it?
5 Don't repair *that old bicycle* again.
It's not worth it.
6 Should I tell the newspapers about it?
Is it any use?

Vocabulary

Noun suffixes *-ity, -acy* and *-ation*

Here are more nouns formed with suffixes. Study them and the notes. Then do the exercise below.

-ity	curiosity, electricity, similarity, familiarity, regularity, (in)ability, originality, respectability, simplicity (Note: poor—poverty)
-acy	accuracy, intimacy, privacy
-ation	justification, identification, simplification, organisation, realisation, legalisation

Note the change of stress from the adjective to the noun, for example:
'curious → ,curi'osity
'simple → sim'plicity
re'spectable → re,specta'bility

and from the verb to the noun, for example:
'justify → ,justifi'cation
'legalise → ,legali'sation

PRACTICE

The word in capitals at the end of each of the following sentences can be used to form a word that fits suitably in the blank space. Supply the correct form of the word.

1 He hit the target with great ______ every time he shot. ACCURATE
2 There is no ______ for paying women less than men if they do the same job. JUSTIFY
3 She shows a great deal of ______ in her drawing and designs. ORIGINAL
4 Millions of people in the world live in dreadful ______. POOR
5 The bank wouldn't change any money for me. I had no means of ______. IDENTIFY
6 He had been waiting for ten minutes when he came to the ______ that he was in the wrong shop. REALISE
7 There is very little ______ if you share a small flat with six others! PRIVATE
8 They say '______ killed the cat', so don't be nosey! CURIOUS
9 There's a certain ______ between them, but I wouldn't really have guessed that they were brother and sister. SIMILAR
10 He showed a surprising ______ to grasp the situation. ABLE

26

Taking the First Certificate Examination

PAPER 1: READING COMPREHENSION

What the Paper consists of

The Reading Comprehension Paper has two Sections, A and B. Section A contains 25 multiple-choice items designed to test vocabulary, structure and usage. Section B contains 15 multiple-choice comprehension questions based on three or more texts. You are given a separate answer sheet on which to indicate your choices, and the time allowed for the whole Paper is one hour.

Some tips on doing the Paper

1 Make sure you understand exactly what you have to do! Read the instructions to all parts very carefully two or three times. Never assume that the instructions are exactly the same as the ones you read in similar practice tests. And make sure that you understand exactly how to indicate your answers on the separate answer sheet. If you are in any doubt, ask the examiner.

2 Work through the Paper as quickly and as carefully as you can.

3 Begin by working through the 25 multiple-choice items in Section A. Read each carefully, mentally 'slotting in' the choices (A, B, C and D) in the blank in the sentence until you know which is the correct choice. Don't waste valuable time thinking about items which you don't understand or know you can't do. Leave them! You may have time to come back to them later. But if you do leave out items, make sure that you mark the following items against the corresponding right numbers on the answer sheet.

4 Move on to Section B. With each text, you might read it once to understand the gist of it, then read the multiple-choice items, and then read the text again before you make your choices. Or some candidates prefer to read the accompanying multiple-choice items first, and then read the text with an eye to the information they are looking for. Whichever procedure you adopt, constantly compare the choices in the items with the text. And again, if you cannot answer certain items, leave them and move on.

5 Work through all the texts and items, answering as many questions as you can.

6 Aim to finish the Paper. This means watching your time rather carefully: for example, if the first half hour has passed and you haven't completed Section A, leave it and go on to Section B.

7 You should aim to complete the whole Paper in 50 minutes. This will give you time to go back and check all of your answers and possibly complete any you might have left unanswered.

TEST: READING COMPREHENSION

Time: 1 hour

Section A

Choose the word or phrase which best completes each sentence.
Write your choice for each (A, B, C or D) on a separate piece of paper.

1 There's ______ in going on a picnic today. Look at the weather!
A no use B pointless C not worth D no point

2 I wish I ______ there for my holiday last year. I didn't enjoy it.
A didn't go B hadn't gone C wouldn't go D would rather go

3 Everybody ______ her for saving the old man from drowning.
A congratulated B accused C praised D prohibited

4 She's a ______ nicer person that I thought she was.
A very B such C quite D much

5 These trousers are much too long, I'm afraid. Can you ______ them for me, please?
A tighten B shorten C loosen D lengthen

6 She has studied so hard for the examination that she's ______ to pass it.
A bound B liable C possible D apt

7 The first thing he did was to ______ his shoelaces and take his shoes off.
A unpack B disconnect C untie D mislead

8 That woman's husband just ______ her one day last year and she hasn't seen him since.
A went back on B grew out of C ran away with D walked out on

9 When he came out of the room, he looked ______ he had seen a ghost.
A if B as though C when D as

10 I've tried ringing three or four times, but I still can't ______ Mr Smith.
A get through to B go on about C get on to D go along with

11 He wouldn't have been arrested if he ______ a car.
A didn't steal B wasn't stealing C wouldn't steal D hadn't stolen

12 I'm ______ at remembering telephone numbers. I can hardly remember my own!
A forgetful B careless C incapable D dreadful

13 Of all the people I know, she drives ______.
A most careful B more careful C most carefully D the most carefully

14 ______ the time the fire brigade got there, the house had burnt down.
A When B As soon as C By D After

15 I must ______ now. I'll call you again at the same time tomorrow.
A ring off B break off C answer back D hang about

16 The last time I came here, that building ______. It looks much better now, doesn't it?
A has been renovated B was renovated C would be renovated D was being renovated

17 I don't suppose I could have a glass of water, ______?
A could I B do I C I suppose D couldn't I

18 It was supposed to be a surprise party, but Bob ______ the game ______.
A gave . . . away B bore . . . out C got . . . across D held . . . up

19 When the soldiers first arrived, they were all supplied ______ a map of the place.
A of B for C with D on

PLEASE TURN OVER

Section A continued

20 Keep going along Station Road until you ______ to a roundabout.
A reach B come C arrive D go

21 It's quite a good road, but you must ______ of heavy traffic near the airport.
A allow B watch out C look out D beware

22 You'd better not leave yet—______ you might miss them.
A if B else C otherwise D unless

23 He spent the whole weekend turning ______ the loft.
A away B out C up D down

24 She's totally ______. She never does anything she promises to do.
A unenthusiastic B disloyal C unreliable D illogical

25 She felt lonely when she first arrived because she had ______ to talk to.
A somebody B anyone C nobody D anybody

Section B

In this section you will find after each of the texts a number of questions or unfinished statements about the text, each with four suggested answers or ways of finishing. You must choose the one which you think fits best. Write your answers (A, B, C or D) on a separate piece of paper. Read each text right through before choosing your answers.

First text

Although the weathermen's forecasts for a month ahead are only a little better than guesswork, they are now making long-term forecasts into the next century with growing confidence. For the dominant trend in the world's climate in the coming decades will, scientists say, be a predictable result of man's activities.

At the start of the industrial revolution nearly two centuries ago, man innocently set off a gigantic experiment in planetary engineering. Unaware of what he was doing, he spared no thought for the consequences. Today the possible outcome is alarmingly clear, but the experiment is unstoppable. Within the lifetimes of many of us, the Earth may become warmer than it has been for a thousand years. By the middle of the next century it may be warmer than it has been since before the last Ice Age. And the century after that may be hotter than any in the past 70 million years.

Superficially, a warmer climate may seem welcome. But it could bring many hazards—disruption of crops in the world's main food-producing regions, famine, economic instability, civil unrest and even war.

In the much longer term, melting of the great ice-caps of Greenland and Antarctica could raise sea-levels throughout the world. The average sea-level has already risen a foot since the turn of the century, and if the ice-caps disappear entirely, it would rise by nearly 200 feet. Complete melting might take many centuries, but even a small increase in sea-level would threaten low-lying parts of the world such as the Netherlands.

The man-made agent of climatic change is the carbon dioxide that has been pouring out of the world's chimneys in ever-increasing quantities since the industrial revolution began. And in the past few years scientists have begun to suspect that there is a second man-made source of carbon dioxide which may be as important as the burning of fossil fuels, namely the steady destruction of the world's great forests. Trees and other vegetation represent a huge stock of carbon removed from circulation, like money in a bank. As the vast tropical forests are cut down, most of the carbon they contain finds its way back into the atmosphere as carbon dioxide.

Section B continued

The amount of CO_2 (carbon dioxide) in the atmosphere is still tiny. But it has climatic effects out of all proportion to its concentration. It acts rather like the glass in a greenhouse, letting through short-wave radiation from the sun, but trapping the longer-wave radiation by which the Earth loses heat to outer space.

Computer studies have suggested that if the concentration of carbon dioxide in the atmosphere were to be twice that of today's, there would be a rise of between 2°C and 3°C in average temperature.

26 Long-term weather forecasts beyond the year 2050 may seem strange because
- A none of us will be alive then!
- B weathermen cannot even forecast next month's weather accurately!
- C weathermen can do much better.
- D no one can stop engineering experiments.

27 Weathermen believe that our future climate will be the direct result of
- A gigantic scientific experiments.
- B clever long-term forecasts.
- C the industrial revolution.
- D planets changing course.

28 One of the results of a warmer world climate could well be
- A an increase in food production.
- B greater co-operation between countries.
- C the death of millions of people from starvation.
- D a reduction in the amount of oil we use.

29 Scientists are fairly sure that, by the year 2050,
- A the sea-level will have risen noticeably.
- B there will have been a third World War.
- C most countries will have been flooded.
- D the polar ice-caps will have melted.

30 How has Man changed the world's climate?
- A By building chimneys.
- B By using up more carbon dioxide.
- C By increasing industrialisation.
- D By destroying forests and by burning fossil fuels.

31 If the amount of CO_2 in the atmosphere increases considerably,
- A we can expect colder weather.
- B plants will tend to grow faster.
- C the world will become warmer.
- D we shall have to cut down more forests.

PLEASE TURN OVER

Section B continued

Second text

(This is an extract from a magazine article *Baths With My Aunt* by Mel Calman.)

Once a week my Aunt would announce, 'I am going to have my Bath today'.

Now most people find it fairly simple to have a bath. You probably remember how it goes. You enter the bathroom, you put the plug in, turn on the hot water, get into the bath, wash, sing, get out, dry yourself and exit. My Aunt's approach was more epic, like one of those long Eisenstein films where people seem to be climbing up the same flight of stairs forever.

My Aunt would first slowly collect her clean linen, so as to have it all ready for changing into after Her Bath. This involved sorting out her linen, which took up most of the morning. Sometimes she would find an old letter buried amongst her linen, become interested in the memories it aroused and have to postpone The Bath until the next day. But if all went well, she would have a bite of lunch and start Phase Two around two o'clock.

Phase Two was Washing Out the Bath. She would wash the bath very thoroughly, rinse it with running cold water, rewash it and then carefully feel the whole surface with her fingers. If there was the slightest blemish, she would clean the whole bath out again. This took about an hour. Then she would fill the bath.

By this time she was feeling a bit hungry and exhausted. So she would put on the kettle for a cup of tea. Several cups of tea and several cream crackers (her favourite food) later, she would go back to the bathroom. And find the water stone cold.

32 According to Calman, most people
- A read film magazines in the bath.
- B make bathtime a special occasion.
- C sing when they are in the bath.
- D have a bath once a week.

33 Calman's Aunt
- A never got used to bathing regularly.
- B always treated bathtime as an event.
- C hated climbing the stairs to the bathroom.
- D would never take longer than anyone else in the bath.

34 How did she use to spend most of the morning?
- A Reading old letters.
- B Preparing lunch.
- C Getting the bath water hot.
- D Sorting out her linen.

35 Why might Calman's Aunt put off bathing until the next day?
- A She might get fascinated by an old letter.
- B She might start ironing the linen.
- C She would sometimes get too tired.
- D She would sometimes have lunch instead.

36 She would never fill the bath until she had
- A cleaned it at least four times.
- B had a cup of tea.
- C polished it inside and out.
- D made sure it was perfectly clean.

37 She would have tea and biscuits
- A before cleaning the bath.
- B while she was rinsing out the bath.
- C after filling the bath.
- D if the water got cold.

Third text

(This is an extract from the information on the back of a record sleeve.)

Most great singing stars have established themselves long before they get to 35, but that is how old Madge Sharp is now, and this is her first record. It will not be her last.

'I've always wanted to be a blues singer,' she says. 'I used to listen to singers like Mahalia Jackson and Ella Fitzgerald and others on record, but my parents would never let me go to a concert. And they never allowed me to sing with a band. The only singing I did for years was in our church choir. Of course I wish I had started in the profession earlier, but I've got something now which a lot of younger singers haven't got—experience and maturity.'

And it's this experience and maturity in her voice which adds a distinct originality to all the tracks on this collection. All the songs may be old, but her versions of classics like *If* and *Georgia* make them sound as if they were written yesterday.

As one critic in *Music Week* magazine wrote: 'We've got so used to listening to rubbish in pop music in recent years that when a new artist like Madge Sharp arrives, it's difficult to believe. She is almost unbelievable: her singing is superb. I just wish she hadn't waited quite so long to make her first record.'

38 Madge Sharp
- A used to sing with a band years ago.
- B was never allowed to sing with Mahalia Jackson.
- C wanted to wait till she was experienced before making a record.
- D made her first record later in her life than most singers.

39 Where did Madge gain most of her (singing) experience?
- A In a church choir.
- B Singing with other mature singers.
- C In a pop group.
- D Imitating Ella Fitzgerald.

40 Madge and the *Music Week* critic agree that
- A she is a superb singer.
- B she should have made a record earlier.
- C she adds originality to old songs.
- D her record will be very successful.

Unit 27

It's easy! Just follow the instructions!

EXAM FOCUS:
Composition

Read and speak

Read these instructions on how to use a Polaroid camera. Then do the exercises on the opposite page.

With a Polaroid camera, just aim and press the button. Your picture ejects automatically and develops before your eyes.

HOW TO TAKE THE PICTURE

Film loading: Your camera uses only Polaroid SX-70 Land film. Each film pack provides ten colour pictures and also contains a battery to power the camera. To load film, push the latch **1** forward to open the film door. Hold the film pack by the edges only **2** and insert it all the way into the camera. Close the film door, keeping your fingers away from the exit slot. The camera will immediately eject the film cover **3**. Remove it.

How to hold the camera: Hold the camera in the palm of your left hand **4**.

Never put your fingers in front of the picture exit slot or the electric eye.

To aim and shoot: Look through the viewfinder. Be sure you can see all four corners of the image area. Position yourself so your subject 'fills' the viewfinder. Don't come closer than 1.2m (4 ft.). Place your right forefinger on the shutter button **5**. The other fingers should be curled into your palm, as shown. To steady the camera, press your right thumb firmly against the picture counter. Hold the camera steady and gently press the shutter button. Hold the button in until the picture comes out of the exit slot. Remove the picture, which will develop by itself, in the light before your eyes. Do not bend, squeeze or cut the picture.

To remove an empty film pack: Open the film door. Pull the pack out by the yellow tab.

INDOOR PICTURES

For indoor pictures, use the Polaroid Electronic Flash No. 2351 or the 10-bulb Polaroid Flashbar. Both are specially designed for your camera. If you use a Flashbar, insert it firmly into the socket on the top of the camera **6**. Always do this with the camera pointing away from you. After the five bulbs on one side have been fired, reverse the Flashbar for five more flashes. When all the bulbs on the side facing the subject have been fired, the camera will not operate, so that you will not waste film. If you should insert a partly used Flashbar, the camera will automatically select the next fresh bulb for the next flash picture.

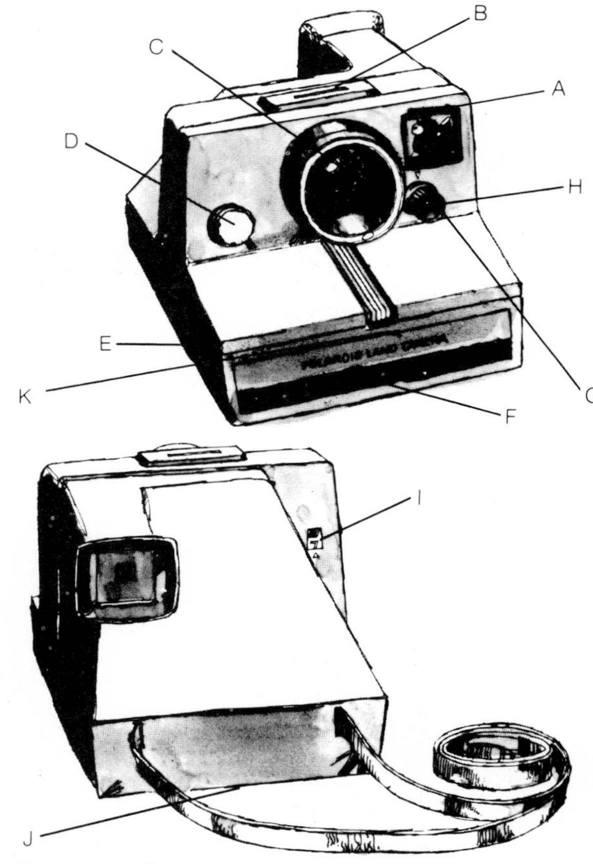

Camera parts

A Viewfinder
B Socket for Electronic Flash No. 2351 and Flashbars
C Lens
D Shutter button
E Film door latch
F Picture exit slot
G Lighten/Darken control
H Electric eye
I Picture counter
J Slot for Tripod Mount
K Serial number (inside camera)

27

1 In pairs, and referring to the instructions and illustrations, ask and tell each other how to use a Polaroid camera.

Ask: How do I/How should I load the film?
or What do I have to do to load the film?
What do I (have to) do to take a picture indoors/in daylight?

Reply: First, . . .; Then (after you've done that), . . .; And finally, ...

2 Referring (as far as possible) only to the illustrations below, explain to another student how to use a Polaroid camera. The other student may ask questions with *Why . . .?* for you to give reasons using *because, so that, to /do/, in order (not) to /do/* or *so as (not) to /do/*.

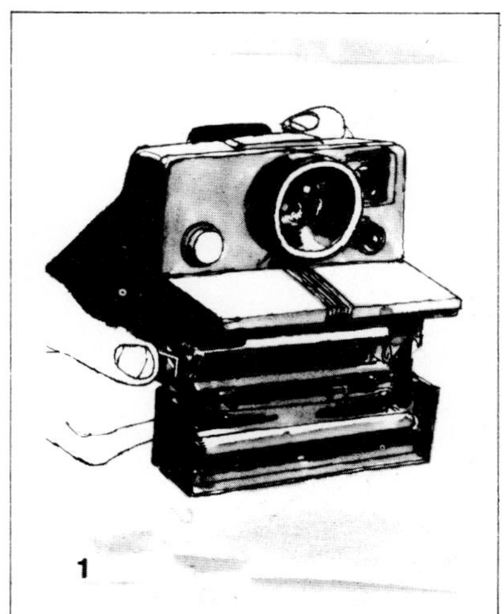

27

Grammar practice 1

Imperative, Present Simple, *have to do* and *should do* for instructions

REVIEW

These sentences refer to using a Polaroid camera (pp 163–164).

> First, { (you) look / you have to/should look } through the viewfinder and position yourself so that your subject fills the viewfinder.
> (*or:* The first thing you (have to/should) do is to look through . . .)
>
> Then { after that, / after you've done that, / as soon as you've done that, } place your right forefinger on the shutter button and press your right thumb against the picture counter.
>
> Next, holding the camera steady, (you have to) press the shutter button and hold it until the picture comes out of the exit slot.
>
> Finally, (you) remove the picture.

ABOUT YOU

Think of something typical from your own country—a national dish, a national (card) game or sport, the public telephone, etc. and write a list of simple instructions under a heading, e.g. *How to make moussaka, How to use a public telephone in Brazil,* etc.
Then, as if giving instructions to an English-speaking visitor, tell another student how to do it. The other student may ask questions, but may not look at your written notes.

Grammar practice 2

Expressing reasons and consequences with *because . . ., so that . . ., to/do/, in order (not) to /do/* and *so as (not) to /do/*

REVIEW

This refers to taking a photo with a Polaroid camera.

> When you place your forefinger on the shutter button, you should curl your other fingers in your palm (like this)—
> { because (otherwise) you might / so that you don't / to make sure (that) you don't / in order not to / so as not to } put a finger in front of the lens.

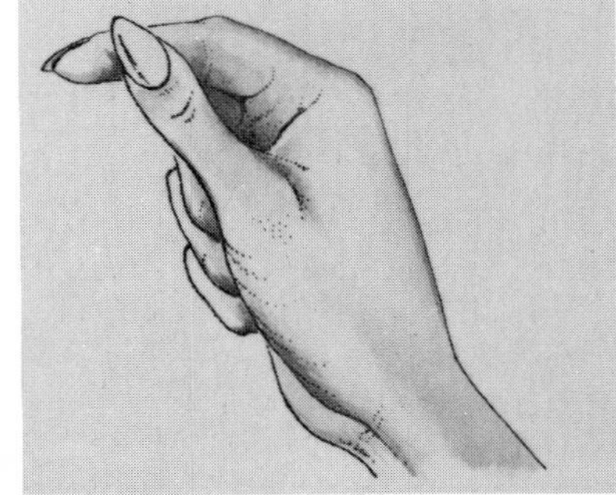

PRACTICE

Refer again to the instructions on how to use a Polaroid camera, and explain to another student what to do, but this time add reasons wherever you can with *because . . .*, *so that . . .*, *so as (not) to*, etc.

ABOUT YOU

1 Think of an indoor game you know well (e.g. a card game) and explain to another student or the class how to play it.

2 Think of a (fairly simple) machine or electric appliance you have at home (e.g. your own camera, an electric iron, etc.) and explain to another student or to the class how to use it.

Vocabulary

Verb prefixes *over, under-, fore-, en-/em-*

Study these verbs carefully and then do the exercise below.

over-	overcook, overdo, oversimplify, overflow, overcharge
under-	undercook, underfeed, undercharge
fore-	foresee, foretell, forewarn, forecast
en-	endanger, enlarge, encourage, enrich, enforce
em-	empower, embitter

Rephrase each of these sentences using a verb from the box above to replace the words in italics.

1 They *charged* me *too much* for the meal.
2 You're *simplifying* the matter *too much.*
3 The meat was *not cooked enough.*
4 They *didn't charge* me *enough.*
5 I can *see in advance* that there's going to be trouble.
6 You will *cause danger to* your health if you drink too much coffee.
7 I was *given courage* to do better.
8 We shall have to *make* the house *larger.*
9 They've been *given power* to arrest people.
10 No one can *tell* the future *in advance.*

Discussion

In small groups, tell each other about the last time you did a job, used a new appliance, etc. and tried to follow the instructions. Say what you did and how well it went—or say what went wrong and why. Try to use the language of instructions you have already practised, for example:
First, I took out the . . . so as not to . . .

And then use some of these phrases:

It wasn't until I had /done/ . . . that I realised . . .
It took a long time/didn't take very long to . . .
The instructions didn't make it very clear what to do . . .
During the time that I was /doing/ . . .
It's (been) some time since I last /did/ . . ., so I thought . . .

27

Taking the First Certificate Examination

PAPER 2: COMPOSITION

What the Paper consists of

In this Paper you are required to write two compositions in 1½ hours. You will be given a choice of five subjects—usually a letter, a narrative, a description, an 'argument' and an optional prescribed text compostion. For each you are expected to write between 120 and 180 words.

Some tips on doing the Paper

1 Read the instructions at the top of the Paper *very* carefully.

2 Read through all the composition subjects carefully and choose the two you think you can do best.

3 For each composition, write a plan and some rough ideas. This will help to ensure that you write on the subject and that you observe the correct form, especially in the letter. Here are some brief reminders about the composition types.

Letter	Make sure that it deals with the topic you have been set. As for form, remember the correct layout for an English letter, and use clear paragraphing.
Narrative	Choose the kind of incident asked for and think of a good story line. You may need to decide whether to use the first or third person. Remember the 'Before the event: the event: after the event' sequence of actions.
Description	Read the topic carefully to see exactly what you have to describe—a person, a scene, a period of your life, etc. There should be a clear introduction, development and conclusion.
Argument	The argument must deal with the topic set and should have a clear introduction, development and conclusion. Remember that this is probably the most difficult type to write.

4 Use language (structures, vocabulary and expressions) that you know. Don't try to 'create' new words or structures in English. It is better to write shorter, correct, well-constructed sentences than sentences which are long and complicated and which may be wrong.

5 Watch the time. With only two compositions to be written in 1½ hours, you can devote the following amounts of time to each: 5 minutes for planning, 35 minutes for writing, and 5 minutes to read through and check.

6 When you have finished each composition, read it through and make any final corrections neatly.

TEST: COMPOSITION

Time: $1\frac{1}{2}$ hours

Write **two only** of the following composition exercises. Your answers must follow exactly the instructions given, and must be of between 120 and 180 words each.

1 An English-speaking pen-friend has written to say that he or she would like to come and stay with you in March next year. Write a letter saying how much you would like to see him or her, but suggesting a more suitable time for you and your family, giving reasons. You should make the beginning and ending as for an ordinary letter, but the address is not to be counted in the number of words.

2 Write a story which ends like this:
'If I had read the instructions more carefully, all of this would not have happened.'

3 'We should all do a lot more for the disabled in our society.' What do you think? If it is worth doing more for the disabled, what do you think should be done?

4 You work for a firm in your own country which is beginning to employ more and more English-speaking people, and you have been asked to write the instructions (in English) for the public telephones in the factory or canteen. Write them clearly.

Unit 28

Soccer violence— What should be done about it?

EXAM FOCUS:
Use of English

Read and speak

Read this opinion column from a newspaper. Then do the exercises.

IN YOUR OPINION

VIOLENCE at professional football matches is not new. As long ago as March, 1969, newspapers in England announced that the Home Secretary, then Mr James Callaghan, had 'declared war on the Saturday afternoon soccer thugs'. The thugs, vandals, hooligans, trouble-makers, or whatever you want to call them, were with us then: they're still with us now—but in greater numbers, at far more football matches, and not only in Britain, either. 'Silence' used to be 'golden': now, it seems, 'Violence is golden'.

But what form does this violence take, and what should be done about it? *In Your Opinion* asked readers: 'What do you think should be done to reduce trouble and violence at soccer matches?'

● Ron Jones, 29, of South London, thought professional football players were to blame for a lot of violence at matches. 'Some players bring the game into disrepute,' he said. 'They should be fined very heavily or banned for a long period for bad behaviour.'

● Janet Green, a computer programmer from Liverpool, felt that the violence had to be stamped out somehow. 'These people ruin everyone's enjoyment,' she said. 'They must be taught a lesson. They should certainly be banned from matches and fined very heavily. Something positive has got to be done soon. It should have been done a long time ago.'

● Susan Saunders, 19, a hairdresser from Coventry, said: 'Something must be done about violence at matches. I think it would help if spectators were forbidden to take alcohol to football matches. If necessary, they should be searched on their way in.'

● Mark Old, a builder from York, thought all football supporters should carry identity cards. He went on: 'Trouble-makers should be arrested, their names ought to be given to the Club, and they should be banned from the ground for life. Football doesn't need people like them.'

● Frank King, 35, of Oxford, said: 'Whenever any of these vandals start a fight or invade the pitch, they ought to be arrested and flung out of the ground. A hundred years ago, such people would have been beaten or even strung up for this sort of hooliganism—but this is the twentieth century.'

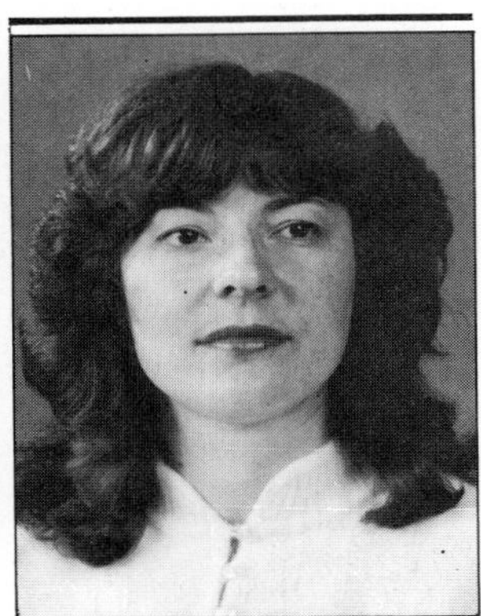

● Housewife Joan Slade of Bristol said: 'I used to enjoy going to football, but I don't go any more. I think these football hooligans should be forced to pay for any damage they do, and then made to do community work. There's no point in fining them or sending them to prison.'

1 In pairs, ask and tell each other

1 who thought it would help if spectators were forbidden to take alcohol into matches.
2 what else she suggested.
3 who said that trouble-makers' names should be given to the Club.
4 what else he said.
5 who thought that players were to blame for violence at matches.
6 how he thought they should be punished.
7 what Joan Slade thought should be done.
8 who felt that violence had to be stamped out.
9 how she thought it could be done.
10 which person you agreed with most, and why.

2 Discussion

In small groups, discuss possible solutions to violence at football matches and other sporting events.

All this violence should be beaten out of people when they're kids..
FOOTBALL VIOLENCE

28

Grammar practice 1

must be done, has/have (got) to be done, should be done **and *ought to be done***

REVIEW

(*Necessity*) People like that	must be have to be have got to be	taught a lesson. arrested. punished. fined heavily sent to prison.
(*Obligation*)	should be ought to be	

ABOUT YOU

What do you think must or should be done to

1 a soccer 'fan' who attacks another 'fan'?
2 a professional footballer who brings the game into disrepute?
3 someone who steals money from an old lady?
4 people who avoid paying bus fares?
5 someone who steals from a shop when he (or she) is unemployed?

Grammar practice 2

ought to/should have been done

REVIEW

Something should have been done about it a long time ago.

They ought to have been banned from the Club.

ABOUT YOU

Read these short newspaper clippings. Then say what you think should have been done in each case.

1 Three of the youths who invaded the pitch during last Saturday's game have each been fined £5.

2 A woman who took a coat from a large store without paying for it has been sent to prison for a month.

3 A man who admitted driving under the influence of alcohol and knocking down and killing an old man was fined £100.

4 A girl who carried new photographic equipment worth £250 through Customs without paying any Duty said she just winked at the Customs Officer and he let her through.

Grammar practice 3

More irregular verbs

REVIEW

Study these verbs and then do the exercise below.

cling	clung	clung	stick	stuck	stuck
dig	dug	dug	sting	stung	stung
fling	flung	flung	strike	struck	struck
hang	hung	hung*	string	strung	strung
sling	slung	slung	swing	swung	swung
spin	spun	spun	win	won	won
			wring	wrung	wrung

*Note that when *hang*='execute', it is regular, for example:
He was hanged at dawn.

PRACTICE

Supply the correct form of the verb given:

1 I've just been (*sting*) by a bee!
2 He (*fling*) his cigarette out of the window as he was driving along.
3 That picture shouldn't have been (*hang*) there. It's in the wrong place.
4 The foundations of the house have to be (*dig*) before they can start building.
5 The girl was (*strike*) by a car which was driven by an old man.
6 The accident happened when one of the racing cars (*spin*) off the track.
7 When he opened the door, it (*swing*) back and hit him in the face.
8 If he hadn't (*cling*) to the branch of the tree, he would have fallen.
9 They've (*string*) lights all along the street ready for the festival.
10 She (*stick*) the broken pieces of the vase together with glue.

DISCUSSION

First, look at these sentence models:

They {should be / ought to be} {forced / compelled / made} to do community work or something else useful.

Such people shouldn't be {allowed / permitted} to go to football matches.

Now, in small groups or as a class, discuss this:
'For most minor crimes, a heavy fine or imprisonment is the wrong punishment.'
Using the models above and other language you have practised in the Unit, say what you think should be done with people who commit minor crimes.

"Hanging's abolished, prisons are overcrowded, so I'm afraid it'll have to be community service."

28

Taking the First Certificate Examination

PAPER 3: USE OF ENGLISH

What the Paper consists of

The Use of English Paper has two Sections, A and B. Section A contains a number (usually four or five) of completion or transformation exercises, while Section B consists of a summary or similar directed writing exercise. The time allowed for the whole paper is two hours.

Some tips on doing the Paper

1 Read the instructions to all parts *very* carefully. Even if exercise or test types look familiar, you *may* have to do something slightly different.

2 Watch the time on this Paper very carefully. It is probably best to work through the Paper as it is, starting with Section A, number 1, and doing as much as you can, leaving something like 40 minutes in which to do Section B. As with the Reading Comprehension Paper, don't waste valuable time thinking about things you can't do: you should have time to come back to them when you have completed most of the Paper.

3 Here are a few reminders of question types in Section A:
- A passage with a number of blanks to be filled in. Read the whole text through before you fill in any blanks. Then re-read it to fill in as many blanks as you can.
- Sentences to be rewritten a different way ('transformations'), for example:
  You'd better not go out tonight→If I were you, I wouldn't go out tonight.
  Read each sentence carefully, and always use the 'starter' given.
- Word formation, for example *encouraged* from *courage.*
- A dialogue with blanks to be filled in. Read the whole dialogue through before trying to fill in the missing sentences or questions.

4 The directed writing test in Section B can take one of many forms. Read the instructions and the passage, text, conversation, advertisement or whatever *very* carefully once or twice before you attempt to write the paragraphs. Always make notes, and try to give yourself time to write a draft version of the summary or paragraphs before you write the final version.

5 When you have finished, you should have time to read through the whole Paper and make any last-minute corrections. Make sure these are neat and can be read easily by the examiner.

TEST: USE OF ENGLISH

Time: 2 hours

Answer all the questions. Write your answers in ink on the paper provided by the teacher.

Section A

1 Fill each of the numbered blanks in the following passage. Use only one word in each space.

I have always admired people like artists, writers and composers ___(1)___ being able to work ___(2)___ their own, with no one else around. Most ___(3)___ my friends all work with other people in shops and so on, and they tell me that they ___(4)___ never get ___(5)___ done if they worked alone. I'm not sure that all artists and writers do, either.

I ___(6)___ born in a small village in the country ___(7)___ everyone knew everyone else: that is, they knew everyone except a writer who kept himself to himself. ___(8)___ the time I was old ___(9)___ to learn people's names, he ___(10)___ been living in the village ___(11)___ at least twenty years, but the villagers still regarded him as a stranger! Every morning he ___(12)___ walk down to the local shops ___(13)___ do his shopping, and although he ___(14)___ to greet everyone he met, only two or three would return his greeting. Just occasionally, someone ___(15)___ feel curious enough to ask him what he ___(16)___ doing, and every time his answer would be the same: 'I'm still writing the book. It ___(17)___ have been finished last year, but I can't get it right.' And that was all we ever learned about him.

Because no one had ever visited his house, either, I remember once ___(18)___ up to the house with three or four other boys to see ___(19)___ we could see what he did. We crept up to the window trembling and looked in, expecting to see our writer typing furiously at his desk. Instead, he was sitting in an armchair ___(20)___ a book.

PLEASE TURN OVER

Section A continued

2 Finish each of the following sentences in such a way that it means exactly the same as the sentence printed before it.

1 He stole the book and should be punished for it.
He ought ....

2 She picked up the glass very carefully so as not to break it.
Because ....

3 I don't like getting up at six in the morning, but I've got used to it.
I've got used ....

4 It's pointless asking him to do anything for you.
There's ....

5 I'd be grateful if you didn't smoke in this room.
I'd rather ....

6 Smoking is forbidden in this compartment.
You ....

7 I have been studying English for five years now, and next year will make it six.
By next year ....

8 I think you ought to deal with the problem soon.
I think it's about time ....

9 I didn't hide those papers, but now I wish I had.
I wish ....

10 They say that he's looking for a new secretary.
He's said ....

3 The word in capitals at the end of each of the following sentences can be used to form a word that fits suitably in the blank space. Fill each blank in this way. Write your answers on a separate piece of paper.

1 No one really seems to know what to do about ______ in society today. VIOLENT

2 A player should be punished for such ______ on the pitch. BEHAVE

3 I think you're ______ the problem: it's far more complex than you imagine. SIMPLE

4 There is no doubt that heavy smoking ______ your health. DANGER

5 He spoke to her with a ______ which told me they had met before. FAMILIAR

6 The receptionist at the desk wanted some ______ before she would allow me into the conference. IDENTIFY

7 There are so many ______ in the country now that for every job offered there are sometimes as many as forty applicants. EMPLOY

8 The only way they could ______ the bridge was to build new supports under it. STRONG

9 Mary's aunt looked at her ______ and said, 'I don't really think you should wear that dress to the dance, do you?' APPROVE

10 The film is one I'll remember for the rest of my life: it's absolutely ______. FORGET

4 Maria and Annie are strangers staying in the same holiday hotel. They have just started chatting to each other. In the following conversation, five questions have been left incomplete. Read the whole conversation first, and then complete the blanks suitably. Write the completed questions (1–5) on a separate piece of paper.

MARIA: (1) Where ....?
ANNIE: From France. Actually, from a small village near Bordeaux. And you?
MARIA: Well, I'm from Scotland originally, but I live near London now. It's nice here, isn't it? (2) Have ....?
ANNIE: No, I haven't. It's my first visit. But it *is* very nice. You're right. I think I shall come here again next year.
MARIA: I hope you don't mind my saying so, but your English is very good. (3) How long ....?
ANNIE: About four years, I think.
MARIA: Is that all? I couldn't learn French that well!
ANNIE: Well, I've studied and practised hard because I need it in my job. I'm a personal assistant to the director of an international company, you see.
MARIA: I see. (4) By the way, when ....?
ANNIE: Well, I've got a flight booked for next Saturday evening, but with these strikes a lot of flights have been cancelled.
MARIA: Yes, I know. (5) What ....?
ANNIE: That's easy. I'll stay on for another week's holiday!

PLEASE TURN OVER

Section B

5 John and Mary Smith want to go to Faliraki on the Greek island of Rhodes for a week's holiday with their two children, James (aged ten) and Debbie (aged seven). They cannot go before 28th June. Using the information taken from a travel brochure, continue each of the three paragraphs opposite. Use no more than 50 words for each paragraph, and write them on a separate piece of paper.

Hotel Faliraki Beach

Location: Faliraki Village, 12 kilometres from Rhodes Town on eastern coast

A marvellous hotel famous for its beauty contest in June, is also ideal for a family holiday because of its amenities and beautiful sandy beach. The Faliraki Beach has just about everything to ensure you have a happy time while on Rhodes. A big, modern building with extensive grounds which feature not only a children's pool and playground but also a small zoo. The hotel offers a babysitting service so that you can relax in the evenings and, if you wish, sample the lively nightlife in the tavernas in the little village of Faliraki, a few minutes' walk down the road. The interior is cool and spacious but we think you'll find it difficult to keep away from the beach, or the superb pool with its wide terraces scattered with loungers, tables and quaint straw sun umbrellas.

Amenities: *Restaurant. Bars. Gift shop. Boutique. Table-tennis. Crazy golf. Water-skiing. Sailing. Windsurfing. Pedaloes. Boat hire. Para-gliding. Volley ball. Tennis. Afandou Golf Course three and a half miles from hotel. Babysitting. Children's playground. CBS Discotheque. Outdoor swimming pool. Children's pool. Pool bar. Snack bar. Taverna.*

Accommodation: *Well-furnished twin-bedded rooms, fully air-conditioned (for July/August only), with shower and w.c., taped music, telephone and side sea view, terrace.*

Official rating: *'A'.*

Price includes: *Half board.*

Cynthia Pension

Location: Half kilometre from Faliraki Village

The Cynthia Pension, set back from the road in very pleasant gardens, is a short walk from the village of Faliraki and its beautiful soft, sandy beach. Recently modernised, it's a very comfortable and friendly little pension and has already proved very popular with Olympic Holidaymakers. Nick Goudis, the hotel owner, speaks good English so you will soon feel at home and you'll find the garden bar a popular meeting place.

Amenities: *Bar. Lounge. Roof garden. Breakfast room.*

Accommodation: *Twin-bedded rooms each with shower, w.c. (some take extra bed).*

Price includes: *Bed and breakfast.*

Cynthia Pension

Faliraki Beach

Yiannis Apartments

Location: Faliraki

The Yiannis Apartments are located on a sand and shingle bay with stunning views of the ocean. This delightful apartment building has beautiful interior furnishings and decoration. The Yiannis is cleaned and linen changed twice a week, but as there are good cooking facilities, residents are left to look after themselves. There are food and general shops in Faliraki village as well as a visiting food van, and a taverna next door. Yiannis residents also have the run of Faliraki Hotel amenities, only about 15 minutes' away along the beach. (Not suitable for children.)

Accommodation: *Ground floor: One apartment for 4 persons with 2 twin-bedded rooms sharing bath, w.c., kitchen, 2 studios with one twin-bedded room with bath, w.c., sharing kitchen.*
First floor: One apartment for 4–6 persons with 2 twin-bedded rooms, bath, w.c., living room (2 extra beds possible) sharing kitchen.

Price includes: *Accommodation only.*

Yiannis Apartments

	Departure dates on or between	Apr 1- Apr 10		Apr 11- Apr 17		Apr 18- May 12		May 13- Jun 5		Jun 6- Jun 27	
Hotel	Ref No.	7	14	7	14	7	14	7	14	7	14
Cynthia	R303	*183	202	166	186	172	191	181	206	191	228
Yiannis	R403	188	208	172	191	177	197	192	211	197	236
Faliraki Beach	R108	236	304	220	287	225	293	237	323	243	328
Child Reduction 2-12 yrs.		20%		25%		50%		25%		30%	

	Departure dates on or between	Jun 28- Jul 11		Jul 12- Jul 18		Jul 19- Sep 7		Sep 8- Sep 20		Sep 21- Oct 11	
Hotel	Ref No.	7	14	7	14	7	14	7	14	7	14
Cynthia	R303	206	244	226	277	237	289	226	277	196	234
Yiannis	R403	212	252	223	272	234	283	223	272	202	242
Faliraki Beach	R108	266	369	277	380	288	391	277	380	266	369
Child Reduction 2-12 yrs.		30%		15%		15%		15%		25%	

* Prices are pounds sterling

If I were John or Mary, I don't think I would . . .

And I think the family would be wise not to . . .

As they're only going for a week, I would recommend . . .

Unit 29

'I can't remember anything at all'

EXAM FOCUS:
Listening Comprehension

Look, listen and speak

You are going to hear an item from a radio news broadcast. First, read the four brief newspaper reports below. Then, as you listen, try to decide which report best corresponds to the information given in the radio news item—A, B, C or D. Then do the exercises below.

A

Third amnesia case

The third man in less than a month suffering from amnesia was found yesterday in Skipton, about 55 miles from Leeds. A police spokesman told reporters that the man had been wandering the hills for days. His wallet contained money, but no identification.

B

Man says: 'I can't remember anything.'

A middle-aged man found wandering in a village in Yorkshire suffering from amnesia said he couldn't remember anything. Police describe him as about 55, about six feet tall, with grey hair, grey beard and glasses.

C

Grassington visited by stranger

A 55-year-old blind man was found yesterday wandering the hills near Skipton in Yorkshire. Well dressed, and apparently well-educated, he is suffering from severe amnesia.

D

Police appeal for help to identify man

Yorkshire police have appealed to the public to help identify a tall man who drove into a Yorkshire village suffering from shock. When he arrived, he was wearing a black suit and grey shirt.

1 Which newspaper report corresponded best to the radio news broadcast? Why? And why were the other three wrong?

2 In pairs, ask and tell each other

1 where the man was found.
2 what he was suffering from.
3 why he couldn't be identified.
4 what the police inspector said the man was wearing.
5 what the inspector said they would be issuing.
6 what the inspector said they thought the man might have been doing.
7 what the inspector said they would do.
8 who the inspector said they would have to rely on.
9 what Mr X told the reporter.
10 what the reporter said about further news.

3 Discussion

Imagine you lost your memory. How do you think you would feel? What would you do about it? What would you say to other people in order to hide any embarrassment you might feel?

Grammar practice 1

Reporting what people said in the past (with modals)

REVIEW

Mr X's actual words were:		When the police interviewed him, Mr X told them/said (that) . . .
'I can't remember anything.'	⟶	he couldn't remember anything.
'I could be anybody.'	⟶	he could be anybody.
'I hope I can (=will be able to) remember something soon.'	⟶	he hoped he would be able to remember something soon.
'I shall/will try to remember something.'	⟶	he would try to remember something.
'I shall be staying in Leeds.'	⟶	he would be staying in Leeds.
'I may/might remember something one day.'	⟶	he might remember something one day.
'I should be able to tell you something.'	⟶	he should be able to tell them something.
'I have to/must find out who I am.'	⟶	he had to find out who he was.
'I must (=will have to) keep on trying to remember who I am.'	⟶	he would have to keep on trying to remember who he was.

PRACTICE

Read carefully this short speech given by a girl who has just won a prize in a music competition. Then tell another student what she said using *She said (that)* . . .

'Ladies and gentlemen,
I'm so excited and so pleased to win the prize that I'm not sure what to say. I must of course thank my music teacher for giving me such expert tuition, and my parents for giving me so much encouragement. I can honestly say that I wouldn't have got this far by myself! But now that I've won the prize, I shall be able to go on with more confidence, and I may make music my career. I would certainly like to.
I can't say anything else. Just, thank you.'

29

Grammar practice 2

Reporting sentences like *We'll get there soon, I hope*

REVIEW

Study this and the list of verbs, and then do the exercise below.

> 'I assume (that) they'll soon find out who the man is,' she said.
> *or* 'They'll soon find out who the man is, I assume,' she said.
>
> Both sentences can be reported in the past as:
> She assumed (that) they would soon find out who the man was.

These verbs can all be used like the verb *assume*:

believe	expect	fancy	gather	hear	hope
imagine	would say	suppose	think	trust	understand

PRACTICE

Report what was said, using the verbs in italics.

1 'I *suppose* they'll come soon,' he said.
2 'I can be there by six, I *think*,' he said.
3 'We *hope* you'll be able to come and see us,' they said.
4 'There'll be a lot of people there, I *gather*,' she said.
5 'I *believe* I'll have to catch an early train,' he said.
6 'I *expect* I'll stay at home,' he said.
7 'I'll have to find a new job, I *fancy*,' she said.
8 'I *understand* I'll have to wait,' she said.
9 'We *assume* John won't be coming with us,' we told them.
10 'You're well, I *trust*,' I said to him.

Listen and discuss

1 A young couple, David and Ann, have just arrived at a theatre for a late evening concert by a pop group, The Ravers. The early evening performance has already finished. Listen and then answer these questions:

1 Why did Ann want to know what was going on?
2 What did David say they'd have to do?
3 What did David find out? Who from?
4 Why did they go to the box office?
5 What did Ann ask the woman if she could tell them?
6 Did David ask the woman if the performance had been cancelled, or just postponed?
7 What did the woman tell them had happened at the first performance?
8 Will they get their money back?
9 How much had they paid for their tickets?
10 What did David think about it all?

2 Now say what you think about the situation. What do you think should be done to the people who went to the first performance? What action do you think the management should take or should have taken? What do you think David and Ann should do? What would you do in their place? Why? etc.

29

Taking the First Certificate Examination

PAPER 4: LISTENING COMPREHENSION

What the Paper consists of

The Listening Comprehension Paper 4 contains three or more *recorded* extracts of spoken English. You will be given a question paper and will have to show that you have understood by answering multiple-choice questions, ticking true/false statements, completing blanks, re-ordering pictures, etc.

Some tips on doing the Paper

1 Listen to the examiner's instructions and read the instructions on your question paper very carefully. Don't hesitate to ask the examiner if you are not sure what to do before the test begins.

2 You will hear each recorded extract twice, so you should have plenty of time to read the relevant questions before, during and after each extract. Don't try to read the *whole* question paper before you start. This is not like the written Papers: here, you will be guided as to what to do and when, and *you* don't have to watch the time.

IMPORTANT: If you cannot hear the recording properly from your position in the examination room, tell the examiner or a monitor immediately. It is no use complaining afterwards.

3 Be prepared to hear the different recordings with slightly different accents. For this reason, it is advisable to listen the first time to get used to the voice and to get the gist of the extract. Then you can begin to make choices, etc., before and during the second playing of the extract.

4 At the end of the test, you cannot really go back and answer any questions you may have missed (as you can in a written Paper) because you can't listen again. But do not leave any questions unanswered. You will get no marks at all for a blank: you might actually gain a mark by ticking 'C', for example, as a guess.

29

TEST: LISTENING COMPREHENSION

Time: approx. 30 minutes

You will hear six extracts of spoken English (each twice on cassette or read by the teacher), and you will be given time to choose your answers to the questions. Before you listen to each extract, read the questions (and suggested answers) carefully. Read or look again as you listen and before the second recording and choose A, B, C or D, mark in the route, or whatever you are asked to do. Check your answers while you are listening for the second time. Write your answers on the paper provided by the teacher.

1 Which is correct?

A The 6.30 train to Little Village and Charlestown has been cancelled.
B The 6.30 train will leave from platform 9 and stop at Little Village and Charlestown.
C The 5.45 train to Hightown will stop at Charlestown and Little Village.
D The 6.30 train will leave from platform 12 and travel non-stop to Hightown.

2 If Jim hadn't gone back to his flat,

A he would have missed his meeting.
B he wouldn't have met the newsreader.
C he would have phoned a neighbour.
D he wouldn't have discovered the fire.

3 The spokesman suggested that people ought to

A learn to relax more at home.
B turn off everything before they leave home.
C use fewer electric fires in flats.
D try to get to work earlier than they do.

4 Which is the correct route by car: A •••••••• B – – – – C —·—·— D oooooooo ?

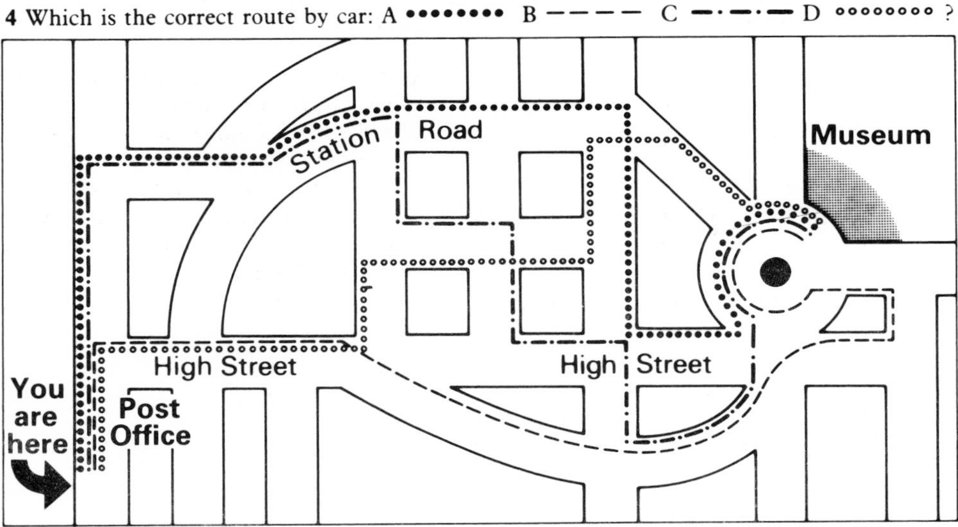

5 What will the weather be like this morning?

A There will be heavy showers of snow.
B It will rain, with some sleet or snow.
C It will remain very cold but dry.
D It will be bright and sunny.

6 This evening

A it will be wet and windy.
B all parts can expect gales.
C there will be a lot more snow.
D it will be clear and dry.

Listen, and complete the blanks in these statements.

7 All the events you hear about are on today. Today is...

8 At the Hayward Gallery there is an exhibition of works by a famous....................................

9 If you want further information, the number of the British Tourist Authority Information Centre is...

10 The changing of the guard outside Buckingham Palace today takes place at ....

11 This evening the London Philharmonic Orchestra are playing at...

12 One of the composers in the programme given by Isaac Stern and Andrew Wolf this evening will be..

13 Of the theatres mentioned, ... are in Charing Cross Road. (How many?)

14 The Royal Shakespeare Company are not performing *Romeo and Juliet*; they are performing ....

15 If you want information about events and activities of interest to children, the number to ring is ....

16 How often did Jamie stay with his grandparents when he was a young boy?
A Once.
B Very rarely.
C Quite often.
D Every weekend.

17 When he stayed with his grandparents, Jamie would
A eat better than at home.
B get up a lot earlier.
C drive his grandfather's car.
D feel more lonely than ever.

18 When he was in Wales, Jamie did not mind
A the noise and bustle.
B being disturbed.
C not being able to go into the hills.
D having to get up very early.

19 What was the noise they all heard?
A A wild animal in pain.
B Some sheep calling to each other.
C A girl screaming.
D They did not know.

20 We must assume that Jamie wished he had stayed at the farm
A because of something that happened later.
B because it was so cold outside.
C because he had not had any breakfast.
D because he was afraid of being pushed onto the train.

Unit 30

A story with a moral

EXAM FOCUS:
Oral Interview

Look, listen and speak

Look at the pictures and listen to the letter. Then do the exercises below.

1 In pairs, ask and tell each other

1. why the man had to call the plasterer/the gasman/the electrician/the glazier.
2. what happened on the way home from the hospital.
3. when the man is going to have the car resprayed.
4. how the man managed to spill tomato soup down the kitchen wall.
5. why the man is going to call the decorator again.

2 In pairs, small groups or around the class, refer to the pictures and tell the story. Begin: 'Mr Helpless was going to redecorate his kitchen himself . . .'

3 Complete this sentence about the events: 'And the moral of the story is . . .'

4 About you

Tell the rest of the class about any occasion when you had something done and it went wrong. What happened?

3
4
7
8
AND THE MORAL
OF THE STORY IS...

5 Where would you go, or who would you go to, to have the following things done:

1 to have a tooth pulled out or filled?
2 to have a piano tuned?
3 to get your eyes tested?
4 to have a dress or coat shortened, lengthened or altered in some way?
5 to have your house painted?
6 to get your car serviced?
7 to have clothes cleaned?
8 to have clothes or linen washed?
9 to get your hair cut or styled?
10 to have something done to the water system in your house?

Game: *What's my line?* (see Teacher's Guide, p 16)

30

Grammar practice

Causative *have/get something done*

REVIEW

Look at these sentences with *have/get something done* in different tenses. Then do the exercises below.

I'm { having/going to have
getting/going to get } my hair cut next week.
I have/get my car serviced regularly.
I've just had/got this suit cleaned.
I had/got my eyes tested last week.
We shall have to have/get the roof repaired soon.
You should have/get those shoes mended.
I really must have/get this coat lengthened.
We might be having/getting the house repainted next year.
It's about time he had/got his hair cut.

Note that the structure *have/get something done* is used when the job or task is done by someone else who is not usually mentioned. For example, *He had his eyes tested last week* means or implies 'by an optician'.

PRACTICE

Look at these pictures and make statements like this:
They ought to have the roof repaired.
It's about time he had his hair cut.

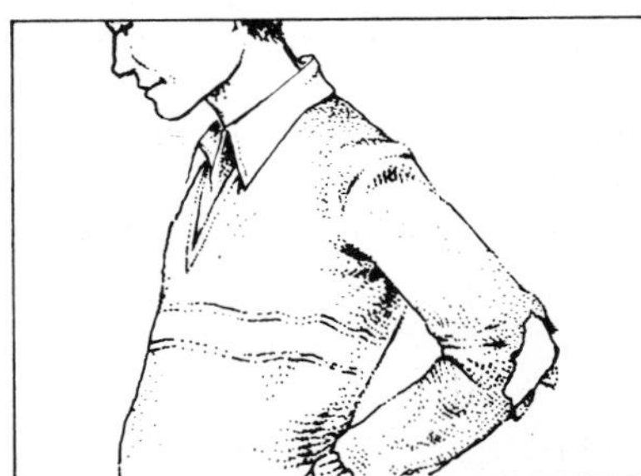

ABOUT YOU

Tell each other about things that you had done in the past, that you have had done recently, and that you will or must have done in the future.

30

Taking the First Certificate Examination

PAPER 5: ORAL INTERVIEW

What the Interview consists of

The Interview consists of three parts.

A A conversation with the examiner about a photograph.

B Reading aloud a short passage—an announcement, part of a letter, instructions, etc.—which you will have time to prepare.

C One of a number of activities: taking part in a role play, giving a short talk on a topic of general interest, taking part in a discussion, etc.

Some tips on what to do and what not to do in the Interview

1 Throughout the Interview, speak as clearly as you can. The examiner wants to hear how well you can speak English, and he or she cannot do that if you mumble or speak so quietly that he or she has to keep saying 'Pardon?'.

2 In the same way, of course, if you don't catch what the examiner says, or don't quite understand what he or she says or what you have to do, ask for a repetition with 'Pardon? I'm sorry, I didn't quite catch that' or 'Pardon? I didn't quite understand (the question)'. And if you can't answer a question, don't be afraid to say so.

3 Reading aloud: you will be given the passage during the interview and will have a few moments to look at it. Read it through quickly to yourself, noting words with difficult pronunciation, noting where to pause, etc. Then, when you are asked to read it, read it out as naturally as you can, that is to say, not too slowly and not too quickly, and showing that you understand what you are reading.

4 In the third part of the Oral, you may be asked to do any one of a number of things. Whichever it is—giving a brief talk, taking part in a role play, joining in a discussion (even perhaps on prescribed books), etc.—make sure that you listen carefully so that you know exactly what you have to do. As in other parts of the Oral, if you do not understand what you have to do, ask.
Then, when you are speaking, try to speak as clearly and as fluently as you can (without too many 'er's' and 'um's'), using language that you have learned throughout your course. The Oral Interview is not the time to start trying to say things in English which you have never learned how to say.

5 Finally, remember that the examiner is trying to find out how well you can understand and speak English, and he or she cannot do that if you answer all the questions with a simple 'Yes' or 'No'.

30

Oral Interview preparation

1 Look at this photo carefully and then answer the questions.

About the photo

1 What are these young men having done? Where and why, do you think?
2 What's the photographer probably saying right at this moment?
3 What do you say in *your* language when you want someone to smile for a photo?
4 What time of year do you think it is? Why?

General

1 Are group school (or college) photos popular in your country?
2 Have you ever been in one? If so, do you ever look at it? Why? When?
3 Do you like having your photo taken? Why?/Why not?
4 When did you last have your photo taken? What was the occasion?

2 Reading aloud

This is part of a letter you have received from an English-speaking friend you met while on holiday. Read it aloud, as if to another friend of yours who was there at the time.

Do you remember that artist we met on the island who said he would paint our picture for almost nothing? I wish we had had it done now. It would have been a beautiful memento of a fabulous holiday. Especially since none of the photos that I took came out. There must be something wrong with my camera, I think. I shall have to have it looked at in our local camera shop. By the way, I don't suppose you could send me some of your photos of the holiday, could you? I'll pay you for them of course.

I think I told you that I would probably have to change my job. Well, there was a letter waiting for me when I got home telling me that they didn't 'require my services' any more. They could at least have told me before my holiday! Still, I've been lucky and I've managed to get another job. I'll tell you all about it in my next letter.

3 Situation for extended role play

An English-speaking friend has just arrived to stay with you for a few weeks. Conduct a conversation between you in which he or she asks and you tell him or her:

- what places of interest he or she should visit
- where he or she should go to buy souvenirs, and what to buy
- where he or she can have his or her hair cut/done
- where best to have the car serviced (because he/she came by car)
- where to have clothes cleaned

4 Topics for individual talks

Choose one of these topics below, write brief notes, and then give a short talk to the class. You should try to talk for up to a minute. When you have finished, the class may ask questions.

- Examinations.
- The advantages and disadvantages of the motor car.
- Keeping fit.
- What should be done to reduce violence in the modern world?
- Space exploration is a waste of time and money—or is it?

Listening Comprehension texts

The following pages contain transcripts of all Listening Comprehension texts used in Presentation and other phases of Units in the book, excluding the texts used in Listening Comprehension Tests, the transcripts of which are to be found in the Teacher's Guide only.

Unit 3

TUTOR: Unit 3. 'Who'll get the job?'
Exercise 2. Jane Langley is being interviewed by Mrs Grey, the Personnel Manager, and Mr Toms. Listen.

MR TOMS: . . . yes, I see. Good. Good.

MRS GREY: Miss Langley, I see that your last employer Mr Carmichael described you as 'conscientious'. Do *you* think you are?

JANE: Well, I certainly try to be. I have a set routine for the day in the office which means that I know exactly all the jobs that I have to do. And if conscientious means being extremely careful and paying attention to detail, then yes, I suppose I'm conscientious.

MR TOMS: But he said too that you could 'adapt quickly to change'. Did you leave because they were making changes, or what?

JANE: No, not at all. They made a lot of changes while I was there. I'm afraid I became unhappy because I wanted something more challenging.

MRS GREY: I assume you wanted something like the job of Senior Secretary that we're offering.

JANE: Yes, that's right.

TUTOR: Exercise 3. Michael James is being interviewed now by the same two people. Listen.

MRS GREY: . . . and according to your last employer, Mr Smith, you 'tend to be a little impatient at times'.

MICHAEL: Well, perhaps I am, perhaps I'm not. Some of the others in the office there were so slow!

MR TOMS: Yes, yes. I like a person who wants to get on with the job.

MRS GREY: Mr James, what I'd like to know is . . .

MR TOMS: Excuse me, Mrs Grey, but I wanted to ask Mr James about his sport. You're a keen footballer, I understand.

MICHAEL: Oh, yes. I play regularly twice a week. And I organised a team at my old place.

MR TOMS: And golf, too, I gather.

MICHAEL: Yes. Actually, I like golf better than football really. That's why I play nearly every morning . . .

TUTOR: Exercise 5. Mrs Grey and Mr Toms are now discussing Jane and Michael after the interviews. Listen.

MRS GREY: . . . so in my view, when you compare the two of them—and this has nothing to do with Jane being a woman—I'd give the job to Jane Langley. She's obviously a better secretary than he is, she's a much better typist, she mixes better with people and is clearly far more polite. We don't even need to discuss *Mr* James.

MR TOMS: Well, we do, because I think he's brighter than Miss Langley. I know he doesn't dress as well or speak as clearly, and he's not as experienced as she is, but he's quicker, more alert. And he's keen on football and golf. I like that. So he gets the job.

MRS GREY: No, I'm sorry, Mr Toms. He doesn't.

MR TOMS: Yes, he does, Mrs Grey. He's the Director's nephew.

Unit 4

TUTOR: Unit 4. 'I hate tidying up'
We interviewed four people in the street on their pet hates—and loves. The first thing we asked them was: 'Have you got any pet hates; things that you hate doing?' Look at page 19 and listen to what they said.

BOY: Yes. I hate having to put things away all the time.
INTERVIEWER: You mean—tidying up?
BOY: Yes. And I don't like family gatherings much. You know, with all the uncles and aunts you haven't seen for years.
INTERVIEWER: Is that all?
BOY: No, there's one more thing. I can't stand having my hair cut.

MAN: Well, I don't like filling in forms much. Um—well, I do a lot of driving, and I hate having to sit in traffic jams.
INTERVIEWER: What about other people?
MAN: I can't stand politicians. I can't bear listening to them or watching them on TV. They either bore me to tears or make me angry.

GIRL: There are a lot of things about school that I don't like, but the thing I hate most is copying out school notes. I don't like waiting for buses much. But I think the thing I detest is other people cracking their knuckles. We've got one girl in our class who does it when she gets nervous. It's horrible.

WOMAN: Pet hates? I don't know. I don't like cleaning up after other people—you know, untidy rooms, or meal things—dirty plates and so on.
INTERVIEWER: What about things that other people do?
WOMAN: Yes. Well, I really hate other people drinking noisily—you know, slurping tea or coffee or soup. I think it's disgusting.

TUTOR: Then we asked the same four what they liked doing most. Listen to what they said.

BOY: What I enjoy doing most is going away on holiday in our caravan. We've been all over the country. I like going somewhere near the sea best because I like swimming a lot.

MAN: I hate to say this because it sounds bad, but I really enjoy breaking things up. My wife thinks I should have been a demolition expert! My private ambition is to break one of those large plate-glass shop windows with a brick. I'd love to do that one day!
INTERVIEWER: I think a lot of people would!—Anything else?
MAN: Yes, I like playing golf—especially with people who are worse than myself.
INTERVIEWER: I'll regret asking this, I expect, but why?
MAN: Because I like winning!

GIRL: I don't know what I like doing *most.* I like going to the cinema. I enjoy reading, listening to music, buying clothes . . . I like wrapping up presents for people: you know, at Christmas or for birthdays. And I love unwrapping presents, too, of course!

WOMAN: What do I enjoy most? No doubt about it: having breakfast in bed! That's my idea of heaven!

Unit 5

TUTOR: Unit 5. 'A Heath Robinson affair'
Look at pages 25 and 26, and listen to this lecture.

LECTURER: If someone makes or mends something, particularly a piece of machinery, with wire and string and so on, and the thing looks ingenious, but perhaps unsafe and a little complicated, an English person may well describe it as 'a Heath Robinson affair' or 'a Heath Robinson contraption'. It's not a very flattering thing for someone to say about something you've made. On the other hand, of course, inventors are just the sort of people who often begin with Heath Robinson contraptions which, when they've been modified and redesigned, turn out to be invaluable items for thousands of people. And we sometimes use the expression, too, almost as an apology, when we've managed to get over a mechanical problem by perhaps tying the thing together with string. 'It's a bit Heath-Robinsonish,' you'll hear someone say, 'but it'll do.'

But who or what is Heath Robinson? William Heath Robinson was in fact an artist—a cartoonist and book-illustrator—who was born in London in May, 1872. His father was an illustrator for the London *Penny Illustrated Paper*, and William took after him. He attended the Islington School of Art and the Royal Academy Schools and then worked for his father for a while in his studio in the Strand in London. William however soon became a well-known book-illustrator and his publications included the Hans Anderson stories, Edgar Allan Poe's poems, Rabelais, Shakespeare's *Twelfth Night*, *The Water Babies*, and many more. But it was for his work as a humorist and cartoonist in magazines like the *Strand Magazine* and the *Illustrated London News* that he became world-famous even before the outbreak of World War I in 1914. Because of his cartoons, like the one on page 26, his name stands for any invention which looks absurdly ingenious and impracticable. Basically, I suppose, he caricatured machinery and inventions in the same way that other cartoonists caricature humans and animals. And you don't need to go into any of his inventions or drawings too deeply to find that they are generally absurd, complicated pieces of machinery designed for totally ridiculous purposes. But his drawings tend to be funny also because they are done in such great detail and with such seriousness, and the people in them always appear so serious.

Heath Robinson died in 1944. He left behind him, in his drawings and cartoons, a kind of humour which people still enjoy, and in the English language, a word which describes almost any contraption or piece of machinery made out of bits of junk held together with bits of string or wire. So if you come across a piece of machinery that looks odd or badly made, with bits of string holding it together, but which actually works, remember we've got a name for it: 'a Heath Robinson affair'.

The drawing on page 26—the *De Luxe Outfit for the Cat Burglar*—is a typical piece. (A cat burglar, by the way, is not a man who steals cats, but is a burglar or thief who enters and leaves a building by climbing up walls and pipes and through windows, like a cat!) Study it very carefully. Then work out what will happen if . . .

Unit 9

TUTOR: Unit 9. 'What I'd really like . . .'
Look at the menu on pages 49 and 50, and listen as the three people discuss it and give their orders to the waitress.

YOUNG MAN: This is not a bad menu, is it?
OLDER MAN: No, it's very good—especially for the price. I've been here before with some friends. It may not look anything special, but their cooking's superb. Anyway, what would you like?
YOUNG MAN: Oh, I think I'll go for the steak and kidney pie.
OLDER MAN: Good choice. It's very good here. But I'm going to have the roast beef.
WOMAN: Well, what I'd really like is just a plain steak. I don't think I can eat three courses in the middle of the day. I wonder if they can do that.

(*Waitress approaches table.*)

WAITRESS: Sorry I've kept you waiting . . .
YOUNG MAN: Not at all.
WAITRESS: May I take your orders now?
OLDER MAN: Yes, I think so. This gentleman and I would like the set menu, but the young lady would like something different. We don't want to mix you up, so perhaps we could give you *our* orders first.
WAITRESS: Yes, fine. What starters would you like?
YOUNG MAN: I'd like soup. What *is* the soup of the day, please?
WAITRESS: Tomato.
YOUNG MAN: Yes, that'll be fine.
OLDER MAN: I'd like fruit juice, I think. Could I have a grapefruit juice, please?
WAITRESS: Of course, sir. And to follow?
YOUNG MAN: Steak and kidney pie for me, please.
OLDER MAN: And roast beef for me. Oh, what vegetables have you got?
WAITRESS: Carrots, courgettes, and boiled potatoes or French fries.
OLDER MAN: Boiled potatoes, please, and the other vegetables, too.
YOUNG MAN: I don't supose I could just have courgettes, could I? No carrots and no potatoes at all.
WAITRESS: Of course, sir. And for you, madam?
WOMAN: What I'd really like is just a plain steak. Do you think I might have just a steak?
WAITRESS: Of course. What kind of steak, madam? Sirloin, rump, T-bone?
WOMAN: Oh, a small sirloin, please.
WAITRESS: And how would you like it?
WOMAN: Medium, please.
WAITRESS: No starter, madam?
WOMAN: No, thank you.
WAITRESS: Good. May I run through your orders again? That was one soup and one grapefruit juice; one steak and kidney pie with courgettes; one roast beef with Yorkshire pudding, carrots, courgettes and boiled potatoes; and one small sirloin steak, medium. Would you like any vegetables with it, madam?
WOMAN: Well, would you by any chance have any green beans?
WAITRESS: Of course, madam. (*pause*) If that's all, I'll get you the wine list.
OLDER MAN: Thank you.

Unit 10

TUTOR: Unit 10. 'A full-time job'
Look at the pictures on pages 55 and 56 and listen to this talk.

MAN: In this short illustrated talk, I'd like to tell you about just some of the things that have to be done every day in a zoo.

First and foremost, all the animals, reptiles, birds, fish and other aquatic animals in a zoo have to be cared for and looked after all the time. Sometimes it's extremely difficult to get this across to the general public, but looking after animals in a zoo is a full-time job—24 hours a day, 7 days a week. All the animals are fed regularly of course and given water, milk or some other liquid. Some are fed and watered every few hours, some every few days. You may have seen the lions, elephants or seals being fed in a zoo somewhere, but feeding time for some animals can be quite different. This *first picture,* for example, was taken in the Seaquarium in Miami. There the dolphins are fed several times a day by a diver.

Sometimes animals born in a zoo are rejected by their parents when still very young and have to be hand-reared by keepers. In *picture two,* a young polar bear is being fed milk from a bottle. And in *picture three,* another young polar bear is being weighed. All young animals have to be weighed regularly to make sure they are being provided with the correct diet and the correct amounts of food. (The stomachs of very young animals are very sensitive.) And of course careful records are kept of their daily progress.

Quite clearly, too, cages and enclosures must be cleaned out regularly, and repaired, repainted or completely renewed from time to time. This repair work is being done all the time by a special maintenance staff: and these are the same people who have to repaint or replace signs around a zoo, as well as collect litter and so on to keep the zoo generally tidy.

And some animals have to be cleaned from time to time, too. *Picture four* shows Chi Chi, the famous female giant panda, being scrubbed by her keeper in London Zoo.

And then, of course, animals—even large dangerous ones—are taken ill and must be treated quickly. And in most zoos they are given the best possible treatment. In *picture five,* a cheetah is being operated on in an operating theatre. The equipment here is as extensive as one would expect in an ordinary hospital, and this operation is being carried out with the same care that would be given to an operation on a human.

It makes me furious when I hear of small zoos where animals are neglected or are kept in poor conditions. Most zoos do everything they can to keep their animals healthy and to cure those that are sick—but if for some reason we are forced to put an animal down, we get it over as quickly and as humanely as possible.

Just one last thing, and this is extremely important: zoos are not places that just keep wild animals locked up for people to go and look at. We are very much concerned with the scientific and educational aspects of looking after animals. To take one example, in many zoos around the world, venom is extracted from snakes and made available to medical researchers and chemists for the production of drugs. *Picture six* was taken at the Serpentarium in Miami. Here the venom is being extracted from the fangs of a puff-adder. Done by an expert, this job is not as dangerous as it might look!

And on the educational side, although children *and* adults can obviously learn a lot about animals by simply walking round a zoo, many now have 'zoo schools'. *Picture seven* shows a class in one in Cologne, Germany, where regular lessons are given in which, among other exhibits, live pythons are shown.

Unit 14

TUTOR: Unit 14. 'How good's your memory?'
Look at page 79 and listen to this talk.

LECTURER: Some people have almost frighteningly good memories: they're brilliant at remembering things. And others are almost unbelievably hopeless at remembering anything at all. What about you? Are you forgetful? Or do you find it relatively easy to remember things?

People often ask me: 'How can I improve my memory?' Unfortunately, I regret to say there's no simple answer. But there are some general points one can make. Firstly, you have to practise. Practise remembering things—all sorts of things: telephone numbers, things you have to do, TV programme times, and so on.

Secondly, *use* your memory. A friend of mine has said to me: 'I'd prefer to make notes all the time rather than rely on my memory.' That's a terrible mistake. I'm sure you actually risk making your memory worse that way. You see, in order to use your memory, you have to be keen to remember—eager to remember, if you like. I've told that friend: 'Stop making notes. If you really *mean* to remember things, you can.' So *use* your memory: avoid making notes which will make you lazy and which can get lost.

And thirdly, I always suggest making associations when you want to remember anything. There are a number of well-established methods of making associations. The example I'm going to give you now uses one kind of 'word-picture' association. Imagine you want to memorise the Grand National winners from 1971 to 1980. You could, I suppose, keep on repeating the list to yourself so that you learn them by rote. But that's difficult and takes a lot of time. Instead, how about making up a story like this? 'I want to tell you about an important man I first met in 1971. He always *specifies* exactly what he wants. Most people consider him a *well-to-do* gentleman. His favourite drink is *Red Rum.* He always has at least two bottles of it in his office—1973 and 1974 vintage. His favourite dish is *L'Escargot* (snails). He made his money in the *Rag Trade.* (This is a slang English expression for the clothes business.) When visitors come to look around his factory, he always offers them some *Red Rum* (1977 vintage) and introduces himself as 'Lucky'. He doesn't like his real first name: *Lucius.* Once a year he goes off camping which he enjoys very much: he even knows how to light a fire by *rubbing sticks* together! And on his camping trip in 1980, he climbed *Ben Nevis.*' Note here that all the names of the horses are in the same order as the years, so having started by mentioning 1971, you only have to remember the sequence of events in the story. And to help a little more, we've added one or two years as well—although that is not always necessary.

I'd be dishonest if I said that you'll remember everything immediately. Just go on practising—with things you have to do over the next few days, relatives' birthdays and so on. To start with, try to find a way of memorising the list of adjectives and prepositions on page 79. You might make up a story about a Mary Fonda who is fond of John Keen, and John Keen is keen on Mary, and so on. Or you might make up a story about the city gentleman. Remember, the story you choose might involve rearranging the words, but that doesn't matter here. The thing is to find the best word-picture association to help you remember the adjectives and prepositions.

When you have memorised both the Grand National winners and the adjectives and prepositions, cover the page and test each other.

Oh, by the way, don't forget to see if you can remember them at the end of the lesson or when you've finished the Unit.

Unit 19

TUTOR: Unit 19. 'Murderer caught "by wireless" '.
Look at page 110 and listen.

READER: The very first time that *radio* was used to catch a criminal was in the case of Dr Crippen back in 1910. Crippen might in fact have got away with murdering his wife if he hadn't come up against an amateur detective —and the very latest thing then in communication, the 'wireless', or radio, as we call it now.

The murder was a particularly horrific one, the sort horror films are made of. The doctor had poisoned, dismembered and then buried his wife in the cellar of their home in Holloway. And he and his mistress and accomplice, Ethel Le Neve, were fleeing to Canada aboard the liner *Montrose.* To avoid being recognised, Crippen had cut off his moustache, removed his glasses and was growing a beard, but he still didn't fool the captain of the liner, Captain Henry Kendall. He was a bit of an amateur detective and had quite quickly come to the conclusion that the wanted murderer was on board. And the appearance of Ethel disguised as a boy aroused Kendall's suspicions as much as anything else.

At 3 p.m. Greenwich Mean Time on Friday, 22nd July, from a position 130 miles west of the Lizard, the Captain sent the now-famous message to Chief Inspector Walter Dew of Scotland Yard. The message read:

> 'Have strong suspicion that Crippen, London cellar murderer, and accomplice are amongst saloon passengers. Moustache taken off. Growing beard. Accomplice dressed as boy: voice, manner and build undoubtedly a girl. Both travelling as Mr and Master Robinson. (Signed) Kendall'

Three days later Kendall sent another wireless message which convinced Chief Inspector Dew that Crippen and Le Neve were indeed on board. This second message read:

> 'More fully convinced it is him. They have no baggage except small cheap grip bought on Continent. Managed to examine his soft grey felt hat while at lunch. Name inside Jackson, Boulevard du Nord. Grey felt hat of accomplice no lining; packed inside band to make fit. Noticed accomplice using safety pins to pants.'

To cut a long story short, Dew caught a faster ship to Canada and before the *Montrose* reached the Canadian coast, Crippen and Ethel Le Neve were arrested. They both stood trial and Crippen was hanged at Pentonville on 23rd November, 1910. Ethel was acquitted, changed her name and lived in London until she died in 1967 at the age of 84.

Unit 20

TUTOR: Unit 20. 'Here is the news . . .'
Look at page 115 and listen.

NEWSREADER: Good evening. Here is the six o'clock news.

Another earthquake, the fifth in three days, hit Japan last night. Hundreds of homes have now been destroyed or badly damaged, and thousands have been made homeless since the earthquakes started. Many of the homeless have begun to make themselves makeshift shelters from the rubble. Electricity, gas and water supplies have also been seriously disrupted. Experts believe that the country will be hit by more quakes during the next 48 hours.

Workmen digging the foundations for a large house not far from York have uncovered an ancient wooden boat thought to be at least 2,500 years old. Archaeologists who have examined it say that the boat has been preserved in the mud and that this is an extremely important discovery. The boat will be removed carefully over the next fortnight and then taken to a museum in London to be examined further.

This year's Book Club Short Story Prize has been awarded to the writer Sonya Johnson. It may come as a surprise to many people that this is the pen-name of Mrs Susan James, who lives near Liverpool. On hearing the news, Mrs James said she had to pinch herself to make sure she wasn't dreaming! The award will be presented to Mrs James at a Book Club Dinner in London next month.

And finally, news is coming in of developments regarding the British hostages. The ten British hostages who have been held by gunmen on an island in the North Atlantic have just been released. They have been held hostage since 3rd November. They were delivered an hour ago to a small airport in the north of Scotland and are being taken to a hospital in Edinburgh where they will be examined by a team of doctors. In a brief interview, one of the hostages said that the public had been misinformed about one thing: they had *not* been maltreated by their captors. But they *had* been bored and for days had kept themselves amused playing cards. We will bring you further news in our ten o'clock bulletin tonight.

Unit 24

TUTOR: Unit 24. 'Forbidden!'
Look at the pictures on page 142 and listen to this radio extract.

ANNOUNCER: The time is now 10.30, time for our 'Letter from America', read this week by Alan Book.

READER: 'The law is an ass—an idiot!' That was the verdict of Mr Bumble in Charles Dickens' novel *Oliver Twist*. And if Mr Bumble had ever visited the young states of North America, he would have found his prejudices more than justified. As in many countries, all kinds of laws were passed years ago, and they have been added to over the years. Some of them, believe it or not, are still in force today, although not surprisingly they are mostly forgotten, and rarely enforced. I say 'rarely', because a man *was* prosecuted a few years ago, under one of these old laws, for slurping his soup in a New Jersey restaurant. You might think that in a free country like the United States you would be allowed to slurp your soup if you want to and if you're enjoying it—but the customer who was prosecuted under this law by the restaurant owner was driving other customers away. The restaurant owner lost the case, by the way, but the publicity was enough to prevent the customer from coming back to the 'scene of his crime'.

The case fascinated me so much that I have begun collecting other old laws like it. For instance, carrying fishing tackle in a cemetery is illegal in Muncie, Indiana. I have not been able to discover why. And in Milwaukee, a man could be prevented from taking his pet elephant for a walk on a public street: he is only permitted to do so if the animal is on a leash. I can only assume that the reason for that is that an elephant did some damage during a circus parade in Milwaukee many years ago. Laws even today have a habit of being made *after* the event.

But back to fish. In Oklahoma, you could still be punished for letting your pet fish get drunk, or for trying to catch a whale in the state's inland waters: both activities are forbidden by law. And insects aren't above the law, either: a strange law in Kirkland, Illinois, actually forbids bees to fly over the town. Although how anyone could stop them from doing so is quite an interesting thought . . .

And finally, to food. I have discovered, during the course of my investigations, that it's forbidden, in Corvallis, Oregon, to buy a cup of coffee after six in the evening. After that, apparently, you have to go without. But with the amount of coffee Americans drink, I can't see that law ever being enforced. Unlike my last example, which concerns barbers in Waterloo, Nebraska, who are not allowed by law to eat onions between 7 a.m. and 7 p.m. It's not difficult to see some sense in a law which forbids one human to breathe onion fumes over another, especially while the one being breathed on is the passive one in the barber-customer situation.

All in all, however, I would agree with Mr Bumble, who can surely be excused for believing that 'the law is an ass'!

Unit 29

TUTOR: Unit 29. 'I can't remember anything at all.'
Look at page 179 and listen to this item from a radio news broadcast.

NEWSREADER: Police today issued an appeal to the public to help identify a man found yesterday wandering around the village of Grassington in Yorkshire suffering from amnesia.
A report from Ron Warrington in Leeds.

WARRINGTON: The sudden appearance of Mr X at 5 a.m. yesterday morning in the village of Grassington, about 8 miles from Skipton, and 35 from Leeds, drew the attention of villagers and greatly disturbed the local police. For this man is the third person suffering from amnesia to be found in this area in the past month. This man, like the previous two, had no means of identification on him—no wallet, no money, no papers, nothing—and all of the labels in his clothes had been cut out. One villager told me that the man was wandering around like a blind man: he had to be led to a house while someone phoned for the police, she said.
When I interviewed the local Inspector of Police, he had this to say:

POLICE INSPECTOR: 'What *is* worrying is that this man seems to be quite well-educated and is wearing expensive clothes, but he can't remember anything. He has no idea who he is or what he is doing in this part of the country. I would like to appeal to anyone who may know him, or anyone who thinks they may know him, to come forward. He's about 55 years old, about 6 feet tall, with glasses, has grey hair and a short grey beard. He's wearing a dark grey suit and black shoes, and a blue striped shirt. We shall be issuing a photograph of him taken just after he was found. From the condition of his clothes, we think he may have been wandering around the hills, but we don't know for sure. Unless someone can recognise him—*and* the two other gentlemen—we have a real mystery on our hands. I can only repeat that we shall do everything we can to discover this man's identity, and shall of course be checking our 'Missing Persons' files, but we shall have to rely very much on the public for help.'

WARRINGTON: In a brief interview, Mr X told me how he felt.

MAN: 'I can't remember anything at all. I wish I could. I could be anybody. I might be single, I might be married and have three or four children. I should probably be at work somewhere right now. But I just don't know. I simply have to find out something about myself. It's like living in a dream world. It's horrible . . .'

WARRINGTON: We shall bring you further news on this mysterious case when we can.
Ron Warrington, Yorkshire.

TUTOR: Unit 29. Listen and discuss.
Look at page 181 and listen.

ANN: What's going on over there outside the theatre?
DAVID: I don't know. We'll have to go over and find out. You try and get to the box office and pick up our tickets, and I'll see what I can find out.

(A few minutes later.)

ANN: Well?
DAVID: I gather the concert's been cancelled.
ANN: Who told you that?
DAVID: One of the people over there.
ANN: I hope it's not right. It can't be, can it?
DAVID: Well, it looks like it. They're not letting anyone in. And there are some rather unpleasant arguments going on. Anyway, now we've got here, let's see what they have to say in the box office.
ANN: Yes, I'll see if I can make the woman hear.
(tapping on box office window) Ah, excuse me. Can you tell us what's happening? We've come to collect our tickets.
WOMAN: *(through box office window)* Pardon?
DAVID: We've come to collect our tickets, but we'd like to know exactly what's happening. We've been told the late performance has been cancelled. Has it?
WOMAN: Yes, I'm afraid it has. The manager's just about to put up a notice outside.
ANN: Well, what's the reason? I mean, why's it been cancelled at such short notice?
WOMAN: It's dreadful. It's never happened here before. I've never known anything like it . . .
ANN: What happened?
WOMAN: I'm sorry to say there were a number of vandals at the first performance and they caused so much trouble and have done so much damage that we just can't . . . well, you know, . . . We'll refund your money, of course.
DAVID: That's all very well, but we've travelled hundreds of miles for this Ravers concert. It's not good enough, is it?
ANN: I suppose there's nothing we can do about it, is there?
WOMAN: No, I'm afraid not.
ANN: Well, if you can refund our money now, we had booked £5 tickets and our name's James.
WOMAN: Thank you. I'll just check.
DAVID: Well, I still don't think they should be allowed to cancel things at short notice like this, especially when a group like this are only here once every three or four years . . .

Unit 30

TUTOR: Unit 30. 'A story with a moral'
Look at the series of pictures on pages 185–186 and listen to this letter to an insurance company.

READER: Dear Sir,

A fortnight ago I arranged to have our kitchen redecorated. The decorator arrived and started preparing the walls. As part of the job, he pulled a little innocent nail out of the wall—and a pile of plaster fell off onto the floor.

So before he could do any work, we had to have the wall completely replastered. The plasterer came the next day and started to knock the rest of the plaster off so that he could replaster the whole wall. However, while he was knocking the old plaster off, he hit a gas pipe and fractured it. There was a dreadful smell of gas, so we turned the supply off at the mains.

Obviously we had to have it mended, so we called the gasman. As it was an emergency, he came straight away, and almost immediately burned through an electric cable (by mistake) with his blowlamp while he was fitting a new gas pipe.

The damage was so bad that it meant having the kitchen rewired, so we called the electrician. He had hardly started work when he put his elbow through the kitchen window. Still, he went on and finished the rewiring while we called the glazier to get the window replaced.

The glazier must have been new at the job because he hadn't been working very long on the window when he cut his hand very badly. So we had to drop everything and take him to the hospital where he had his hand sewn up.

On the way back from the hospital in the car, we were waiting at some traffic lights, and I must have been thinking about something else, I suppose, because the moment the lights turned to green, I started off. The driver in front of me, however, was not quite so quick. So I had to take the car to the nearest garage to have the bumper straightened. (The front of the car will have to be resprayed, too. I shall be getting that done when the kitchen has been finished.)

By the time we finally got home and the glazier had left (after arranging for someone else to come and finish fitting the window the next day), no one was in a mood to cook a proper meal. So I opened a tin of tomato soup. And it was when the dog rushed past me—we've got a large sheep dog, by the way—that the soup spilt all down one wall. So now we've got to have that wall repainted, and I am about to ring the decorator up again.

Since I would like your company to deal with one series of claims at a time, however, I enclose all the receipted accounts from the garage and from the different men who did the work—and who caused all the damage.

I look forward to hearing from you.

Yours faithfully,

I.M. Helpless

Acknowledgements

We are grateful to the following for permission to reproduce copyright textual material:

British Tourist Authority for an extract from 'What's On'; John Clare Books for an adapted extract from 'Mike Yarwood' from *Could Do Better* edited by Mark Barker; James Ellis for his article 'Windsurfing Chose Me . . .'; Brian Ford and John Gribbin for their help with 'The Tour of the Century'; London and Express News and Feature Services for an adapted extract from 'The Unthinkable' by Jonathan Dimbleby from *TV Times* November 1–7 1980; Meteorological Office for an extract from the weather forecast taken from the telephone Crown Copyright 1981; National Holidays for an adapted extract from *National Holidays In Great Britain and Europe* March–November 1981; The National Trust for Places of Historic Interest or Natural Beauty for an adapted extract from '60 Miles Round London' *Touring Guide* 1981; Octopus Books Ltd for an adapted extract from *The World's Greatest Mistakes* edited by Nigel Blundell; Penguin Books Ltd for an adapted extract p25 'Baths with my Aunt' from *The New Penguin Calman* by Mel Calman (Penguin Books 1977) © Mel Calman 1963, 1967, 1968, 1972, 1974, 1977; Routledge and Kegan Paul Ltd for an adapted extract from *Loch Ness Monster* by Tim Dinsdale and adapted extracts from *The Book of Heroic Failures* by Stephen Pile; Syndication International Ltd for an extract from 'How far do you let your children go' by Jill Guyte *Woman's Own* February 22nd 1975; The Times for adapted extracts from 'A Life In the Day of Buchi Emecheta' by Buchi Emecheta *Sunday Times Magazine* March 23rd 1980, article by John Barnes *Sunday Times* May 25th 1980, 'This Little Monkey is Nursemaid to a Man' by David Blundy *Sunday Times Magazine* August 30th 1981 and 'Here is the weather forecast for the next century' by Brian Silcock *Sunday Times* January 4th 1981; the author's agents for an adapted extract from 'Pawley's Peepholes' *The Seeds of Time* by John Wyndham.

We are grateful to the following for permission to reproduce copyright photographic material:

Aspect Picture Library Ltd. for page 30; Associated Press Ltd. for page 98; Alternative Routes In Britain, published by the Automobile Association for page 31 (right); Barnabys Picture Library for page 45; British Tourist Authority for page 24 (bottom right); Calman, HELP!, Methuen London Ltd. for page 170 (bottom); Calman/Sunday Times 9.12.1979 for page 72; Camera Press Ltd. for page 55 (bottom right); Colorific Photo Library Ltd. for page 8 (top) & 8 (middle); Daily Express for page 22 (bottom); D.D. Lamson Ltd. for pages 89/90; James Ellis for page 61; M.C. Escher, Self Portrait: '© S.P.A.D.E.M. Paris, 1982' for page 103 (top); M.C. Escher, Day and Night: '© S.P.A.D.E.M. Paris, 1982' for page 103 (bottom); M.C. Escher, Belvedere: '© S.P.A.D.E.M. Paris, 1982' for page 104 (left); M.C. Escher, The Impossible Triangle: '© S.P.A.D.E.M. Paris, 1982' for page 104 (right); Feature Pix Colour Library for page 24 (bottom left); General Accident for page 148 (bottom); Geographia Ltd. Crown Copyright Reserved for page 33; Sally & Richard Greenhill for page 169 (top left); Kenneth Griffiths/Sunday Times 23.3.1980 for page 2; Louise Gubb/Sunday Times 30.8.1982 for pages 135 & 136; Heath Robinson, Inventions, Gerald Duckworth & Co. Ltd. for page 26; Hilton Hotels for page 49 (left) & 50 (right); John Topham Picture Library for page 115 (middle left); Keystone Press Agency Ltd. for page 115 (bottom right); David Langdon for page 172; Lochness Monster by Tim Dinsdale, sketches by Torquil Macleod, Routledge & Kegan Paul Ltd. for page 44; London Daily Mail for page 43; Longman Group Ltd. for page 141; Longman Photographic Unit for pages 13, 14, 19, 115 (bottom left), 143, 169 (top right), 169 (bottom left), 169 (bottom middle), 169 (bottom right) & 170 (top); Miami Seaquarium for page 55 (top); Miami Serpentarium Laboratories for page 56 (bottom left); National Holidays for page 93 (left); The National Maritime Museum, London for page 115 (middle right); National Zoological Gardens, Pretoria for page 56 (top left); Olympic Holidays Ltd. for pages 177 & 178 (top); Paul Popper Ltd. for page 56 (top right); Picturepoint Ltd. for pages 8 (bottom), 24 (top middle), 24 (top right) & 60; The Commissioner of Police Metropolis for pages 86 & 119; Polaroid (U.K.) Ltd. for pages 163 & 164; Rex Features Ltd. for page 147 and for permission to reproduce the illustration on page 79, from a copyright photograph by D. McEnery; Spectrum Colour Library for page 24 (top left); Paddy Summerfield for page 189; The Sunday Times for page 169 (bottom); Susan Griggs Agency Ltd. for page 97; Syndication International Ltd. for pages 37 & 110 (top); Times Newspapers Ltd. for page 110 (bottom); Norman Thelwell: This Desirable Plot, Methuen London Ltd. for pages 150 & 151; Janine Wiedel for page 148 (top); Zefa Picture Library (UK) Ltd. for pages 24 (bottom middle) & 115 (top); Zoologischer Garten, Koeln for page 56 (bottom right); The Zoological Society of London for page 55 (bottom left).

Illustrations by: Ann Axworthy, Peter Bailey, Bill Le Fever, Maggi Ling, Tony Morris, Chris Ryley, John Woodcock, and Chartwell Illustrators.